Baedeker

W9-CXN-637

New York

www.baedeker.com

Verlag Karl Baedeker

SIGHTSEEING HIGHLIGHTS ✶✶

Giant skyscrapers, the Statue of Liberty, the Empire State Building, Grand Central Terminal, Fifth Avenue, Central Park, Brooklyn Bridge and world famous museums – who doesn't know New York's main attractions. There are a few others, too, not quite as well known, but no less worthwhile.

✶✶ American Museum of Natural History
The largest museum of natural history tells the story of the origins of the universe.
▶ page 172

✶✶ Brooklyn Bridge
A guaranteed eye-catcher with its 532m/582yd freely suspended deck ▶ page 199

✶✶ Brooklyn Museum
The second largest museum in New York has a unique Egyptian collection. ▶ page 199

✶✶ Central Park
The green oasis in the middle of Manhattan provides an idyllic contrast to the adjacent skyscrapers. ▶ page 203

✶✶ Chinatown
The largest Chinese city outside China ▶ page 212

✶✶ Chrysler Building
One of the most beautiful buildings in the city ▶ page 215

✶✶ Empire State Building
The tallest and most famous building in New York ▶ page 232

✶✶ Fifth Avenue
The sinfully expensive boulevard is a shopper's paradise. ▶ page 233

✶✶ Frick Collection
The collection of old masters is in a grandiose city villa. ▶ page 245

✶✶ Grand Central Terminal
Commuter trains stop in this masterpiece of Beaux-Arts style. ▶ page 248

Brooklyn Bridge
The famous Manhattan skyline is in the background

There is much to discover

Statue of Liberty
»Lady Liberty«, a gift from France

BAEDEKER'S BEST TIPS

We've collected the most interesting of the numerous Baedeker tips in this book for you here. Experience and enjoy the best that New York has to offer!

⚠ Sunsets
We'll reveal where you can best watch the sun go down. ▶ **page 39**

⚠ Open Rehearsals
Most of the New York Philharmonic Orchestra's rehearsals are open to the public. ▶ **page 48**

⚠ Street parties
New Yorkers love to party in the streets. ▶ **page 88**

⚠ Eat at reasonable prices
Lunches and pre-theatre dinners are cheaper. ▶ **page 95**

⚠ Room brokers
Reserve your room via a room broker and save up to 45%. ▶ **page 65**

⚠ Fair fares in New York
The MetroCard is valid on all subways and buses. ▶ **page 144**

⚠ Halloween Parade
On the last Sunday in October the Avenue of the Americas becomes »Magical Sixth Avenue«. The colourful parade has a different theme every year. ▶ **page 175**

⚠ New Yorkers on the waterfront
In the summer fashionably dressed office workers, picnicking families and tourists populate the plaza down by the river side. ▶ **page 179**

⚠ Historic Diner
The best chips in a classic 1940s diner ▶ **page 183**

⚠ Fine dining with a view
Luxury restaurant with a view or a chamber music concert on a barge. ▶ **page 195**

⚠ Nathan's culinary invention
The best hot dogs are served where they were invented. ▶ **page 198**

Esplanade
The promenade along the Hudson invites a stroll

Harlem
Sunday is gospel day

🔳 Float across the East River
A cable car in New York ► **page 181**

🔳 Open air
Free SummerStage concerts, Shakespeare performances, live jazz, salsa and funk
► **page 206**

🔳 Excellent lunch address
The organic supermarket »Whole Foods« lets customers chose tasty dishes and salads and eat them in the adjacent restaurant. ► **page 233**

🔳 Excellent lunch address
The organic supermarket »Whole Foods« lets customers chose tasty dishes and salads and eat them in the adjacent restaurant. ► **page 233**

🔳 Bed & breakfast
Family atmosphere, homemade breakfast as well as tips for sightseeing
► **page 256**

🔳 Hearty homecooking
Probably the best soul food outside of the South in an authentic restaurant. The fried chicken is legendary. The walls are decorated with Harlem folk art.
► **page 258**

🔳 Gospel
Infectious music: gospel choirs in Harlem's churches ► **page 261**

🔳 A museum with a view
The roof terrace of the Metropolitan Museum: art and magnificent views
► **page 278**

🔳 Summer parties
Young architects and designers transform the courtyard of the P.S.1 into an abstract playground. ► **page 295**

🔳 New Year's Eve on Times Square
On 31 December Times Square becomes a fairground; the show starts at 6pm.
► **page 318**

BACKGROUND

PRACTICALITIES

The subway connects all parts of the city
► page 145

TOURS

Downtown Manhattan: the skyline is famous all over the world
► page 267

*Chinatown: the largest
Chinese city outside China*
► page 212

SIGHTS FROM A to Z

Fifth Avenue:
New York's glamour street
▶ **page 233**

Chrysler Building: for a year, it was the
tallest building in the city
▶ **page 216**

BACKGROUND

NEW YORK IS A CITY OF SUPERLATIVES.
HERE, IN BRIEF, IS ALL YOU NEED
TO KNOW ABOUT ITS RESIDENTS,
ECONOMY, POLITICS AND HISTORY.

PLANET NEW YORK

No question about it: New York City is one of the most exciting travel destinations on earth. The city of eight million is a symbol of urban life worldwide. Even though it's one hundred percent American, New York is seen by the whole world as the absolute metropolis, as the mother of all large cities and as a laboratory for lifestyle and urban trends.

Everyone knows New York inside and out – even if he has never been there. No other metropolis is internationally so well known: Manhattan, Wall Street, Ground Zero – who in the world does not know that the World Trade Centre was located there before 11 September 2001? Who doesn't know the Statue of Liberty or couldn't place

names like Central Park, Fifth Avenue, the Empire State Building and Broadway in New York City? We have accompanied generations of Hollywood actors, from Charlie Chaplin to Woody Allen and Tom Hanks, on their adventures in these urban canyons, charming diners and sinfully expensive apartments.

New York City boasts the most daring examples of modern architecture, and it would take years – some even say a whole lifetime – to even begin to savour the art scene in the way it deserves. And it's worth savouring, too, because it has a style of its own.

Brooklyn
In May the cherry trees in the Japanese Garden are in their full glory

Where America's Heart Beats

New York is not America, but the country's heart beats loudest here. This multi-ethnic city has the country's best restaurants, the best theatres (40 Broadway stages alone), the most beautiful parks, the best shopping: if it can't be found here, it's certainly not to be found anywhere else.

But it would be frivolous to call New York City a paradise – even if there has been an unparalleled boom since the 1970s, when whole neighbourhoods threatened to decay and the city led the country's statistics on catastrophes. Today New York's crime rate is well below the national average and formerly uncontrollable neighbourhoods like the Bronx have become model inner-city areas.

Confidence
Harlem, the neighbourhood in northern Manhattan, is going through its second renaissance.

Twin beams of remembrance
The towers of the World Trade Center characterized nhattan's skyline for almost 30 years. Every September two columns of light commemorate the events of 9/11.

Street life
New York City has more than 8 million residents, and almost all races and nations are represented. This unique variety can best be experienced in the streets.

Chinatown
More than 150,000 ethnic Chinese live in the city within the city south of Canal Street.

I love New York
Not just the opinion of the young ladies in the t-shirts, but also of the more than 40 million visitors every year.

Patriotism
The terrorist attacks of 11 September 2001 have changed America.

New York is *the* global capital of finance and assets. Its soaring sky-scrapers are symbols of its unbroken faith in the values of the Western world, even though the terrorist attacks of 11 September 2001 have changed the city (and the rest of the world). New Yorkers shrug off the increased security measures that cause delays and inconveniences in many places, as well as the five million dollars that the guarding of bridges, tunnels, public transport and significant buildings costs. The message to the friends as well as the enemies of New York is »now more than ever«, and this attitude impresses and inspires the visitor, too.

The City that Never Sleeps

New York, situated in the state of the same name on the northeastern coast of the USA, is spread out over numerous islands. It comprises five boroughs (city districts) and has an area of 781 sq km/301 sq mi. Manhattan is the tourist centre, where Broadway, Central Park, the financial centre and the most important museums are to be found, as well as most of the towering skyscrapers. It is impossible to get to know New York in one trip: the city is huge and overwhelming. Its more than eight million inhabitants are visited by millions of people from all over the world every year. Its many facets would suit a middle-sized country, and the city is characterized by such noise and bustle that the newcomer to New York may at first be ill-at-ease.

New York
Megacity, and moloch

»The city that never sleeps« applies as much today as it did yesterday: New Yorkers don't walk, they run; taxi drivers never help with baggage; sales staff let their customers know that they don't have all day. The city is a dizzying mix of select styles, fin-de-siècle romanticism and tastelessness. New York both repels and attracts. The apparently inexhaustible supply of creativity inspires, while the lack of tolerance for losers can be shocking. New York may be many things, but one thing is certain: the great city on the Hudson is never boring. Welcome to the city that never sleeps!

Facts

New York City is the largest city in the USA today. But it developed only slowly at first. Around 1800, scarcely 66,000 people lived in Manhattan. It was mass immigration in the second half of the 19th century that made New York a city of millions – and by 1900 the population had already risen to over three million.

Population · Politics · Economy

A Colourful Ethnic Mixture

With a little over 8.4 million residents New York is the largest American city, but it developed only slowly in the first 200 years after its founding in 1621. At the beginning of the 18th century only 5,000 people lived in Manhattan, by 1790 it had reached 33,000, and by around 1800 the number had almost doubled. But it was only the **mass immigration** in the second half of the 19th century that made New York a city of millions – by 1900 the population had climbed to over three million (►Baedeker Special p.313).

Development

Immigration has lead to an unusual variety of ethnic groups in New York, many of which live in their own areas, the typical **neighbourhoods**. Thus the Chinese live in Chinatown, the Poles and Ukrainians in the East Village, the Hungarians and Czechs on the East Side, the African Americans in Harlem, the Dominicans and Cubans in Washington Heights, while East Harlem and the Bronx are mainly Latin American. In Brooklyn, near Atlantic Avenue, live Arabs, mainly Syrians and Lebanese; orthodox Jews are concentrated in two Brooklyn neighbourhoods, Crown Heights and Williamsburg, and Danes and Norwegians in Bay Ridge. Astoria, the Queens neighbourhood, has a large Greek colony, and many Colombians have found a new home in Jackson Heights. All of these groups have their own shops, restaurants and often their own churches. But the opposite trend is also apparent: apart from the trattoria and ristoranti on Mulberry Street not much is left of Little Italy, and the former German colonies in East Village and on 86th Street have disappeared completely.

> **? DID YOU KNOW ...?**
>
> ■ Presently 35% of the New Yorkers are of European, 23% African American, 28% Latin-American and 10% Asian descent. Only one third were born in the city. There are still American Indians among the residents: in 2008 there were 16,300 Native Americans.

The ethnic richness can also be seen in the variety of languages: about 120 – some sources even say 200 – languages are spoken in the city! Some estimates state that about 4.2 million residents of New York speak English poorly or not at all, and approximately 1.5 million speak only Spanish. 30% of all school-aged children in New York speak a language other than English at home. But it works both ways: New York University teaches 25 different foreign languages, one of the most diverse programmes in the country.

Language variety

←*Prospect Park in the heart of Brooklyn is a popular site for the residents of the »suburb«*

In Brighton Beach, Brooklyn, there is an eastern European neighbourhood with a flair all its own

Economy

Even though New York has been financially ruined several times already, the city has always managed to recover. It is still the **financial capital** of the world, and the **media capital** of the United States. In 1949 New York was still one of the largest industrial centres in the country, but three in five jobs in this sector had been lost by the end of the 1970s. Only the textile industry has remained: located in the Garment District in Chelsea, it employs about a quarter of a million people. Today, about 85% of jobs in New York are in the **service sector**, above all the retail, finance and real estate sectors as well as in health and education. CHASE (Manhattan) and Citibank, two of the largest banks in the USA, are headquartered in New York, along with six of the world's largest insurance companies and three of the largest American newspapers, the *New York Times*, the *Wall Street Journal* and the *Daily News*. The headquarters of the three largest television networks, CBS, ABC and

Facts and Figures *New York*

New York city

► Metropolis of the state of New York and largest US city; the capital and governor's seat however is Albany, situated 250km/155mi upriver on the Hudson.

Location and climate

► On the north-eastern seacoast of the USA, in the south-east corner of New York State, where the Hudson and East Rivers flow into New York Bay.

► 40° 42' north latitude and 74° west longitude
(by comparison: Naples lies on 40°).

► Average temperature:
in January 32°F (0°C)
in July 76.5°F (24.7°C)

Size and population

► Area: 782 sq km/301 sq mi
(by comparison: Greater London covers 1579 sq km/610 sq mi)

► Population: 8 million in 5 boroughs:
Manhattan 58 sq km/22 sq mi, population 1.5 million
Bronx 106 sq km/41 sq mi, population 1.3 million
Staten Island 150 sq km/58 sq mi, population 0.4 million
Brooklyn 154 sq km/60 sq mi, population 2.5 million
Queens 313 sq km/121 sq mi, population 2.2 million

Religion

► More than 100 different religious communities with about 6,000 places of worship, temples and synagogues

► About 40% of New Yorkers are Roman Catholic, about 30% are Protestant and 3.5% are Muslim.

► With approximately 1.75 million individuals, New York has the largest Jewish community outside Israel.

Language

► American English

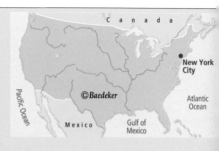

Economy

► New York City is the world's financial capital, and the US media capital. Largest employer: services sector.

► Unemployment: under 10%

Government

► The mayor is the head of the government, which also includes the City Council with 51 members.

Security

► New York is currently America's safest major city.

? DID YOU KNOW ...?

■ how the city got its nickname »The Big Apple«? According to the official explanation the term was used for the first time on 18 February 1924 by the horse racing journalist John FitzGerald in a column in the *The Morning Telegraph*. He had picked up the term from stable boys in New Orleans and then applied it to New York. A second version states that the term comes from the jazz musicians of the 1920s and 1930s, who apparently used to say: »The tree of success has many apples on it, but when you pick New York you pick the biggest of them all, the Big Apple.« In 1971 the president of the New York City Bureau of Tourism heard the nickname and since then the image has had huge success as the city logo.

NBC, are in New York, and the largest number of hotels, theatres, museums, publishers and advertising agencies are located here. **Tourism** is also very important, with about 700,000 people working in this sector. In 2009 New York was host to about 46 million visitors, of which approximately 9 million came from abroad, most of them from Great Britain, Canada, Japan and Germany.

The problems of a cosmopolitan city

But the »world's capital« has some big problems as well. The reconstruction taking place at Ground Zero with its exploding costs is straining the city. In the past decades the city has only been able to meet its obligations with help from the state and federal governments, and in exchange has had to give up part of its financial autonomy.

The unemployment rate is presently about 9.6% (national average: 9.5%); with more and more businesses leaving the city it is on the increase. The distribution of unemployment also reveals social inequality: almost twice as many Hispanics are unemployed as whites. Of the African Americans between 16 and 19 years old, almost every other one is unemployed, and 50% of adult African Americans and 43% of Hispanics have no income. Overall, every sixth New Yorker is on welfare. Despite the difficult financial situation, significant investment is necessary to counter the neglect which threatens some urban fringe areas, to create jobs in problem areas and for cheap housing. The state schools are in need of repair: people who can afford it avoid sending their children to them. The renovation of the approximately 860 bridges over the Hudson and East River is very expensive, as is the around 6,000 miles of sewerage, which is 100 years old. Improvements in the infrastructure are overdue: the city is collapsing under street traffic, public transport needs to be expanded and a proportion of the delivery of goods would be better carried out by rail. A large problem

Boroughs

Long Island Sound
Manhasset Bay
Hudson River
BRONX
Little Neck Bay
NASSAU
East River
MANHATTAN
QUEENS
New Jersey
Jamaica Bay
BROOKLYN
Upper New York Bay
Newark Bay
Lower New York Bay
STATEN ISLAND
Atlantic Ocean
N
3 mi
5 km
©Baedeker

Seat of the city government and the mayor: City Hall

here is the deep gap between rich and poor: this city of extremes has the most open trade, the greatest works of art, the world's highest buildings – and the poorest of America's poor.

Transport

Thanks to its location, New York was once an important seaport. Manhattan was bordered by piers up to about 100th Street, where up to the middle of the 20th century both shipping and passenger traffic were handled. Once the entrance to the New World, their importance declined with the arrival of the container ships – today these dock mostly on the New Jersey side of New York Bay – and the aeroplane as a means of mass transportation. New York has three airports. The largest and at 26km/16.2mi away the furthest from the centre of town is John F. Kennedy Airport (JFK), where predominantly international traffic and national flights to the western United States are handled. La Guardia (LGA), handling exclusively domestic traffic, is only 13km/8.1mi from the centre. Newark (EWR) is about 25km/15.5mi away in neighbouring New Jersey: both international and national airlines fly there. Amtrak long-distance trains depart from Pennsylvania (Penn) Station. This is also the terminal for trains of the New Jersey Transit and the Long Island Railroad, the commuter trains with the largest number of passengers in America. Grand Central Terminal is significant for suburban traffic. The most important means of transportation in New York are the subway, busses and ferries (▶Practicalities, Transport).

History of the City

How did a Native American village named Manhattan become a modern city of millions? Who were the first New Yorkers? Where did the city get its name? Find out here how a small Dutch settlement became one of the most important centres of the Western world.

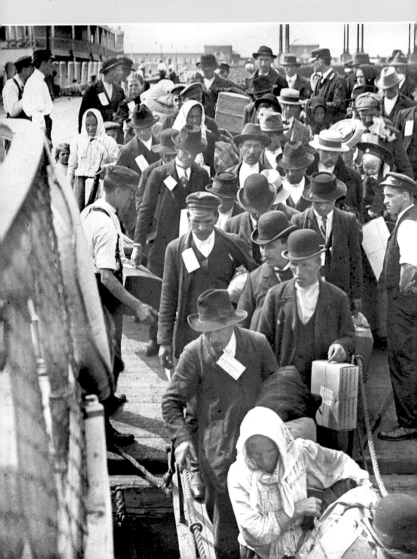

New York's Beginnings

9500 BC	The first American Indians settle the area of what is now New York
1609	Europeans settle on the island
1626	Nieuw Amsterdam founded

About 11,500 years ago the area of today's Manhattan was settled by the Algonquin tribe. They called their territory Manhattan, Manhattes, Manhata or Manhatans, which means »island of hills«. In 1524 Giovanni da Verrazzano from Florence sailed at the command of the French king Francis I along the American east coast and was the first European to reach the Bay of Manhattan, today's New York Bay. But it was over 80 years later, in the year 1609, that the Englishman Henry Hudson set foot on the southern point of Manhattan. He explored the Hudson River, which was later named after him, on behalf of the Dutch East India Company. After that more and more Dutch and Walloons emigrants settled on Manhattan. In 1626 the first governor of the town, Peter Minnewit from Wesel on the Rhine, bought the island of Manhattan from the Native Americans living there for cloth and glass beads worth about 60 guilders and called the settlement Nieuw Amsterdam. In 1653 Governor Peter Stuyvesant, a man known for his strictness, had a wall built in the north of the city – which had a population of about 1,000 at that time – between the Hudson and East Rivers; Wall Street, which got its name from this wall, runs along here today.

England Conquers the City

1664	England takes Nieuw Amsterdam
1689–1691	Rebellion in the English colonies
1735	The birth of freedom of the press in America

During the second Anglo-Dutch War (1664/1665 until 1667) the English took Nieuw Amsterdam without a fight.
The English king gave the colony to his brother, the Duke of York, and Nieuw Amsterdam, which in the meantime had a population of 1,500, was renamed New York in his honour. The Glorious Revolution – the overthrow in 1688 of James II of England by Parliament – spread to the colonies in 1689. In New York the German business-

← *Prospective immigrants on a ferry off Manhattan*

man Jacob Leisler led the rebellion, ruling the city for two years. To the very end, he refused to turn the city over to the incoming English governor. He was finally captured and sentenced to death.

In 1733 Johann Peter Zenger, who had emigrated from the Palatinate and founded the *New York Weekly Journal*, was imprisoned after criticizing the governor. He was released in 1735 after a sensational trial. This event is considered to be the birth of freedom of the press in America.

By 1709 there was a slave market at the end of Wall Street, and within 34 years around 2,000 black slaves were living in New York.

The War of Independence

1775–1783	War of Independence against England
1776	Declaration of Independence of New York
1783	England recognizes Independence
1784	New York is made capital of the USA
1789	George Washington takes oath of office

New York's population numbered 25,000 at the beginning of the War of Independence of the American colonies, and its harbour handled more cargo than Boston's or Philadelphia's.

The headquarters of England's troops was in New York. In order to raise money the English parliament decided in 1764 to impose customs duties on trade goods. In 1765 the **Stamp Act** (every business transaction required a stamp which was liable to a fee) provoked the New Yorkers' protest. The Sons of Liberty, a secret organization which stirred up resistance to the Stamp Act and the English crown, was formed with its motto »no taxation without representation«. The taxation of tea resulted in the Boston Tea Party in December 1773 and in April 1774 the lesser-known New York Tea Party: as in Boston, rebels dressed as American Indians dumped crates of tea that was to be taxed into the harbour. New York signed the Declaration of Independence in 1776, and George Washington, commander in chief of the Continental Army, moved his headquarters from Boston to New York in April of that year. England sent almost 500 ships with 32,000 occupying troops as reinforcements, which set up camp on Staten Island. On 27 August British and American troops clashed at Brooklyn Heights: in the so-called Battle of Long Island the American troops were at a disadvantage and had to withdraw. New York was left to the British until peace was declared, and the British developed it into their military centre. Over 10,000 American prisoners of war died on ships that had been converted to prisons on the East River.

After the English troops surrendered on 19 October 1781 the British crown recognized the independence of their colonies in the Peace of Paris treaty in 1783. New York had been plundered by the British after the long occupation and partially destroyed by fire. Nevertheless the city was named the capital of the young nation until Philadelphia took its place in 1790. In 1789 George Washington took his oath of office as the first president of the United States in Federal Hall in New York. The population grew to over 30,000, and the city became capital of the state of the same name until Albany took over that function in 1797. In the same year the most important stock exchange of the financial world was founded. In 1811 the city fathers showed great foresight: even though only the southern tip of Manhattan was inhabited they developed »the grid«, the pattern of 12 avenues that run from south to north and 155 (today 220) numbered cross streets.

George Washington monument in front of Federal Hall

The Civil War

1827	The city of New York abolishes slavery
from 1850	First mass immigration
1861–1865	Civil War between the North and the South

After the opening of the Erie Canal in 1825, which connected New York with the Great Lakes, the city flourished as a seaport. With over 150,000 residents it became the largest city in the country in 1820. When the state of New York abolished slavery in 1827, around 14,000 African Americans were living in New York City. A large fire in 1835 destroyed over 700 houses. From 1850 hundreds of thousands of Germans and Irish fled from poverty and persecution in Europe to New York. In the 1880s Jews from Eastern Europe and Italians streamed into the city (►Baedeker Special p.313), and New York's population passed the half-million mark.

In February 1860 Abraham Lincoln delivered his famous speech against slavery. When he was elected president in November, 13 states seceded from the union and formed the Confederate States of America.

On 12 April 1861 the **Civil War** began, the North fighting against the defected South. Since the city's traders did business with the South, New York at first remained quiet. Then Lincoln enacted a new law on military conscription: it became possible to buy release from military duty for $300. This led to great dissatisfaction among the Irish especially, because they could not raise this much money. The second military draft on 13 July 1863 in New York led to the »draft riots«. An angry mob attacked the police, plundered homes and hunted abolitionists. The hate turned in the end against the African American residents of New York, who as the source of cheap labour were the biggest competition on the job market. When the riots were over 105 people had been killed in what is considered to be the bloodiest uprising in America to this day.

From the Civil War to the Stock Market Crash

1870	New York's population exceeds one million
1883	The Brooklyn Bridge is completed
1886	Inauguration of the Statue of Liberty
1898	Greater New York City is formed
1904	The first subway runs

After the Civil War, New York became the starting point of industrialization. The large banking houses were founded, and Wall Street developed into the main business centre of the Western world. The city experienced a building boom. In 1883 the Metropolitan Opera and the Brooklyn Bridge were opened; in 1886 the Statue of Liberty, a gift from France, was erected at the entrance to the harbour. In the 1880s a **second wave of immigration** began, when particularly Jews from Eastern Europe and Italians streamed into the city. Until 1919, Ellis Island was the gateway into the »Land of Opportunity« for 17 million Europeans (►Baedeker Special p.313).

Greater New York City   In 1898 the five until then independent communities of New York – Manhattan, Queens, Brooklyn, Bronx, Staten Island – united to form

Greater New York City. With 3.5 million people, this was the world's second-largest city after London. In 1904 the 14.6km/9.1mi-long first segment of the subway from City Hall in south Manhattan up to 145th Street was opened (►Baedeker Special p.145).

1930s until today

1929	Black Friday on the stock exchange causes world-wide depression
1932	Opening of the Empire State Building
1939	World's Fair in Flushing Meadows
1954	Ellis Island is closed
11.09.2001	Attack on the World Trade Center
2008	US financial bank crisis

The boom was only stopped by the crash on Wall Street on »Black Friday« in 1929, heralding an almost ten-year long depression and sending many residents of New York plummeting into poverty. Around 1930 New York's population had grown to 6.9 million; Harlem with its 220,000 residents was the largest community of African Americans in the USA. It was during the depression – when every fourth New Yorker was unemployed – that the 381m/1,250ft Empire State Building was opened in 1932. For a long time it was the tallest building in the world; today it is still an office building for 25,000 people and a major Manhattan landmark. In the same time period the Chrysler Building, the RCA Building and the George Washington Bridge across the Hudson were built.

New York's recovery began under the Republican mayor Fiorello H. LaGuardia. During his time in office (1932–1945) the city's infrastructure was expanded and social housing was promoted. New York's second World's Fair in Flushing Meadows in 1939/40 attracted 44 million visitors. Between 1933 and 1945 countless Jews, intellectuals, artists, scientists and political refugees fled to the United States; they influenced the development of architecture and art in New York. In 1941 the USA entered the Second World War. In 1946, when New York became the seat of the United Nations, the city had more than 7 million residents.

New York's recovery

In the 1960s and 1970s New York experienced racial riots, the assassination of the African American politician Malcolm X (1965) and the first wave of emigration: more than one million whites left the city and moved to the suburbs. In their place came a new wave of im-

September 11, 2001: the Twin Towers burn

migrants from Puerto Rico, Central America and the South. During the third New York World's Fair in 1965 there was a 16-hour blackout: nine months later there was an unusually high birth rate. In 1973 the 420m/1377ft-high twin towers of the World Trade Center in the financial district of Manhattan were opened. Many businesses moved out of Manhattan because of the rising cost of real estate. In 1975 New York was not able to pay its bonds; a temporary loan from the federal government prevented **insolvency**, and since then the city has been under a strict austerity programme.

In July 1977 New York experienced a second power blackout, which lasted 27 hours. In 1987 »Black Monday« on Wall Street brought about a 30% loss in value of all stocks traded.

David Dinkins was the first African American to become mayor of the city and took office on 1 January 1990. In 1994 he was replaced by Rudolph Giuliani, whose »zero tolerance« politics (until 2001) led to an enormous reduction in crime level. Booming stocks brought in increased tax revenue, which were immediately spent on overdue repairs and beautification of the city. But stocks fell shortly afterwards and the city is again close to insolvency.

9/11 On **September 11, 2001** the city experienced its greatest catastrophe: two planes flown by terrorists flew into the twin towers of the World Trade Center and caused them to collapse, killing more than 2,800 people. On the fourth of July 2004 the cornerstone of a new building was laid at the site, which is known as **Ground Zero**. The 20t »symbol of American strength and confidence« (George Pataki, governor of the State of New York) made of grey-black granite comes from the Adirondack Mountains, cost $14,000 and was painstakingly carved out by hand, chiselled (it bears the inscription: »to the enduring spirit of freedom«) and polished in order to be buried under 20m/66ft of cement and concrete. The planned height of the so-called **Freedom Tower**, 541m/1776 feet, symbolizes the year (1776) of the American Declaration of Independence.

Jeanne-Claude and Christo: »The Gates«, art in Central Park, February 2005

In February 2005 the married artist team Christo and Jeanne-Claude realized the project that they had been planning since 1979, entitled **»The Gates«**: for 16 days saffron-coloured cloth panels coloured 7,500 gates in Central Park. More than four million people streamed into the park to see the art project.

The **worst worldwide financial crisis** since 1929 began in January 2008 when several large American banks admitted to gambling away billions of dollars on speculations. In September the Lehmann Brothers investment bank went broke and let the crisis overflow onto the rest of the world. The complete collapse of the system could only be prevented through bail-out packages worth several billion dollars.

Arts and Culture

How did the »vertical city« (the description comes from the French Swiss architect Le Corbusier) come about? What do the theatres on Broadway or the playhouses in the village have to offer? What treasures are waiting to be discovered in the famous museums?

City Development and Architecture

New York's spectacular skyline with about 200 skyscrapers is a gigantic panopticon of historical building styles – from New York's first skyscraper, the Flatiron Building, through the neo-gothic Woolworth Building, the Art Deco ornaments of the Chrysler Building and the rationality of the Seagram Building by Mies van der Rohe, to the figurative neo-renaissance of Philip Johnson's AT T Building.

The Rise to International City

New York's rise to become an international city began at the end of the 18th century after declaring its independence from England. At that time the city covered an area from the southern tip of Manhattan to around today's Canal Street, largely still on the street map that had been designed by the Dutch. Because of the rapid rise in population (New York was in 1800 already the largest city of the still young USA) the growth of the city threatened to get out of control. In order to make up for the lack of building land, landfills were created early on around the southern tip of Manhattan. Thus, for instance, the round **Castle Clinton** in today's Battery Park was built at that time only 100m/110yd from the shoreline in the harbour. In the same way, today's Water Street near South Street Seaport got its name because it was originally right next to the water. Even though New York only took up the southern tip of Manhattan, the city council developed a plan in 1811 that was supposed to control the future development of Manhattan. The **street grid** covers the whole island like a net with its twelve avenues running north to south and the cross streets numbered 1 to 220. Only the older parts of the city south of 14th Street and the path of today's Broadway, which was already established by the Algonquin Indians as a hunting trail, were integrated into the plan.

The decision for this quite regular grid was the consequence on the one hand of economic pragmatism (in the sale of plots of land there were to be no »good« or »bad« locations), but also of democratic convictions: the city was supposed to offer all of its residents the same living conditions.

Manhattan grew quickly and by 1864 more than half of the population of the island lived north of **14th Street**. As a consequence of the expansion northwards the centre of the city shifted away from the southern tip. This was possible due to the improvement of the inner

The city centre shifts away

← Solomon R. Guggenheim Museum: idiosyncratic spiral construction by Frank Lloyd Wright

The Woolworth Building under construction, 1913

city means of transportation (at first horse-drawn trams, later streetcars and subways). After the completion of **Central Park** around 1870 its southern edge (the northern part of the park was in an area that was for the most part undeveloped) quickly became a centre for building projects and encouraged the city to expand northwards. During the second half of the 19th century 14th Street became the meeting point for elegant New York society: Tiffany's jeweller's shop was located on Union Square, and the city opera house, the Academy of Music, was a few blocks away. By the turn of the century the centre of activity had already shifted. The construction of the Flatiron Building (1902) and the Metropolitan Life Tower (1909) on Madison Square hinted at this development. In the 1930s and 1940s **42nd Street** developed into a centre for theatre and nightlife, and at the same time **Fifth Avenue** changed from a sleepy side street to a city boulevard. In the meantime the construction of luxury hotels like the Plaza or the Savoy had changed the southern edge of Central Park to a centre for the elegant world of New York. As of the 1960s the most expensive shops in the city can be found on **58th Street** as well as on **Fifth** and **Madison Avenue**. The two areas with the greatest density of skyscrapers today are the southern edge of Central Park (**Midtown**) as well as the southern tip of Manhattan (**Downtown**). This concentration in two places can above all be attributed, next to the already described city development, to the character of the ground: in both of these areas the massive bedrock is directly at the surface of the ground and thus guarantees the secure foundation of very tall buildings.

Four Generations of Skyscrapers

Ancestry   With the invention of the skyscraper towards the end of the 19th century American architecture began to free itself from the until then dominant European influence. The skyscraper has been the symbol of American entrepreneurial spirit and optimism ever since. This development was made possible by two decisive technical innovations: **steel skeleton construction** and the improved security of the **elevator** which had been developed earlier (the New York engineer Elisha Otis proved the reliability of his new security system in 1853 at the New York World's Fair in a spectacular experiment on himself).

While the first skyscrapers needed especially thick supporting walls, with steel skeleton construction the façade was simply hung in front of the supporting steel frame like a curtain. This light and stable building method allowed buildings to be erected in heights that had never been reached before. Shortly after the turn of the century the use of steel concrete also gave new stimulus to construction. The centres of this development were the cities New York and Chicago. After the Great Fire of 1871 a building boom began in Chicago which led to a series of new buildings, among them the first skyscraper with a steel frame, built in the year 1884. Inspired by these buil-

Competition for height

Luxurious foyer of the Woolworth Building

dings the first towers began to grow into the heavens in New York as well. Yet the first New York skyscraper was imported from Chicago: in 1897 the Chicago architect Louis Sullivan built the **Bayard Building**, 65 Bleecker Street, a 12-storey steel frame with a terracotta façade. From then on the two cities entered into a competition for height that still continues today (though in the meantime the tallest buildings in the world are found in Southeast Asia).

Tendency for decoration

The architectural style of the early skyscrapers in New York is clearly different from that of the buildings in Chicago. While a modern and functional style predominated in the latter quite early on, New York buildings imitated traditional European models for a long time. A typical example of this tendency for decoration is the neo-gothic **Woolworth Building** of 1913 (Cass Gilbert) or the **Metropolitan Life Tower** (on Madison Square) of 1909, which is styled after the campanile on Saint Mark's Square in Venice. The sight of these towers may be romantic, but it should not be forgotten that there is a modern steel skeleton and building technology inside. Perhaps the most famous of the early skyscrapers is the 200m/657ft-tall **Singer Tower** built in 1908 in the Beaux-Arts style on lower Broadway, the tallest building in the world at that time. In spite of great protest it was torn down in 1970 in order to build 1 Liberty Plaza (incidentally, it is to this day the tallest building ever torn down, a task presenting considerable technical problems).

1916 Zoning Law

As early as 1916 the growing number of skyscrapers was beginning to disturb the residents of New York. The reason was the completion of the **Equitable Building** (120 Broadway, near Wall Street), which rises 39 storeys in a massive block on a small lot and completely overshadows lower Broadway. In order to preserve air and light in the streets the city fathers passed the Zoning Law, the first building regulation. From then on, newly constructed buildings had to taper off after a certain height. This model for skyscrapers made architectural history.

1920s Art Deco

In the middle of the 1920s, in the jazz period, New York discovered its love for Art Deco. During this time the elegant **Chrysler Building** (William van Alen, 1930) was built, which appears to be the embodiment of speed and energy with its shining steel tip and the gigantic waterspouts in the form of eagle heads. After its completion the 319m/1047ft Chrysler Building was for a few weeks the tallest building in the world until the title was taken by the **Empire State Building**, which was under construction at the same time. The Empire State captivates less through stylistic detail than its measurements. It stands more or less unobstructed and thus its tower dominates the Midtown skyline and is visible throughout the entire city in ever changing profiles. With its slowly receding stories from a broad base (like a wedding cake) and the slender point set onto the tower, the

Art Deco detail on the Fuller Building, built in 1929

building is the definitive New York skyscraper. The steel point was incidentally conceived as the anchor point for airships, and a small lobby for airship passengers was even provided. For reasons of safety (Hindenburg-catastrophe in Lakehurst) the installation was never used.

Further highlights of New York Art Deco are the **Waldorf Astoria Hotel** on Park Avenue or the Radio City Music Hall complex in the **Rockefeller Center**, whose foyer and hall are furnished with extravagant ornaments and the most exquisite materials. The Rockefeller Center, which was conceived in 1927, is especially significant in the development of the skyscraper, since for the first time towers are joined together instead of being built separately, forming a »city in the city«. The buildings of the central area (the last buildings of the Rockefeller were only completed toward the end of the 1960s) already point to the abandoning of the romantic skyscraper of earlier years. With its cubic forms and the relatively undecorated facades, the central **RCA** (today GE) Building, designed by Raymond Hood, already foreshadows the period of architectural rationalism.

City in the city

International Style

From the middle of the 1930s European modernism also began to gain influence in New York architecture. The exhibition initiated by Philip Johnson in 1931, *The International Style* in the Museum of Modern Art, was the first to introduce the American public to the architectural tendencies of the European avant-garde. The exhibition catalogue introduced the principles of modern architecture: »Not symmetry but order are to give clarity to the design, instead of arbitrarily applied decoration the natural elegance of the material, the technical perfection and the proportions appear«. No longer decorative inclination but **functionality** and **progress** were the new leitmotifs. In the following years many architects of the Bauhaus (among others Walter Gropius, Mies van der Rohe) and other European schools of architecture emigrated to the United States and began to work there. For many it was the first opportunity to realize their designs.

Curtain wall 1950s

The decisive technical innovation of this time was the so-called curtain wall or curtain façade, in which the stone covering of the steel skeleton structures used up to this point was replaced by a light outer skin of glass and steel. The first skyscraper in New York with a curtain wall was the **United Nations Headquarters** on the East River with its covering of green glass designed in 1950 by an international group of architects under the leadership of W. K. Harrison (based on the concept of Le Corbusier). The **Lever House** on Park Avenue, built two years later by Gordon Bunshaft (from the office of Skid more, Merrill & Owings), is clearly inspired by the UN Building. Next to the light and elegant façade the slab-shaped high-rise Lever House is an innovation primarily because of its setting. Instead of occupying the entire (very expensive) plot area the building leaves an open area on Park Avenue which is surrounded by arcades.

Only a few blocks away, an indisputable masterpiece of the late 1950s is the **Seagram Building** by Mies van der Rohe and Philip Johnson, from the year 1958. With its elegant façade of vertical bronze profiles and the glass-covered two-storey entrance hall, the beverage company Seagram's simple 38-storey tower is a classic example of Mies van der Rohe's architectural minimalism. Its location, set back from Park Avenue, allows the viewer »room to breathe«. This type of building was copied countless times in New York in the following years, but only rarely were the delicacy and elegance of the original attained.

1960s and 1970s

Inspired by the Seagram, the New York city planners decided to revise the Zoning Law of 1916. This allowed additional storeys if the constructors created **public spaces** in return. Whoever wanted to build higher had to construct a so-called plaza on his property, and it was in this way that most of the large open areas in the city came about. At the end of the 1950s the era of the skyscrapers seemed to be finished: only a few large projects were completed. In addition to economic reasons, attitudes toward the »dinosaurs« of architecture had changed. The harsh public criticism of the **Pan-Am Building** completed in 1963 (today the **MetLife Building**), in which Walter Gropius also took part, seems to exemplify the altered zeitgeist. The Pan Am Tower, which rises over Grand Central Terminal, was accused primarily of overshadowing the entire area as well as distorting the view along Park Avenue (the building is the only Manhattan high-rise on a street corner). New York had bid farewell to the boundless 1930s enthusiasm for its towers and now viewed them much more critically. Nevertheless in 1973 the largest building complex of the city to date, the **World Trade Center** with its smooth, 420m/1377ft-high twin towers, was opened. In the course of the 1970s, when the city was close to bankruptcy, construction all but stopped in Manhattan.

It was only in the **boom of the 1980s** that the climate for the building of new high rises seemed to improve. New paths of form were followed as well: Philip Johnson's **AT&T** Building (1984; today **Sony**) with its meanwhile famous Chippendale gable clearly marks the end of the simple, pragmatic »box with glass curtain façade« that had predominated in New York for decades. Other buildings from that time are the **Lipstick Building** (1985; also by Johnson) or the silver **Citicorp Tower** with its concise triangle as a concluding element (1977; both on Lexington Avenue), the Trump Tower (1983) and the **World Financial Center** in Battery Park City. The curious side

Style mix: Trump Tower behind the point of the Crown Building, with the Sony Building on the right

of the boom is the fact that many owners of lower buildings sold the air rights over their buildings to the owners of skyscrapers, in doing so accepting a shadowy existence in exchange for financial reward. In this way the Museum of Modern Art among others financed the

◄ Trade in air rights

The most famous skyline in the world with the Citycorp Tower seen from Queens. In the foreground is the monument protected Pepsi logo

building of the Museum Tower (architect: Cesar Pelli) in 1984, which is attached to the main building.

After some years of economic stagnation a boom caused in large part by the new medium of the internet began in the middle of the 1990s, giving the architectural development of New York new momentum. The markedly reduced crime rate and the increased involvement of the city fathers in the renovation of the subway as well as countless parks and squares (Bryant Park went from a notorious drug dealing site to a green oasis in a few years) provided the city with a breathtaking boom in real estate. Even the ensuing collapse in profits in the internet industry, as well as the tragic events of 11 September 2001, only temporarily weakened this development. The **Time Warner Center** on Columbus Circle (architect: S.O.M.), completed in 2004, is the most spectacular construction of the internet age. With its two angled-off glass towers, the building both continues the course of Broadway and at the same time continues the tradition of the double towers on the western edge of Central Park. Another project from this time is the 48-storey tower of the publishing house **Condé Nast** (4 Times Square; architects: Fox & Fowle) completed in 1999. The building is noteworthy above all for its energy-saving building engineering, which set new standards worldwide. The transformation of **Times Square** and **42nd Street** between Seventh and Eighth Avenues, furthered for the most part by Disney, points to Manhattan's newest large civic project: the development of the long neglected West Side between 42nd and 34th Street. So for example the *New York Times* gave up its headquarters on Times Square (which gave it its name) and moved into a

! *Baedeker* TIP

Sunset

Christopher Street Pier in the West Village (Greenwich Village) on Manhattan's West Side is an especially good place to watch the sun set. Simply follow Christopher Street to the Hudson. Two former piers, numbers 45 and 46, have been converted to parks, and their lawns, promenades and playgrounds are attractive places to spend some time.

highly modern publishing house on Eighth Avenue, corner 42nd Street (Renzo Piano in cooperation with Fox & Fowle). This tower is a further architectural development of Piano's buildings for Daimler Chrysler on Potsdam Square in Berlin.

Pushing westward

Further south the new push westward is manifest in the plans for **Penn Station**. The former main post office on Eighth Avenue is to be transformed into the new entrance to Pennsylvania Station. The main element of the entrance (architects: S.O.M.) is a fan-shaped, 40m/132ft-high glass hall. There are plans to convert Penn Station's former train yards to anything from a new stadium (originally conceived as a possible site for the Olympic Games in 2012, before London was awarded the games in the IOC vote) to a new convention centre. A further element to the renewal of the West Side is the partially fulfilled vision of a **green corridor** between Battery Park in the south and Riverside Park in the north: new piers have been made out of the harbours and docks opposite Greenwich Village, which with their lawns and playgrounds give stressed New Yorkers an opportunity to relax.

◄ Christopher Street Pier

New World Trade Center

The **Financial District**, hit especially hard by the attacks of 11 September 2001, is turning the tragic event into a chance to solve some structural problems that already existed before 2001. The new buildings at Ground Zero and the new transportation terminal, which will improve the connections between various subway routes (architect: Santiago Calatrava), will contribute to making the formerly purely business district into an residential area of apartments and cultural facilities. The new buildings at **Ground Zero** will be constructed according to the architect Daniel Libeskind's master plan. The main elements are the five high rises set in a crescent open towards the west, which increase in height from south to north. The building furthest to the north, the 541m/1776ft-high (a reference to the year of American independence) Freedom Tower (architect: Daniel Libeskind with David Childs of S.O.M.) will be the tallest building in the world when it is completed in 2009. However only half of the height will be usable for a building; the top will be an open steel construction with integrated wind turbines. The remaining towers of the new WTC will be designed by various architects in order to lend variety to the overall impression. In the centre of the new complex the new **National September 11 Memorial & Museum** (architect: Michael Arad) will be embedded in a park: two lowered pools will be shaped in the form of the two former Twin Towers.

Preservation of Historical Monuments

In 1963 the Pennsylvania Railroad Company had its train station, a masterpiece by McKim, Mead White, torn down. The broad public outrage led to the Landmark Preservation Act of 1965, in which 900 buildings and 55 so-called historical districts with 18,000 houses were placed under preservation orders.

The Landmarks Preservation Commission, which has been founded in the meantime, keeps strict watch over New York's architectural heritage. Thus the historic **Grand Central Terminal** can be admired in its original state since the detailed renovation was completed in 1998. With its many shops and restaurants the train station now functions both as a hub of transportation and a shopping mall in historical garb. But not only is the architecture of the turn of the century being preserved; buildings of the modern age, the 1950s and 1960s, which for a long time had gone unnoticed, are also being placed under protection, now considered to be of historical value at the beginning of the 21st century.

New York – City of Culture

With two opera houses, around 250 theatres, several orchestras, ballet and dance companies, more than 150 museums and 400 art galleries, cinemas, universities and colleges, New York is the **cultural centre of the USA**. Most of the US publishing houses are here and the publishers of almost all large US periodicals. Alongside the public library, incidentally the second largest library in the USA, there are many smaller libraries for every field of interest. More than 50 cable programmes provide television for New Yorkers.

There are about 130 **universities**, schools of higher learning and **colleges** with around 300,000 students. The oldest and perhaps best known is Columbia University, founded in 1754 as King's College, and the largest is New York University with more than 40,000 students, which was founded more than 150 years ago.

Music and Theatre in New York

New York's music and theatrical life with its opera houses, theatres, concert halls and jazz bars takes the indisputable lead in the USA and is an important economic factor: behind the scenes is the machinery of organizations, unions, agents, producers and an industry that meets the stage's every need. The aforementioned 250 **theatres** are divided into the 40 established Broadway theatres north of Times Square (between 40th and 50th Streets) and the remaining playhouses, the so-called Off-Broadway and Off-Off-Broadway theatres, of which most have settled in Greenwich Village or Chelsea. There are around 600 premieres every season.

Spoilt for choice here, too: musicals

NEW YORK – CITY OF CINEMA

Could it be that you fully expect to come across a rampaging gorilla or a screaming lady in white on the Empire State Building? If you have to describe the view from a skyscraper on Manhattan, do you imagine that you're on top of the Chrysler Building with its stainless steel waterspouts? Do you imagine your taxi being driven by Robert de Niro, and is the quintessence of Manhattan for you the black and white Queensboro Bridge in the fog? Do you think of the Marilyn Monroe's blowing white chiffon dress when you walk over the grating of subway shafts, and does the name Tiffany's remind you not of lamps but of Audrey Hepburn's almond eyes?

If the answer to these questions is yes, then you are like all cinema lovers: New York lives in your mind predominantly through cinema images burned into the brain. Not only the most famous movies like *King Kong*, *The Bonfire of the Vanities*, *Taxi Driver*, *Manhattan*, *The Seven-Year Itch* and *Breakfast at Tiffany's*, but also countless other movies that take place in New York have left a lasting impression on their audiences. At any moment a feeling of déjà vu might come over you on the streets of New York. At www.newyorkinthemovies.com you can find out why.

A Setting in Demand

With more than **40,000 approved locations** New York is the most sought-after cinema setting in the world. More than 1,500 films play in the Big Apple, most of them in the streets of Manhattan. In the meantime

Scene from the film »King Kong« from the year 1930

it has become common to film the location shots in New York and the rest of the scenes in the studio in Hollywood. It was all rather different when the nickelodeon was still young. In April 1896, a few months after cinema history had begun with the Lumière brothers' presentation in the Grand Café in Paris, **the first film was shown** on the American continent in Koster and Bial's Music Hall in New York. New York remained the centre of the American film industry until the First World War. Soon the producers – with Thomas A. Edison leading the way – tried to control the quickly growing market: they founded a trust in 1908, the Motion Picture Patents Company, that did everything to secure a monopoly. Although even mafia tactics could not get the better of independents in the cinema industry – among them Charlie Chaplin, Douglas Fairbanks, William Fox, Samuel Goldwyn, Carl Laemmle and

Mary Pickford – the future studio bosses chose to move their places of work to the quieter and sunny California, where they found ideal production conditions. New York's commercial film scene dwindled.

Independent Movies

Away from the mainstream along the Hudson River however, one of the most important centres of **underground films** developed. What today is known as ethnic film became established as early as the 1920s: Jewish films came from the Lower East Side and Harlem became the centre of black cinema. After 1945 New York moved on to be the international **capital of avant-garde cinema**. The New York school of filmmakers fea-tures names like Maya Deren, Jonas Mekas, Michael Snow, Robert Crumb with Fritz the Cat and of course **Andy Warhol**, who dedicated one of his static 24-hour films to the

In »West Side Story« two youth gangs, the Jets and the Sharks, fight for power in the streets

Empire State Building. Since 1955, the New York periodical *Film Culture* has accompanied the various movements of independent film. Representative of the intellectual role that New York plays in the film industry is the fact that the **Museum of Modern Art** began to build a collection of films in the early 1940s, a collection which contains more than 22,000 films today.

Hollywood Musicals

If films were produced in New York after 1920 then it had something to do with the inexhaustible dramatic potential of **Broadway**. Moreover, Hollywood's producers were fascinated by the success and the aesthetics of the extravagantly staged musicals. A new film genre was born: the Hollywood musical. And – how could it be any different – some of the best took place in New York. In *42nd Street* (1933) Busby Berkeley made Manhattan's skyline dance. *On the Town* in 1949 – three sailors on shore-leave in town – conveyed the euphoric post-war mood and was also the first Hollywood musical which was not filmed only in a studio but also on location in New York. *West Side Story* turned attention to the backyards of Manhattan in 1960, and in 1977 *Hair* showed that flower power didn't just exist in San Francisco.

Indeed, the declarations of love to New York just don't stop flickering across the screen: they existed as early as 1928 when Josef von Sternberg, in the exquisitely shot silent film *The Docks of New York*, immersed the dark harbour scenery into soft, transfiguring light. They lie in the small everyday gestures, when every morning Harvey Keitel in *Smoke* (1994) steps in front of his tobacco shop in Brooklyn and photographs the opposite street corner. Spike Lee's *Do the Right Thing* (1988) is another declara-

tion of love, in which he makes the atmosphere of a humid summer day in black Brooklyn so thick that you can smell the pizza, tap your foot to the rap and feel the brooding heat, romantic as the city he loved. Behind his black rimmed glasses was the coiled sexual power of a jungle cat… New York was his town, and it always would be«.

> »*Behind his black rimmed glasses was the coiled sexual power of a jungle cat… New York was his town, and it always would be.*«

and – like the kids in the film enjoy – the cool water when the fire hydrant is opened. They are full of poetry like the brilliant opening scene in Woody Allen's *Manhattan*: set against breathtaking black-and-white pictures of New York, with Gershwin's *Rhapsody in Blue* in the background, a New Yorker offscreen tries to formulate his relationship to his city. He hovers between kitsch, pathos and irony: »Chapter One: He was as tough and

Recently the producer Martin Scorsese, with his powerful and violent historical epic film *Gangs of New York* (2002), illustrated how in the middle of the 18th century the development of the city was also shaped by violence and crime.

The **American Museum of the Moving Image** in Brooklyn, the first ever American museum of film, has information on the history of American cinema.

Drama The theatre tradition goes back to the time when New York was slowly growing to be one of the largest cities in North America. In the first half of the 18th century only amateur groups played in temporary buildings. In 1750 the first professional performance took place, of Shakespeare's *Richard III* in the New Theatre in Nassau Street. At the beginning of the 19th century a popularization began, which finds its culmination in today's perfectly marketed mainstream musicals. 200 years ago **melodramas**, **variety shows**, **Vaudeville shows** and **acts from fairs** dominated the stages. When the wave of immigrants increased at the end of the 19th century, the **theatre** offered the immigrants an ideal home: thus Jewish theatre and Irish **musicals** were established. In the years after the First World War the dramas were about the unique

> **? DID YOU KNOW …?**
>
> ■ In New York there are about 40 Broadway, 20 Off-Broadway and over 200 Off-Off-Broadway theatres. While on Broadway between 41st and 53rd Street the long-running successes (especially musicals) are on the bill, the more unusual productions are at home Off-Broadway, and the completely experimental pieces in the Off-Off-Broadway theatres. But boundaries are flexible: the one or other successful Off-Broadway play has already made the jump from one of the theatres in Midtown or the Village to Broadway.

ethnic variety in New York. After the years of war, which were marked by patriotic restorative tendencies, new avant-garde streams could only prevail again in the 1950s and 1960s. Acting societies, among them the »Living Theatre«, took to the streets with their pieces, making political theatre and creating the world of **Off-Broadway**. Soon, in the 1960s, more experimental stages formed, the so-called **Off-Off-Broadway**, which presented completely new forms of theatre: performances, happenings and improvisations.

Musicals Nowadays, the musical predominates on Broadway: after all, the form was born here. Elements of variety shows and melodrama, minstrel shows, ballad opera and borrowings from America's own music, ragtime and jazz, have all contributed to this glamorous form of musical theatre. The **first real musical** was *The Black Crook* (1866). Shining with spectacular effects, the mixture of song, dance and entertainment was performed 475 times in a row. The boom on Broadway made the city on the Hudson River the music and theatre centre of the United States. The real success only came in the 1930s, when underscoring was introduced and more modern music such as jazz entered into the productions. The scores were made simpler, the texts more meaningful and dance became a regular part of the narrated story. After the Second World War the musical scene boomed: many musicals whose melodies we still hear today were box office successes in the 1940s and 1950s, among them *Annie Get Your Gun* (1946), *Kiss me Kate* (1948), *Guys and Dolls* (1950) and *My Fair Lady* (1956), which broke all records. Finally the critical and meaningful musical found its place on Broadway: *West Side Story* opened at the

Winter Garden Theatre in 1957, in which Leonard Bernstein carried the story of Romeo and Juliet over to the world of the Puerto Ricans in New York.

Presently significantly more musicals than dramas are being performed in Broadway theatres. 33 of the theatres belong to three men, the so-called landlords, who make all decisions and collect all profits in their theatres. The producer of the show is actually just a tenant. Broadway musicals like *Cats*, *Phantom of the Opera*, *Miss Saigon*, *The Lion King* or *42nd Street* suffer from their immense technical and financial complexity and radiate an almost sterile perfection. Moreover they can also be seen on musical stages in London, Toronto or Sydney. Insiders say that only two of every ten shows make a profit. The actual profit is made on tours through the USA and in royalties – including the soundtracks and film rights.

Musical scene from »The Lion King«

Those who would rather indulge in the pleasures of a **concert** are spoilt for choice in this city. Concert halls like Carnegie Hall, where the crème de la crème of classical music meets, or Radio City Music Hall – here lighter tastes are satisfied – and of course Lincoln Center with Avery Fisher Hall, the home of the New York Philharmonic Orchestra, are all near Broadway, north of 50th Street.

New York had the first permanent symphony orchestra in the USA, the Philharmonic Society founded in 1842. But not only the large orchestra is promoted here – anything goes: choir concerts, gospel music, chamber music, every kind of avant-garde music and a rich selection for children and young people, a tradition in which Leonard Bernstein, long time conductor of the New York Philharmonic Orchestra, with his »Young People's Concerts«, played a pivotal role.

The glittering highlight of classical music is the opera. Performed at **Opera** many locations in New York, above all it has the most significant stage in the New World at its disposal: the Met. When the opera

!   *Baedeker* TIP

Open Rehearsals
Most of the New York Philharmonic Orchestra's rehearsals are open to the public. They generally start at 9.45am and last until about 12.30pm; times and programme are available on tel. 212-875-5656 or at www.nyphilharmonic.org.

house befitting their social class, the Academy of Music, became too small for the wealthy families of John Pierpont Morgan and William H. Vanderbilt, they remedied the situation as only the rich can: by having the Metropolitan Opera House built – with enough boxes – on 40th Street in 1883. In 1966 the Met moved to the new Lincoln Center. The Met has no real competition in the city but there are numerous ensembles that offer unusual programmes, of which the New York City Opera (also in Lincoln Center) has managed to establish itself.

Ballet   In the 20th century New York also became a metropolis of ballet. Isadora Duncan, Ruth Saint Denis and Martha Graham developed expressive dance into its American form, modern dance. Later innovators in ballet were George Balanchine, who in 1934 founded the School of American Ballet – which later developed into the New York City Ballet (Lincoln Center) – and Merce Cunningham. He and his ensemble worked closely with contemporary composers and painters from 1952. There is also a broad scene of ethnic dance, in which dancing styles from all over the world are represented.

Jazz   The USA's real autonomous contribution to musical history is jazz, an art form which developed out of the tension between oppression, pressure to assimilate and self-awareness: the music of African Americans. Even though jazz had its first strongholds in New Orleans and Chicago, New York quickly became the focal point at the beginning of the 20th century, and the first jazz phonograph record was produced here in 1917. However it took another 20 years for the music to become successful in its pure form. Until then jazz was either reviled as »negro music«, abused as dance music or treated as a curiosity in minstrel shows, in which white people with blackened faces played supposedly black music for exclusively white audiences.

Jazz finally became an avant-garde art form in the 1940s: in New York, jazz saxophonist Charlie Parker and trumpeter Dizzy Gillespie created the nervous and technically brilliant bebop, making the city the world's jazz capital. The various styles existed alongside each other; even New Orleans jazz was dusted off again. In one single street, 52nd Street, also called Swing Street or simply »the Street«, one could find a bar for every variety of jazz. At the end of the decade the trumpeter Miles Davis transformed bebop to what he called cool jazz. Even though it was first developed in New York and studio recordings made here, this new direction was less important for the city. The cool jazz scene moved to the West Coast; in 1959 the jazz saxophonist Ornette Coleman came from there and brought free jazz

Dee Dee Bridgewater in the legendary Blue Note in Greenwich Village, said to be »the world's finest jazz club«

to New York. In the legendary **Village Vanguard**, a lively venue in Greenwich Village that still exists today, he and John Coltrane became the stars of the scene. Jazz became accepted by the establishment when in 1991 the Lincoln Center opened a separate department within the performing arts. Since 2004, jazz events have been taking place at Jazz at Lincoln Center, a venue designed especially for the purpose. Meanwhile hip hop, born in the ghettos of the Bronx, has become one of the important means of musical expression for African Americans. The DJs Grandmaster Flash, Kool Herc and Africa Bambaataa mixed records in the middle of the 1970s and moved them back and forth by hand on the turntable, a method known as »scratching«. Their raps or rhymes were as rhythmic as possible: spoonerisms, lyrics from former slave camps and prisons, later also verses about sex and violence. The background of these new sounds were the gang wars in the ghettos that were supposedly playfully enacted in song form – instead of with weapons. It was at the beginning of the 1980s when *Rapper's Delight* from the Sugarhill Gang initiated the worldwide debut of hip hop.

Art in New York

America, and Europe's fascination with it, was long defined by clichés in which the country's cultural efforts were of little importance. American fine arts tried to gain their independence from 1900 on, but attained this goal only after 1945 with **abstract expressionism**, an art movement that not only did away with the European influenced concept of a picture, but also took the leading role in artistic events in the Western world with New York as the centre. This autonomous development in art looks back on a long process of assimilating European influences. At the same time the interaction remained between progressive and conservative tendencies, the repression of the art and culture of North American Indians, the devaluation of the so-called secondary culture of the African Americans and the preference for the European-dominated art created by white artists.

With about 150 **museums**, some among the best in the world, such as the Metropolitan Museum, the Museum of Modern Art, the Guggenheim, the Frick Collection, the Brooklyn Museum and the American Museum of Natural History, as well as more than 400 art galleries and cultural institutes of European, Asian and African countries, New York is today one of the most important – if not the most important – **art centres of the Western world**.

From the Beginning to the End of the 19th Century

17th and 18th centuries
In the 17th century, mostly anonymous **folk art** was produced, whose character is often determined by a certain world view (for example Quaker) and is more rational and functional. In the 18th century artists in New York, as in other American cities, earned their living by painting **portraits** of wealthy citizens. As in English painting of the time the person portrayed was depicted in front of a landscape background. Along with artists living in New York, John Singleton Copley, who lived and painted here for a short time, is worthy of note as well as Charles Wilson Peale and Gilbert Stuart in the time after the Civil War, who both represented a romantic realism. Just like J. S. Copley, Benjamin West, who played a significant role in the emergence of the American history painting, went to Europe; he was successful in England and became the successor to J. Reynolds as president of the Royal Academy. After returning from France, John Vanderlyn settled in New York and with *Ariadne* created the first nude painting in America, which promptly provoked the resistance of the Puritans.

19th century
The invention of daguerreotype in around 1839 meant that portrait painting receded into the background in favour of animal and still life painting. Some New York painters (N. G. Wall, N. Calyo, among

others) used **cityscapes** as motifs. The conquest of the country and the expansion to the west and south-west led to a stronger interest in **landscapes**. In the dramatically growing city, bankers, businessmen and railway directors promoted painters of the **Hudson River School**, for example Thomas Cole, Frederic E. Church and Th. W. Whittredge; other Romantic landscape painters were Albert Bierstadt who took part in expeditions westward, George Catlin, a painter of Native American life, and G. C. Bingham. In part – as with Bingham – **landscape and genre painting** pervade their work, whereby the genre was able to succeed as a form of its own from 1850 and artists who learned in London, Paris and Düsseldorf, such as J. G. Brown and Eastman Johnson, were able to combine European technique with American subjects. Thus Winslow Homer, whose pictures with their realistic painting of light are a high-point of the second half of the 19th century, found his subjects in the events of the Civil War. The painters George Inness and Morris Hunt, through contact with Corot and the Barbizon School, became important guides on the way from Romanticism to Realism and along with Thomas Eakins prepared the way for Pleinairism. However the realistic landscape and moralizing genre painting contradicted Impressionism, which had been imported from France, and the attitude of »art for art's sake« that accompanied it. To promote the new movements **Impressionism** and **Symbolism** the Society of American Artists was founded, which organized exhibitions with William Meritt Chase, Julian Alden Weir and John Singer Sargent among others.

! Baedeker TIP

Guide to Art
The Metropolitan Museum of Art is a universal museum which spans a broad range of works from the beginnings of art until the present. The Guggenheim also shows modern art in its spiral building, but it cannot compete with the collection of the world famous MoMA. The Whitney has committed itself completely to American art, while the Frick Collection is a phenomenal collection of old masters.

Other branches of the arts began to emerge: free and applied **graphics** became an important factor, and the **Arts and Crafts Initiative**, based on the English model, reformed artistic craftsmanship – above all in the production of glass and metal (L. C. **Tiffany**). Three main streams could be distinguished in the arts at the end of 19th century: the Romantic with Rader and R. Blakelock, the Impressionist with Chase and Childe Hassam, the academic-neo-classicist with Blashfield and Cox.

20th Century

The basis for **American Realism** as the counterpoint to Impressionism and academic art was created by the group **The Eight** in New York under the leadership of Robert Henri – also called the Ashcan School by opponents – whose members exhibited in 1908 in the

Macbeth Gallery. George Luks, William James Glackens, John Sloan, Everett Shinn, Arthur B. Davies, Ernest Lawson and Maurice Brazil Prendergast chose as their subjects the lives of simple people and the depiction of American urban life, while George Bellows produced socio-critical milieu studies and anti-militaristic pictures. Superficial, flattering and idealized forms are alien to them.

The legendary **Armory Show**, with over 1,500 works of art, was held in 1913 in New York in order to bring modern art to North America. One third of the exhibits, among them pictures by Cézanne, Braque, Picasso, Matisse, Léger, Kandinsky and Duchamp, were of European origin and belonged to the avant-garde. But the Cubism, Constructivism and Dadaism movements of the 1920s were, despite vehement discussion, without great effect; even though »New York Dada« with Francis Picabia, Man Ray and Marcel Duchamp built the foundation for developments in art after 1945. Some painters carried orphean, futuristic tendencies further (for example Joseph Stella), others processed cubistic influences (Arthur Dove, Max Weber) or carried them out in a precisionist style that showed clear lines and reduced forms (Charles Demuth, Charles Sheeler, Niles Spencer).

1930s In the 1930s the effort to suppress European avant-garde influences and to create **American painting** led to a retrospective of traditional themes and forms, and to the school of the Regionalists Grant Wood, Charles Burchfield and Thomas Hart Benton. The realistic style of painting showed other variations as well: while Edward Hopper represented a completely unique, modern style of **new concreteness**, painters like Milton Avery, by withdrawing into a personal world, found their way to a **connection between realism and mysticism**. By contrast the Depression caused by »Black Friday« caused many artists in New York to become politically active. They organized themselves in the John Reed Club, published the *Art Front* and demanded **art by the people and for the people** with revolutionary zeal.

Aaron Douglas and Charles Alston painted murals that combined African or African American ideas with modern techniques; Jacob Lawrence took his motifs from African American history. The New York sculptress Gertrude Vanderbilt Whitney promoted artists and gave them important opportunities to exhibit, eventually in 1930 founding the **Whitney Museum of American Art**.

WPA and foreign influences During the worldwide Depression a programme was created for artists (WPA, Work Progress Administration). The work they carried out on public buildings was influenced by the murals of the Mexican artists José Clemente Orozco and Diego Rivera who lived in New York. Many artists who took part in the WPA project were European emigrants – Willem de Kooning from Holland, Arshile Gorky from Armenia, Mark Rothko from Russia, Hans Hofmann and Josef Hofmann, Lyonel Feininger from Germany, Piet Mondrian – and they brought the ideas of Bauhaus, Picasso and Surrealism to America.

Jackson Pollock, master of the legendary »dripping« technique

Abstract art

Since the Museum of Modern Art's exhibitions in the 1930s and 1940s of abstract, cubist and surrealist art simply passed over American abstracts, it organized itself in the group American Abstract Artists, which declined in importance with the breakthrough of Abstract Expressionism. At the beginning of the 1940s the **surrealist movement** in New York was strengthened by the immigrant artists André Breton, Yves Tanguy, André Masson and Max Ernst as well by the exhibits of the gallery owner Peggy Guggenheim, who was married to Ernst. At about the same time in New York and Paris, around 1946/47, a style of painting developed called **l'art informel** or Tachism, which rejected geometric abstraction and promoted the total freedom of colour and form. The automatism of the surrealists – in America represented especially by Matta and Arshile Gorky – served as the source and the abstract-expressive style of Wassily Kandinsky. In contrast to Europe, **Action Painting** was predominant in the USA. Prominent representatives of the New York school of Abstract Expressionism were Jackson Pollock and Willem de Kooning, along with Arshile Gorky, Franz Kline, Robert Motherwell, Sam Francis and Cliffort Still. **Jackson Pollock** played the leading role as the master of the legendary »dripping«, the unconventional drop technique in which the artist apparently drips the runny colour on the canvas at random. A reaction to the emotionally charged Abstract Expressionism are the works of the painters who use »colour as colour«. Here, with the artists of the so-called **Colour Field Painting** and **Hard Edge** (simple geometric figures with clearly limited colour zones), the pure, homogenously used colour can either become a space for meditation (Mark Rothko, Barnett Newman, Ad Reinhardt) or be used as an unemotional rational structure (Frank Stella, Kenneth Noland, Ellsworth Kelly, Jules Olitsky). A lyrical variation is represented by Helen Frankenthaler. This painting finds its equivalent in three dimensions in **Minimal Art**, in the geometric, sober sculptures – often lined up next to each other – of Carl André, Donald Judd, or Sol LeWitt of the 1960s.

New Realists The contraposition to abstract art grew into a new interest in depicting reality as with the New Realists like Robert Rauschenberg and Jasper Johns, who anticipated the later Pop Art. The methods of acquiring reality in readymade and objet trouvé, which had been developed from Dadaism, led to the forms of expression called combined painting, environment – represented by George Segal and Edward Kienholz – and object art; the Dadaist action and the action charged painting of Abstract Expressionism led to a new form of art, **Action Art** in the forms Happening (Alan Kaprow), Fluxus (George Macunias) and Performance.

Pop Art In the mid-1950s in England and in the USA, Pop Art, which had urban culture, consumerism and mass media as its subjects, was taken up in New York by Richard Lindner, James Rosenquist, Roy Lichtenstein and Andy Warhol. The goal of the **photorealists** (for example Richard Estes) was to make people conscious of reality as a consequence of perception processes; as with pictures a corresponding over-sharpness can also be seen in the hyperrealistic sculptures of Duane Hanson. The realistic tendencies were continued in the work of Alex Kath and Janet Fish.

Present Growing wealth encouraged the formation of a market for contemporary art; in New York hundreds of galleries sprouted like mushrooms, and the city became the centre of the art trade. But the huge boom in art and the desire of the artists for their own programme created a split into many styles. More than ever before, gallerists and the market influenced aesthetic reception. That led to analyzing forms of art at the end of the 1960s, which left gesture and its effect completely to the material, in which the creative act or the idea gained more attention than the work of art. These include, along with the already mentioned Minimal Art, the **Land Art** of Walter de Maria, whose objects in remote areas can for the most part only be conveyed by the media, and **Conceptual Art**. This advocates »art in the head«, which will no longer be realized or which deals with everyday experiences. Conceptual tendencies are evident in the work of Lawrence Weiner, James Lee Byars, Jeff Koons, Joseph Kosuth, who uses art as a method of perception, Jenny Holzer, whose medium is language, and the process-oriented artists Eva Hesse and Don Graham. In three dimensions, Richard Serra represents a post-minimalist direction, John Chamberlain's objects work like painting that has been frozen in metal, and Dan Flavin's light installations – neon tubes which make the space perceivable as a space – are concrete minimalism.

The answer to the reserved Minimal Art followed with massive vehemence and emotional energy with the **neoexpressionists** Susan Rothenberg, Julian Schnabel and Jean Michel Basquiat, the latter being close to the graffiti art of Keith Haring.

The high value placed on **photo art** in New York is in the tradition of Alfred Stieglitz: in this context, Cindy Sherman and Robert Mapplethorpe should be mentioned, as well as the expansion to video art by Dan Graham and Gay Hill, while Action Art finds its echo with J. L. Byars and David Hammons. Within this pluralism of style Miriam Shapiro represented »Pattern and Decoration«, Nancy Spero and her husband Leon Golub took a socio-critical direction.

With the arrival of post-modern culture in the 1980s, in the time of the **Trans-Avant-Garde** with artists like Jonathan Borofsky, Jeff Koons, Haim Steinbach and Robert Longo among others, a decentralization of the art trade appears. Increased mobility and improved communication make it easier for Europe to connect again and to become an equal partner in the art scene.

Robert Longo and his wife Barbara Sukowa in his studio

Famous People

What links John Jacob Astor, one of America's first entrepreneurs, with Martha Graham, the main representative of American Modern Dance? Here are a few monuments in miniature to some well known – and some lesser known – personalities who have influenced New York's reputation or who are connected with the city.

Woody Allen (born 1.12.1935)

There are neurotics in every city, but New York boasts the most famous neurotic of all: Woody Allen, producer and actor, whose films are almost all declarations of love to his home town on the Hudson River.

Woody Allen was born Allen Stewart Konigsberg on 1 December 1935 in the New York borough Brooklyn. He earned his first wage as a joke writer for newspapers under the pseudonym Woody Allen, and then wrote gags for American films and television shows, eventually working in cabarets and nightclubs as an entertainer from 1961 on. In 1965 he had his first contact with films, as author of and actor in the comedy *What's New, Pussycat?*. At the latest since his film *Annie Hall* (1977), for which he received three Oscars, Allen has been regarded as the most

Producer, actor and clarinet player: Woody Allen

important comedian of more recent American film, and is an idol of intellectual cinema audiences throughout the world. In further works like *Manhattan* (1978), *Hannah and Her Sisters* (1986) and *Mighty Aphrodite* (1995) he elected to expound on his city and on the lives of the better-off, often neurotic, bizarre New Yorkers – but never on the social problems of this giant.

Woody Allen lives on Fifth Avenue, in fact on the mundane Upper East Side. He plays clarinet almost every Monday in the Carlyle (about $100 admission, 35 East 76th Street, tel. 212-744-1600).

John Jacob Astor (1763–1848)

John Jacob Astor, originally from Walldorf near Heidelberg in Germany, was one of the first great American entrepreneurial personalities. He came to New York at the age of 20 and was initially a dealer in musical instruments, but later traded the instruments for furs. In the year 1809 he started the American Fur Company, which was followed by two other fur companies in the following years, resulting

Entrepreneur

← *The dancer and choreographer Martha Graham as Judith, 1957*

in a near monopoly in the USA. The greatest part of his enormous wealth however came from real estate speculation, in which he bought countless plots of land, above all in Manhattan. When he died his estate was estimated at 25 million dollars, making him the richest man in America. Shortly before his death he founded the Astor Library in New York with a donation of 400,000 dollars, the first public library in America.

George Gershwin (1898–1937)

Composer

George Gershwin was born Jacob Gershowitz on 26 September 1898 in Brooklyn, New York. The son of Russian-Jewish immigrants, he grew up with two brothers, Arthur and Ira, and a sister, Francis, on Manhattan's Lower East Side. It was in fact Ira who first wanted to study piano, but the young George took to the instrument immediately and began to play by ear, so his parents arranged lessons for him from the age of twelve.

By the time he was fifteen, George was already setting out on a professional career in his first job as a pianist in Tin Pan Alley, the legendary 28th Street, home to New York's music publishers. Aspiring composers and songwriters would present new songs here in the hope of selling their tunes, and Gershwin, apparently able to identify what made a song successful, soon began composing himself. In 1919, at the age of 20, he wrote *La, La, Lucille*, his first complete Broadway musical. The following year, his song *Swanee* was a huge success for Al Jolson, and after that came a string of hits, usually with his brother Ira as lyricist.

Gershwin was also a successful composer of music for the concert hall, in 1924 premiering *Rhapsody in Blue*. It is said that the piece was composed in three weeks, George having forgotten all about his promise to bandleader Paul Whiteman to write it until he read an advertisement in the press announcing an exciting new Gershwin composition. It became his most famous work. There followed *An American in Paris*, written in part on a trip to Europe, and the opera *Porgy and Bess* (1935), which centred on the lives and loves of the poor African American people of South Carolina. Though today the most successful opera ever written by an American, it only became a success after Gershwin's death in 1937 at the age of thirty-eight.

Martha Graham (1894–1991)

Dancer and choreographer

Martha Graham, who came from a doctor's family in Allegheny, Pennsylvania, is regarded as the leading figure of American Modern Dance. She grew up in Santa Barbara, California and was one of the early members of Denishawn, Ruth St. Denis' and Ted Shawn's school, which in Los Angeles was to play an important role in the development of modern American dance. At the age of 22 she made her debut in New York with her first solo programme; in 1917 she had already opened her own school, to this day internationally re-garded as one of the most renowned establishments in its field. Martha Graham had a career as a dancer as well as choreographer and teacher. As almost no other teacher of dance in the 20th century she succeeded in developing a strictly codified system of teaching for non-classical dance, whose special technique rested on the contrast between tensing and relaxing the body. Her film *A Dancer's World* presents an impressive picture of her dance aesthetics.

Alexander Hamilton (1757–1804)

Founding Father

A close confidant of Goerge Washington, Alexander Hamilton advocated the federal government assumption of debts accumulated during the War of Independence. As the first secretary of the treasury of the United States (1789–1793) he set important economic impulses by founding the Bank of New York and by playing a significant role in the establishment of the New York Stock Exchange. He was a major contributor to the constitution of the United States. It was mainly thanks to him that New York City was voted to be the first United States capital. His portrait is on the US ten dollar bank note.

Edward Hopper (1882–1967)

Painter

The career of the painter and graphic artist Edward Hopper, who for decades had a studio on Washington Square in New York, started slowly. Hopper depended on his work as an illustrator to earn his living until the 1920s. The influence of his work on American art or on the formation of the nation's artistic identity was considered to be groundbreaking. He observed his environment as no other artist, creating paintings of the life of the city, its streets, its people and their isolation. His estate contained more than 2,000 oil paintings, aquarelles, drawings and graphics for the **Whitney Museum of American Art**, which held the first exhaustive retrospective in 1980.

Archer Huntington (1870–1955)

Museum founder

The adopted son of the railway magnate Collis P. Huntington, born in New York, wanted to found a museum when he was only twelve years old: specifically a miniature Spain in North America. He pursued this goal with enthusiasm and devotion. In 1904 he founded the Hispanic Society of America, whose aim was to disseminate and study Iberian language and culture. Four years later the society – half museum, half library – began its work. One of the most spectacular successes was the discovery of the »painter of light« from Valencia, Joaquín Sorolla Y Bastida (1863–1923), by whom the Hispanic Society has a large number of paintings. In addition works by Velázques, El Greco, Goya, Rivera, Murillo and modern Spanish painters as well as archaeological finds, gold objects and Islamic art can be seen.

Louise Nevelson (1899–1988)

Artist   Alongside Georgia O'Keeffe, Louise Nevelson was one of the grand dames of American art. Born in Kiev, she came to New York at the

age of six with her parents, where she studied art, religious studies and philosophy from 1929 until 1931. After studying for a while in Munich with the painter Hans Hofmann she became the assistant of Diego Rivera in Mexico City from 1932 to 1938. She found her own artistic expression in the 1950s with her wood sculptures, which she created from wooden objects, table legs, off-cuts and driftwood and painted mono-chrome black, white or gold. Her mysterious, totem-like, even threa-tening shrines and altars, often lar-ger than life, soon gained her entry into the most important museums in the world. The high point of Louise Nevelson's career was three rooms which she conceived for the American pavilion in the Biennale

Louise Nevelson

in 1962 and her work for the Documenta in Kassel, Germany in 1964. Her works decorate countless squares and buildings in New York and all over America.

Adolph S. Ochs (1858–1935)

Publisher   The newspaper publisher Adolph S. Ochs was born in Knoxville, Tennessee, the son of a German-Jewish immigrant. He began his career at the age of eleven as a newspaper boy in his home town and was an apprentice typesetter until 1875. He then went to Chattanooga, Tennessee, where three years later, at the age of 20, he bought the *Times* newspaper and in four years transformed it into a generally respected newspaper. He landed his greatest coup in 1896, when he bought the *New York Times* for 75,000 dollars. The paper had been founded 45 years earlier and had survived only with difficulty amongst the bitter competition of the New York press, but by the time of his retirement in 1993 Ochs had made it the most important newspaper in America, with its motto: »All the news that's fit to print«.

The newspaper, which has since grown into a corporation with publishing house, paper factory, periodicals, radio and television stations, is now a stock corporation, but is still run by Adolph S.

Ochs' heirs: the present publisher, who took over in January 1992, is Arthur Ochs Sulzberger jr., a great grandson of Adolph S. Ochs.

Cornelius Vanderbilt (1794–1877)

Entrepreneur

At only twelve years old, Vanderbilt would help his father to ferry passengers and baggage from Staten Island to New York. Four years later he had his own boat, after eight years he became the executive of a steamship line, and after another ten years he founded his own steamship line, with which he brought gold diggers to California via Nicaragua in 1849. He eventually entered into transatlantic traffic, but when the competition of the British and German lines became too strong he changed to railway lines. In 1863 he bought his first railway company, the New York and Harlem Railway; others were added. When Vanderbilt died, the »Commodore«, as he was called, left a fortune of 105 million dollars, an inconceivable sum for his time. His son William Henry expanded the empire within eight years to 50 railway lines with 25,000km/15,530mi of track. The Vanderbilts were the richest family in the USA. For some, Cornelius Vanderbilt is the definitive American self-made man; for others he is a monstrosity of capitalism, who gained his wealth through deception, exploitation, bribery and merciless competition – though it is said his competitors were no different.

Andy Warhol (1928–1987)

Artist

Probably the most famous representative of Pop Art was actually called Andrew Warhola and was originally a graphic artist. At the beginning of the 1960s he painted his first pictures, and then turned more and more to screen printing, with which he reproduced photographs from mass media and printed them in series. As motifs he chose everyday items like dollar bills or soup cans (*200 Campbell's Soup Cans*) and mass idols like Elvis Presley, Elizabeth Taylor or Marilyn Monroe (*Marilyn Diptych*). The goal of his artistic work was the radical integration of art in the mechanical work process. From 1963 he turned to film (*Sleep*, *Blue Movie*, *Flesh*); only in the 1970s did he again produce prints (*Willy Brandt*). He created his works in a collective with the members of his living and working group, the »Factory«. With increasing fame Warhol himself became an idol and object of his own art. As well as possessing incontestable artistic talent, Warhol had a great ability to market himself; his concept of art extended so far that he declared the large number of objects and antiques that he acquired to have become part of his own existence through his act of purchasing them, and argued that they could thus themselves be viewed as art.

Practicalities

HOW DO YOU GET FROM THE AIRPORT INTO
TOWN? WHICH SUBWAY GOES TO
BROOKLYN? WHERE DO YOU BUY
TICKETS TO MUSICALS OR A GOOD
JAZZ CONCERT? LOOK IT UP HERE –
PREFERABLY BEFORE THE TRIP!

Accommodation

In New York – and the following applies only to Manhattan – there are hundreds of hotels, from luxury establishments to very simple hostels located away from the expensive parts of the city. The average price of a room is $180, and rooms under $150 are rare. As is usual in the USA, the advertised rates are per room and not per person: if two people share a double room, it doesn't cost any more than a single person in that room. It is advisable to book early – by telephone or online with a credit card.

Breakfast is almost never included in the room price. The guest is not obliged to eat breakfast in the hotel, rather he can go to a nearby diner, lunch room etc. Almost all hotels, and particularly the larger ones have one or more restaurants; the price range corresponds, more or less, to the accommodation. All hotels have safes where you can keep jewellery and cash as well as other valuables. The room key is usually not left at reception but taken along. 14.75% accommodation tax and $3.50/day room tax are added to the price of the room.

Hotel Guide The New York Convention & Visitors Bureau publishes the helpful *The NY Official Travel Planner* (tel. 1-800-NYC-VISIT, 212-582-3352; fax 212-924-7935; www.nycgo.com).

The Waldorf-Astoria

Countless luxury hotels and other hotels offer special rates at weekends. Reservations are required for these low rates, which are worth asking about. The agency Crossways Travel Inc. offers hotel rooms and suites in nine selected city hotels with discounts of up to 50%: Fax 1-516-921-0359.

Quikbook also offers hotel rooms up to 50% cheaper (Tel. 212-779-7666, Fax 212-532-4556, www.quikbook.com).

> ! **Baedeker TIP**
>
> **Hotel room broker**
>
> With a bit of luck you can save up to 45% of the normal rate if you contact a hotel room broker, who buys up large blocks of rooms at a discount in advance and passes on part of the savings to the customer. Various online brokers, such as www.hotelroomssearchengine.com, www.alpharooms.com and www.cityandshow.com, offer discount prices.

Rising hotel costs have made bed-and-breakfasts and apartments increasingly popular. Agents offer various possibilities from apartments to rooms in a family home. The prices vary; the average is about $100.

Bed & breakfast

 RECOMMENDED HOTELS

▶ ① etc. ▶maps pp. 104 –107
Entries without a number are not on the map.

▶ **Price categories per double room**
Luxury: over $300
Mid-range: $180 to 300
Budget: up to $180

LUXURY

▶ ① **Carlyle**
35 E 76th St.
(between Madison and Park Ave.)
Tel. 212-744-1600
Fax 212-717-4682
www.thecarlyle.com
180 rooms. Many critics consider the Carlyle to be »the best run hotel in New York«. The five-star hotel has attracted famous guests since its opening in 1930. The staff, always present but unobtrusive, are so discrete that even two members of the Beatles, who stayed here after the group sepa-

rated, did not know that the other was there. Only about 20% of the luxurious rooms are set aside for tourists and other travellers. The rest are leased long-term.

▶ ② **Four Seasons**
57 E 57th St.
(between Madison and Park Ave.)
Tel. 212-758-5700
Fax 212-758-5711
www.fourseasons.com
364 rooms. With 52 floors, the Four Seasons is New York's tallest hotel at 208m/681ft, and the rooms in Art Deco style are the biggest in the city. The bathtubs fill very quickly (in about 60 seconds).

▶ ③ **Pierre**
61st St./Fifth Ave.
Tel. 212-838-8000
Fax 212-940-8109
www.fourseasons.com/pierre
236 rooms. The painter Salvador

Artists and art lovers relax in the lobby of the Chelsea Hotel

WHO SLEEPS WHERE...

Liz Taylor, the Dalai Lama, Prince Rainier and Princess Grace of Monaco – the list of prominent guests who have stayed at the Waldorf Astoria is endless. To this day, only the rich and famous stay here.

It was ever thus, ever since the hotel was opened in 1931. In 1893 the multimillionaire William Astor, a descendant of German immigrants from Waldorf, near Heidelberg, opened the Hotel Waldorf on Fifth Avenue. Another member of the family then opened the Astoria Hotel next door. Four years later the two hotels merged, but in 1929 they had to make room for the Empire State Building. In 1931 the hotel celebrated its reopening on Park Avenue near 50th Street. With 42 floors and 1,380 rooms it was at that time the largest hotel in the world; it is still the most famous hotel in New York. If the luxurious rooms and suites are too expensive, it is still possible to enjoy the atmosphere of the Art Deco hotel in the lobby, in the shops, bars and restaurants on the lower floors. But those looking for the elegance and exclusive atmosphere that a hotel like this one promises have to go to the top – and that applies to the prices, too. Waldorf Towers, between the 28th and 42nd floor, is run like a separate hotel – with 106 deluxe suites and 85 luxury rooms, where nume-

rous permanent guests choose to stay, like the composer Cole Porter did in days past. Even the president stays here when he pays the city on the Hudson a visit. The price for a night in the president's suite? $3,000.

The Chelsea

Ernest Hemingway, Arthur Miller, Sarah Bernhardt, Mark Twain, Bob Dylan, John Lennon, Andy Warhol, Jimi Hendrix – the Chelsea also has famous names to offer. But crowned heads of state and statesmen did not and do not count among the guests of the ten-storey Victorian red brick house on 23rd Street. Erected in 1884 as an apartment building, at that time the Chelsea was the tallest building in Manhattan and gave the neighbourhood its name. In 1903 it was converted into a hotel. It quickly attracted artists who lived here for months or even years, and who not uncommonly were inspired to produce masterpieces, like Thomas Wolfe who wrote *You Can't Go Home Again* here. The saddest kind of fame came to room 100 where the punk musician Sid Vicious of the Sex Pistols stabbed

his girlfriend. The hotel still houses many artists, or those who think they are, as permanent guests. About 100 of the 400 rooms and apartments are available for tourists. They aren't exactly cheap: in order to keep the rents low for the long-term guests, the short-term guest has to pay more than $130 – for a small, pretty shabby room.

But for all that the hotel, which has been classified as a historical monument since 1984, offers much that is original and bizarre in the way of atmosphere: the lobby for example, with its paintings, photos and other exhibits, as well as rooms that were designed by the artists who lived here.

The Leo House

Illustrious names in the Leo House? Difficult question! But here, too, a part of the clientele comes from a certain segment of society. The hotel on 23rd St. is often frequented by catholic clergy; the Leo House is a catholic establishment. But they won't ask for your religious affiliation when you reserve a room – every guest is welcome here. The Leo House origi-

nally stood in New York's Battery Park. The hotel was opened in 1899 by the St Raphael Society, a society of German clergy, who wanted to help German immigrants find work or relatives in the New World. During the end of the 19th century and the beginning of the 20th century the charitable society helped thousands of new arrivals get started in the USA. In the middle of the 1920s the Leo House moved to 23rd Street where there are now over 100 beds on eight floors available to guests: in single, double and so-called family rooms for up to six people. Even though the Leo House is still a »Catholic hospice« for travelling catholic clergy, these by no means make up the entire clientele anymore, and all profit from the low prices and the clean accommodation. A double room with toilet and sink (showers in the hall) costs a scant $70. The excellent breakfast buffet is also inexpensive – served daily except for Sunday, the Lord's Day. Non-English speakers are also catered for: the receptionists speak both English and Spanish, and one of the managers even speaks German.

! **Baedeker TIP**

Good to rest

Waldorf Astoria: one of the most famous hotels in the world
Metro: With a view of the Empire State Building
Leo House: Catholic hostel with affordable prices

Dalí felt at home in this hotel, which was opened in 1929 and still features old-fashioned luxury and elegant, European-style ambience. One night costs over $300. The singer Madonna pays $2,900 per night for two suites – one for sleeping in and the other for her weights and other fitness machines.

▸ ④ **Mandarin Oriental**
80 Columbus Circle
Tel. 212-805-8800
Fax 212-805-8882
www.mandarinoriental.com
203 rooms. New York's newest luxury hotel is located between the 37th and 53rd floor of the Time Warner Center, which was opened in 2004. The rooms offer guests spectacular views of Central Park, the Hudson or Manhattan's skyline.

▸ ⑤ **St Regis**
2 E 55th St. / Fifth Ave.
Tel. 212-753-4500
Fax 212-787-3447
www.stregis.com
315 rooms. The flagship of the luxury division of ITT Sheraton, a former townhouse, was built from 1902 to 1904 by John Jacob Astor, who drowned in 1912 when the Titanic sank. The hotel impresses

with its perfect service. The associated restaurant Lespinasse with its sophisticated cuisine is one of New York's foremost attractions for gourmets. Of course there has been no lack of big names at this hotel: these include Liza Minelli, Leonard Bernstein and Marlene Dietrich, who was a welcome guest in the King Cole Bar.

▸ ⑥ **Waldorf Astoria**
301 Park Ave. / 50th St.
Tel. 212-355-3000
Fax 212-872-7272
www.waldorfastoria.com
1,380 rooms. ▸Baedeker Special p.66

▸ ⑦ **Hotel Gansevoort**
18 Ninth Ave., near 13th St.
Tel. 212-206-6700
Fax 212-255-5858
www.hotelgansevoort.com
187 rooms. An ultra-hip hotel in the middle of the trendy Meatpacking District. The roof area with a 15m/16.4yd glassed-in pool (with underwater music!) and the fantastic views cannot fail to impress; so too do the often very original room designs and the exquisite interior – marble dressing tables, bedding made of Egyptian linen, mobile phones and so on.

▸ ⑰ **Millenium Broadway**
145 West 44th St. (near Sixth Avenue), Tel. 212-768-4400
Fax 212-768-0847
www.milleniumhotels.com
The cultivated Art Deco hotel is only two blocks away from Times Square and attracts with numerous extras like larger beds, more comfortable covers and free internet access.

▶ ⑧ **Algonquin**
59 W 44th St.
(between Fifth and Sixth Ave.)
Tel. 212-840-6800
Fax 212-944-1419
www.thealgonquin.net
Opened in 1902, the Algonquin
hosted the famous round-table
meetings of Dorothy Parker, Robert Benchley and James Thurber
among others in the 1920s and
1930s, where they pondered the
decline of Western civilization.
Today's hotel owners are Japanese
and have restored it with great
care. The rooms are tiny but nicely
decorated, the panelled lobby has a
living-room atmosphere.

▶ ⑭ **Mercer**
147 Mercer St. / Prince St.
Tel. 212-966-6060
Fax 212-965-3838
www.mercerhotel.com
The archetype of arty: André
Balazs, wealthy night-owl city-
celebrity, has had an interesting
mixture of atelier, café and living
room built in the middle of trendy
SoHo. The corridors are lit by
changing pastel lights; star designer Christian Liaigre designed
the rooms (often with a French
balcony). Leonardo di Caprio re-
laxes here on a regular basis.

MID_RANGE

▶ ⑨ **Ameritania**
1701 Broadway, near 54th St.
Tel. 212-247-5000
Fax 212-247-3313
www.nychotels.com/
ameritania.html
The hotel's A-logo is futuristic, as
is the entrance hall. But the rooms
are furnished more traditionally in
this 1930s building, located on
Broadway right next to the Ed

Sullivan Theater where the *Late
Show* with David Letterman takes
place. The hotel is an ideal base for
guests who love theatre and musicals. Those travelling alone
should ask for a single room,
which costs just over $100.

▶ ⑩ **Box Tree**
250 E 49th St.
(between Second and Third Ave.)
Tel. 212-758-8320
Fax 212-308-3899
Kitsch as kitsch can: there are
canopy beds and fireplaces even in
the standard rooms. Pure romanticism – which has already attracted guests such as Robert De
Niro and Barbra Streisand.

▶ **The Franklin**
164 E 87th St.
(between Lexington and Third
Ave.)
Tel. 212-369-1000
Fax 212-369-8000
www.franklinhotel.com
92 rooms. Very small rooms
tastefully furnished, where you
can enjoy luxury at an affordable
price. Small breakfast and parking
included in the price. This elegant
hotel is near the Museum Mile,
and the international boutiques on
Madison Avenue as well as first-
class restaurants are not far away.
The Franklin is the preferred
accommodation of fashion
models.

▶ ⑫ **Radisson Lexington**
511 Lexington Ave. / 48th St.
Tel. 212-755-4400
Fax 212-751-4091
www.radisson.com
700 rooms. Because of its central
location – near Grand Central
Terminal and the United Na-

tions – the 27-floor hotel is especially popular among business travellers and shoppers. There are two in-house restaurants – Italian and Chinese.

▶ ⑬ **Belleclaire**
250 West 77th St
Tel. 212-362-7700
Fax 212-362-1004
www.hotelbelleclaire.com. Almost posh, nevertheless affordable house – built in 1903 in Beaux-Art style, recently restored – on the Upper West Side. The cheapest rooms cost only a little more than $100 (without bathroom), but they run to over $400. Furnished very nicely and comfortably. There are many ethnic restaurants and trendy cafés nearby, or just go to Zabar's.

▶ ⑮ **Metro**
45 W 35th St.
(between Fifth and Sixth Ave.)
Tel. 212-947-2500
Fax 212-279-1310
www.hotelmetronyc.com
179 rooms. The hotel has small, tastefully furnished rooms and a nice rooftop terrace with a view of the Empire State Building. It is conveniently located, therefore also popular among business people. Breakfast is included and recently a restaurant was opened.

▶ ⑯ **Paramount**
235 W 46th St.
(between Broadway and Eighth Ave.)
Tel. 212-764-5500
Fax 212-354-5237
www.somelia.com
610 rooms. This used to be a tourist hotel. After being completely redesigned by the success-

ful French designer Philippe Starck it has become a popular place to go in the theatre district. The rooms are very small, but have all the necessities. The hotel offers a coffee shop, a restaurant, a fitness room and the Whiskey Bar.

▶ **Hotel Wales**
1295 Madison Ave (near 92nd Street), Tel. 212-876-6000
www.hotelwalesnyc.com
The rooms were furnished with care and everything fits to the last detail. Th atmosphere is homey and the European bedding only makes it more comfortable. The fitness room and business centre are modern. Continental breakfast is included in the price.

▶ ㉕ **The Lucerne**
201 West 79th Street (corner of Amsterdam Ave.), Tel. 212-875-1000, www.newyorkhotel.com
The historic hotel was built already in 1903 as a dormitory for the university. But with elaborate remodeling in 1995 it was converted to a comfortable and European-style boutique hotel. It is surprisingly affordable for being on the Upper West Side. The rooms have wireless internet and numerous extras.

BUDGET

▶ ⑱ **Chelsea Hotel**
222 W 23rd St.
(between Seventh and Eighth Ave.)
Tel. 212-243-3700
Fax 212-974-7502
www.hotelchelsea.com
▶Baedeker Special p.66

▶ ⑲ **Salisbury Hotel**
123 West 57th St.

Tel. 212-246-1300
Fax 212-977-7752
www.nycsalisbury.com
This basic hotel is located opposite Carnegie Hall and only a few minutes from the shops on Fifth Avenue. The rooms are surprisingly big for a budget hotel. There are »corporate rooms« available with computer ports etc. for business travellers.

► ⑳ **Gershwin**
7 E 27th St.
Tel. 212-545-8000
Fax 212-684-5546
www.gershwinhotel.com
150 rooms. Somewhat crazy but very nice (recently renovated) hotel near Fifth Ave. and the Empire State Building. Rooms from very cheap (with bunk beds) to family suite.

► ㉑ **Leo House**
332 W 23rd St. (between Eighth and Ninth Ave.), Tel. 212-929-1010, fax 212-366-6801; 100 beds
►Baedeker Special p.66

► ㉒ **Riverview Hotel**
113 Jane St. (between 12th and 14th St.), Tel. 212-929-0060
Fax 212-675-8581
www.hotelriverview.com
208 rooms. Low budget hotel on the Hudson River in Greenwich with simple, clean rooms.

► ㉓ **Milford Plaza**
270 W 45th St. / Eighth Ave.
Tel. 212-869-3600
www.mildfordplaza.com
1,310 rooms. This pre-war high rise is an easy walk from all of the Broadway theatres. The rooms have all been renovated, are comfortably furnished and very clean.

There is a fitness room available to guests.

► ㉔ **Seafarers and International House**
123 E 15th St.
Tel. 212-677-4800
www.sihnyc.org
First opened 35 years ago as a home for poor sailors, today the hotel provides some of the cheapest accommodation in New York with small but clean rooms.

OTHER ACCOMMODATION

► ㉖ **Vanderbilt YMCA**
224 E 47th Street
(between Second and Third Ave.)
Tel. 212-756-9600
Fax 212-752-0210
www.hostelworld.com
430 single to four-bed rooms. This centrally located former youth hostel has been converted into a low-price hotel. Some rooms are very small. A fitness room and two pools are available for the guests.

► ⑪ **West Side YMCA**
5 W 63rd St.
(between C. Park West and Broadway)
Tel. 212-787-4400
Fax 212-875-4273
www.ymcanyc.org
525 rooms. This youth hostel is located near Lincoln Center and Central Park. The rooms are simple but clean.

► ㉗ **East Village Bed & Coffee**
110 Avenue C
Tel. 917-816-0071
www.bedandcoffee.com
Ideal location but without breakfast! But the location has anough on offer.

► **Regina's Bed & Breakfast**
16 Fort Green Place, Brooklyn
Tel. 718-834-9253, www.home.
earthlink.net/~remanski
Pretty rooms in a listed brownstone house.

**BED & BREAKFAST ·
APARTMENTS · SUBLET**

► **Private homes**
Alternatives to hotels are in fashion, including bed & breakfast,
apartments or flatsor subletting.
The price varies with the furnishings, number of rooms and location. Booking online is simplest:
www.urbanlivingny.com

www.newyork.craigslist.org
http://newyorkcity.sublet.com

Others:
City Lights, Tel. 212-737-7049
www.citylightsbandb.com
Abode Bed & Breakfast
Tel. 212-472-2000
www.abodenyc.com
Bed & Breakfast Network of New
York, Tel. 800-900-8134
www.bedandbreakfastnetny.com
NY Apartment Petra Loewen LLC
Tel. 718-373-2226, www.aptpl.com
Affordable New York
Tel. 212-533-4001
www.affordablenewyorkcity.com

Arrival · Before the Journey

How to Get to New York

By air Most visitors arrive in New York by air. There are scheduled and
charter flights from all major airports in the UK, Ireland, Australia,
New Zealand, and of course from
other airports in the USA. The **flying time** from London is around 7
hours. Keen competition results in
lucrative special offers, but the pri-
cing system can appear impene-
trable. Information is available in
travel agents, from the internet or
in travel magazines such as *National Geographic Traveler* (www.
nationalgeographic.com). The
website www.cheapflights.co.uk allows you to compare prices.
All three of New York's **airports** are
outside the city centre. The traveller can get information on how to
get into town or to another airport at the Ground Transportation
Centers.

! *Baedeker* TIP

Carry cash!

It is advisable to carry a small amount of cash
(both notes and coins) at all times. Taxis and
museums, for example, only accept cash, and
bus drivers do not give change. Moreover, taxi
drivers are not required to accept notes over $20
and owners of small shops and stores can rarely
be persuaded to provide change.

By ship Apart from cruises New York can only be reached with one passenger ship line: the Cunard Line (Cunard Seabourn Ltd, Mountbatten

ARRIVAL INFORMATION

AIRPORTS

▶ **J. F. Kennedy International Airport – JFK**
Location: 26km/16.2mi outside of town, on Jamaica Bay (Queens)
Information: Tel. 718-244-4444
Lost and found: 718-244-4225
www.panynj.gov
Airtrain: Connection between various airport terminals (free of charge) and the subway stations Howard Beach and Jamaica Center ($5); continue on lines A and E to Penn Station in Manhattan ($2); travel time approx. 90min.
Shuttle: Supershuttle runs minibuses from JFK to Manhattan ($20–30).
Taxi: From JFK to Manhattan: $50 flat rate plus $3.50 tunnel toll as well as tip. Travel time approx. 1hr
New York Airport Service: Bus service from 6:15am until 1am every 15 to 30min between the airport terminals and Manhattan (Grand Central Terminal, Penn Station, Port Authority Bus Terminal – Eighth Ave. / 42nd St. – and many hotels); tel. 718-706-9658; fare $13; travel time approx. 1hr
Helicopter Flight Services: Tel. 212-355-0801, www.heliny.com

▶ **LaGuardia Airport – LGA**
Location: 13km/8.1mi outside the city centre, in the north of Queens
Information: tel. 718-533-3400
www.laguardiaairport.com
New York Airport Service: The New York Airport Service buses travel between the terminals of La Guardia and Manhattan, ▶JFK; fare $10; travel time approx. 45min
Taxi: fare approx. $30, plus bridge

and tunnel toll and tip; travel time approx. 45min
Bus: M60 (New York City Transit Authority, 5am–1am) via 125th to 106th St. / Broadway with connection to subway lines.
Helicopter: ▶JFK

▶ **Newark Liberty International Airport – EWR**
Location: 24km/14.9mi south-west in New Jersey
Information: tel. 973-961-6000
www.newarkairport.com
Airtrain: Transfer (included in NJ Transit or Amtrack ticket) between terminals and Newark Penn Station; from here continue with the trains PATH, NY Transit or Amtrak to Penn Station in Manhattan; travel time approx. 30 min.
Taxi: about $60 plus bridge and tunnel toll and tip
Airport Express: Buses (6am–1am every 15 or 30 min.) to stations in Manhattan (Port Authority Bus Terminal, Fifth Ave. /Bryant Park, Grand Central Terminal); travel time 40–50 min., $15.
Express bus: SuperShuttle from door to door; fare $15–20; travel time 40–50 min. to Manhattan, Tel. 800-258-3826
Helicopter:▶JFK

AIRLINES

Direct flights from London to New York City: Virgin Atlantic
tel. 1 800 821 5438 (from USA)
tel. 08705 747 747 (from UK)
www.virgin-atlantic.com

British Airways
tel. 1-800-AIRWAYS (from USA)
0870 850 9 850 (from UK)
www.ba.com

American Airlines
tel. 1-800-433-7300 (from USA)
08457 789 789 (from UK)
www.aa.com

Delta Airlines
tel. 1-800-241-4141 (international), tel. 1-800-221-1212 (inland)
www.delta.com

Continental Airlines, tel. 1-800-352-8637, 212-661-9382
www.continental.com

Non-direct flights: United Airlines, Lufthansa, Air France, Swiss, AUA, KLM, SAS and Iberia.

RAILWAY STATIONS

► **Grand Central Terminal**
42nd St. / Park Ave.
Information: tel. 212-340-2210
www.grandcentralterminal.com

Open: Daily 5.30am–1.30am
Main station for the commuter trains going north and east of New York, to Connecticut and West-chester County. There is a subway station in the lower floor, and bus stops outside.

► **Penn (Pennsylvania) Station**
Seventh Ave. / 33rd St.
Information: Tel. 212-630-6401
Open: Daily 5.45am–11.30pm
Station under Madison Square Garden, commuter trains go from here, and trains to New Jersey and Amtrak trains. There are subway stations in the lower floor, and bus stops outside.

► **Port Authority Bus Terminal**
42nd St. / Eighth Ave.
Information:
Tel. 212-564-8484

House, Grosvenor Square, Southampton, SO15 2BF; tel.: +44 (0)23 8071 6500, fax: +44 (0)23 80225843, www.cunard.co.uk) sails the luxury liner *Queen Elizabeth 2* (*Queen Victoria* from 2008) from April to November once to three times a month in five days from Southampton via Cherbourg to New York.

It is not advisable to drive to New York in a hire car. Parking spaces are extremely rare, and hotels charge up to $25 for 2 hours in parking spaces in car parks, while towing costs at least $200 plus the fine. It is also not unlikely that the car will be stolen.

By train   There are two railway stations in Manhattan, Grand Central Terminal and Pennsylvania Station. There are subway stations directly under the railway stations, and bus stations directly outside. **Amtrak**, the state-owned railway, can be contacted in the USA on tel. 1-800-872-7245; in the UK, contact Leisurail (tel.: (0800) 698 7545 or (0870) 750 0222 / 443 4483, www.leisurail.co.uk).

The main hall of Grand Central Terminal impresses through sheer size

If a visit to New York City is part of a USA holiday, the **Greyhound** bus line (tel. 1-800-229-9424, www.greyhound.com) can be used to connect to the largest cities. The »Ameripass« is an all-inclusive ticket which can be purchased for 4, 7, 10, 15, 21, 30, 45 or 60 consecutive days. The passes cost significantly less for foreign visitors than for Americans, but they need to be bought in Europe. Seat reservations are not accepted but if the bus is full an additional bus is provided.

By bus or coach

Arrival and Departure Regulations

As a consequence of the attacks on 11 September 2001 the USA have made their arrival regulations stricter. Thus also visitors not required to have visas are photographed and fingerprinted upon arrival. Further information is available at the Department of Homeland Security under www.dhs.gov and at the places listed under ►Information.

Note

To enter the USA (for a stay of up to 90 days) UK citizens require a machine readable passport with at least 6 months validity remaining. Children need their own machine readable passport. Young people especially will often be asked to produce a return air ticket before being granted entry. A visa is required for those planning to remain in the USA for more than 90 days, or wishing to study or work there.

Travel documents

Further information: ▶Information or at the Immigration and Naturalization Service, 2401 E St., Washington, D.C. 20520, tel. 202-514-4330, www.formdomain.com. At present a full national **driving licence** from most countries is accepted in the USA for up to one year. An international driving license is not required, but helpful when travelling in remore areas. It is a good idea to check on the requirements of car hire companies before renting a car in New York.

Customs regulations
Entry ▶
Adults over 21 may bring one litre of wine or spirits and 200 cigarettes or 50 cigars (but not from Cuba) or 1300g/46oz of tobacco duty free. Children and adults may bring along gifts worth up to $100/£50 duty free. Meat, plants, fruit and obscene articles and publications may not be brought in. Up to $10,000/£5,000 may be carried upon arrival. Visitors who need medication containing drugs should bring a sufficient supply along with a doctor's attestation of the need (in English) in order to prevent the possible suspicion of drug smuggling. The same applies to injection needles for diabetics. Information is available at consulates or U.S. Customs, 1301 Constitution Ave. NW, Washington D.C. 20229, tel. 202-927-6724.

Departure ▶
In general the customs regulations of the country of destination apply. As a member of the EU, the following may be brought into the UK (from the age of 17 upwards): tobacco (200 cigarettes, 100 cigarillos, 50 cigars, 250g/8.8oz loose tobacco), alcohol (1l high-proof spirits), coffee (500g/17.6oz coffee and 200g/7oz instant coffee), scent (50g/1.8oz perfume and 0.25l/9fl oz eau de toilette), medicines for personal use and all other goods up to a value of €430/£380, excluding articles for personal use.

Travel insurance
Travel insurance is preferable for a visit to New York, since all medical costs must be paid in cash or with a credit card. The costs will be reimbursed when the receipts are presented to the insurance company. It is advisable to see to it that diagnoses, prescriptions and costs are listed in detail.

Beaches

Beaches in New York
The beaches known as **The Rockaways** in the south of Queens, **Coney Island** in Brooklyn and **South Beach** on Staten Island are very popular; during the peak season from the end of June to the beginning of September they are unfortunately often overcrowded. South Beach lies under the Verrazano Bridge and is said to have the fourth longest beach promenadein the world (more than 4km/2.5mi).
Jones Beach on Long Island is also easy to reach. It stretches about 10km/6.2mi along the Atlantic Ocean and offers mini golf courses and other attractions (directions: from end of May until beginning /

mid-September take the Long Island Railroad, LIRR, from Penn Station to Jones Beach; www.mta.info/lirr, tel. 718-217-5477; information on events at Jones Beach Theater: tel. 1-866-375-7591).

The 50km/31mi-long beach at **Fire Island**, one of a narrow chain of islands that lies off the southern coast of Long Island, is a good place for fishing, swimming and hiking (directions: Long Island Railroad, LIRR, from Penn Station, Brooklyn and Queens to Bayshore or Sayville, where ferries from Manhattan dock as well; information: www.fireislandferries.com, www.islanderstravel.com, www.sayville ferry. com).

Children in New York

The Friday *New York Times* has a »For Children« page in the *Weekend* section with tips on where kids can have fun in New York over the whole week. Tips can also be found under »Children's Events« or »Activities for Children« in *New York Magazine. Frommer's New York City with Kids*, available in bookshops, also provides information. There follow a few suggestions; the ones marked with an arrow (►) are described in the section ►Sights from A to Z.

Activities with children

Children examine the animals in the Bronx Zoo at close quarters – there is also a children's zoo here

In ▶**Central Park** with its many playgrounds, children can play, ice skate, roller skate, ride bikes, etc. In the old harbour, the ▶**South Street Seaport** on the East River, there are historical sailing ships. The boat trips around Manhattan or to Staten Island, or city tours on double-decker buses are fun.

The ▶**American Museum of Natural History** is considered to be the most popular museum in New York; among other things there are very impressive dinosaur skeletons here. In the **Brooklyn Children's**

▶ HITS FOR KIDS

▶ Central Park Carousel

A colourful carousel has been turning on this site ever since the first one was built in 1871. It is located in a round building that protects it from wind and weather. Just like at the county fairs of the first half of the 20th century, children ride on large hand-carved wooden horses. (Central Park near 66th Street, tel. 212-879-0244; summers daily from 10.30am until 6pm, winters until 5pm

▶ Blessing the animals in St John the Divine

Certainly a highlight for kids and other animal lovers: the annual blessing of the animals in the ▶Cathedral of St John the Divine. On the first Sunday in October at 11am camels, elephants, donkeys, dogs, cats, birds and other repre- sentatives of the city's fauna gather to be blessed for the coming church year. Free tickets are avail- able from 9am; come early, as the queue is long.

▶ Children's Museum of Manhattan

The children's museum invites children to join in: in an inter- active computer department, for example, bikes learn to fly and robots to speak; children can draw, colour or scribble on various computer monitors. (212 W 83rd St., between Amsterdam Ave. and Broadway; tel. 212-721-1234; www.cmom.org; Wed–Sat 10am–5pm.) Similar active muse- ums: Snug Harbour (▶Staten Island) and in ▶Brooklyn.

▶ Scott's Pizza Tours

Just the thing for pizza lovers: the NYC Pizza Bus Tour by Scott's Pizza Tours goes to four of the best pizzerias in New York. Enroute the history of the pizza is explained; watch pizzas being made in the pizzerias. Of course, there are also free samples and at the end a goody bag to take along. (Spring Street, tel. 212-209-3370; www.scottspizzatours.com; Sun 11am–3.30pm, adults $55 or $60, children (aged 4–12) $50

▶ New York Aquarium

In the New York Aquarium (▶ Brooklyn) children can admire hundreds of kinds of exotic fish – and hunt for Nemo, the little clownfish. The appearance of the family of Beluga whales and the acrobatics of the sea lions are especially popular.

Museum children can touch, try out and play with all the exhibits (►
Brooklyn). In **FAO Schwartz** (767 Fifth Ave./59th St.), it is possible
to buy anything a child's heart desires. Here, be prepared to spend
lots of time – and money. The interesting space and sea travel museum, the **Intrepid Sea, Air & Space Museum**, is situated on an aircraft
carrier on the Hudson (►Practicalities, Museums). The ►**Bronx Zoo**
is one of the most beautiful zoos in the world with artificial jungles,
huge open areas for animals, a children's zoo and a monorail. The
Little Orchestra Society (»Happy Concerts for Young People«) in
Avery Fisher Hall in the ► Lincoln Center offers **classical music** for
children. When Handel's *Water Music* is played the conductor appears in a diving suit (always on Saturday afternoons, times vary).
The **Big Apple Circus** performs in Damrosch Park along with the
Metropolitan Opera from October to January (62nd St., between
Columbus and Amsterdam Ave., tel. 212-268-2500, www.bigapple
circus.com).

Electricity

The mains supply is 110 Volts AC. Those bringing European norm
(set switch to 110!) electrical appliances need an adaptor which can
be purchased at the airport or department stores, but also at large local department stores.

110 Volts
AC

Emergency

► **Ambulance, police, fire department**
Tel. 911

Entertainment

New York is the undisputed world capital of nightlife. The selection
is huge: music events, rock, pop and Latin concerts, both in halls
and the open air, jazz clubs, pubs with live music, comedy shows, cinema, Broadway shows, clubs, dance, studio theatre – and so on.
Which clubs or discos are currently coming into fashion is almost

Spoilt for choice

impossible to predict. The magazine *Village Voice* has a good ear for the trendy, especially when it comes to modern music, and the weekly *Time Out New York* is also well-informed. The gay and lesbian scene is covered by journals like *Gay City News* and *Go!* Since 9/11 security is much tighter in New York, so it is best to carry identification at all times. Very important: the drinking ages is 21. Anyone younger will not be served alcohol.

Programmes and costs

The clubs' programmes vary. There is music, live or mixed by DJs, theatre, cabaret and also poetry readings. The terms (entrance or minimum charge, reservations, time etc.) vary from programme to programme. A (very rough) rule of thumb: the price of a live show with known stars is between $30 and $120 (or more), and a drink costs from $6.50. Live performances rarely begin before 9pm or 10pm, though there are exceptions including brunch sessions at jazz clubs at weekends. Discos open at midnight, but things don't start to swing before the early hours.

In the Coral Room discotheque visitors can dive into strange worlds

Information on individual clubs and bars is available at www.club-planet.com. Links to the homepages of the clubs are found here as well, and they often offer special deals – in the form of coupons that have to be printed out.

Since March 2003 New York's nightlife has one ritual less – at least according to the smokers: whether in clubs or bars, smoking is now prohibited, so smokers have to go outside in order to indulge, or use nicotine patches.

Nightlife rituals

New York's real nightlife, incidentally, takes place on weekdays – Thursdays, Fridays and Saturdays, the so-called Bridge and Tunnel days, belong to the suburbanites from New Jersey, who come in via tunnels and bridges, or to those visitors who still believe there is such a thing as »Saturday night fever«.

It's not always easy to get past the bouncer's velvet rope: black clothing is advised – though even khaki green is allowed, along with a good bit of self-confidence and the fact that dollars are more important at the till than an elite image, which won't pay the club manager's bills. Arriving very early, at 10pm, or very late, after 3am, gives you a good chance of being let in. Putting your name on the club's guest list online is also worthwhile.

The fact that few kids can be seen in Midtown has to do with the fact that the area north of 30th Street is considered to be forty-something territory, for the older and more well-behaved night-owls. Trendy areas lie south of 14th Street: the area around Tompkins Square Park or the Lower East Side and the Meatpacking District, the former meat market around Gansevoort Street.

Trendsetter's territory

Cinema

Film premieres generally take place in the city cinemas (exceptions prove this rule). The **largest central cinemas** are in the area around Times Square, further west of Broadway between 50th and 60th St. and east between 50th and 70th St., and on the Upper East Side on East 34th St. near Third Ave. The rest of the large cinemas are in Greenwich Village. The daily papers and the magazines *The New Yorker* and *New York* print the current programmes in their issues. Smaller cinemas can be found all over town; some have specialized in certain types of films such as classics, cultural films or experimental films.

 Baedeker TIP

For cinema lovers

The Lincoln Center is the site of the annual New York Film Festival (p. 262).

Foreign and independent productions can be seen at BAM Rose Cinemas in the Brooklyn Academy of Music, 30 Lafayette Ave., Brooklyn, tel. 718-636-4100.

The ultimate cinema venue in the summer is the Bryant Park Film Festival behind the Public Library, 42nd Street. For information: tel. 212-512-5700, or www.bryantpark.org.

⏵ A FEW ADDRESSES

▶ ① etc. ▶**Maps p. 104 – 107**
No number: not on map

**LOUNGE BARS ·
DISCOTHEQUES**

▶ ① **Avalon**
660 Sixth Ave.
(between 20th and 21st St.)
Tel. 212-807-7780
Recently re-opened disco in a
former church – once home of the
legendary New York Limelight
Club. First class sound.

▶ **Bailey's Corner Pub**
1607 York Ave. (corner of 85th St.)
Tel. 212-650-1341
This pub has been one of the best
after-work addresses on the Upper
East Side since 1951. The rustic
bar comes from a 19th-century
tavern. Not surprisingly, real Gui-
ness is served here, but the whisky
is from the Emerald Isle

▶ ② **Blue Bar/Algonquin**
59 W 44th St.
(between Fifth and Sixth Ave.)
Classic New York bar in the lounge
of the former New York literary
hotel.

▶ ③ **bOb**
235 Eldrige St.
(between Houston and Stanton
St.) Tel. 212-777-0588
Witty, sparsely furnished lounge
with terrarium feeling, which also
serves as an art gallery. As well as
hip hop, exotic world music is also
played here.

▶ ④ **Bubble Lounge**
228 W Broadway/White St.
Tel. 212-431-3433
The only champagne bar in New
York. Eric Benn and Eric Macaire
serve over 250 types of sparkling
wine and champagne. Until 4am
classy snacks and hors d'oevres
can be ordered, too.

▶ ⑥ **230 Fifth**
230 Fifth Ave./27th St.
Tel. 212-725-4300
Huge roof terrace bar on Fifth
Avenue with a view that includes
the Empire State Building.

▶ ⑦ **Gramercy Tavern**
42 E 20th St.
(between Park Ave. South and
Broadway)
Tel. 212-477-0777
Sophisticated bar, which also
serves excellent food

▶ ⑧ **Kaña**
324 Spring St. (between Greenwich and Washington St.)
Tel. 212-343-8180
This tapas lounge is a good place
to end the evening.

▶ ⑨ **Momofuku**
163 1st Ave./10th St.
Tel. 212-475-7899
Hip noodle bar in the East Village
offering American-Asian dishes
made from products from small
local farms

▶ ⑩ **Mc Sorley's
Old Ale House**
15 E 7th St. (between Second
and Third Ave.)
Tel. 212-473-9148
Earthy Irish pub from 1854 – the
oldest in Manhattan. Good beer,
but unfortunately only mediocre
food.

▶ **Saloon**
1584 York Ave.
(near 84th St.)
Tel. 212-570-5454
Thirtysomethings and older are welcome – if they can dance. Dance on a giant dancefloor to the top-40s tunes and the sound of (average) cover bands. The wrong place for under-30s

▶ **South Street Seaport**
19 Fulton St.
Pier 17 in front of the restaurants is a popular gathering place on warm summer evenings.

▶ ⑫ **Webster Hall**
125 E 11th St.
(between Third and Fourth Ave.)
Tel. 212-353-1600
Friendly, large disco with three (unfortunately airless) dance floors. The music ranges from rock and pop to house.

▶ ⑬ **Zum Schneider**
107 - 109 Ave. C / 7th St.
Tel. 212-598-1098
Whether German bankers taking part in an exchange programme, German business people or just beer fans – here everyone feasts on genuine Bavarian wheat beer, with twelve kinds on draught.

JAZZ

▶ **Apollo Theater**
253 W 125th Street
Amateur nights, where beginners long to be discovered, are held on Wednesdays in this legendary club, in which the careers of many jazz musicians began.

▶ ⑭ **Birdland**
315 W 44th St.

(between Eighth and Ninth Ave.)
Tel. 212-581-3080
The Upper West Side's answer to the Village jazz scene: live jazz and excellent cuisine, seven days a week. There are no big names here, but rather a professional mainstream, often with local artists. The audience: decided jazz lovers and students.

▶ **Big Apple Jazz/EZ's**
2236 Adam Clayton Powell Jr. Blvd. (between 131st and 132nd St.), tel. 212-283-5299
www.bigapplejazz.com
Small café in Harlem: scene meeting place and source for the latest news.

▶ **Bill's Place**
148 W 133rd St.
(between Lenox and A.C. Powell Jr. Blvd.), tel. 212-281-0707
Bill Saxton, the legendary saxophone player, opens his basement on Friday nights at 10pm. Reservations necessary!

▶ ⑮ **Blue Note**
131 W 3rd St.
(between Sixth Ave. and Mac-Dougal St.)
Tel. 212-475-8592
Four of the most famous jazz clubs are at home in the West Village. The Blue Note has been full to bursting every weekend for years; the very best mainstream jazz is offered here – from the greats of jazz history to the stars of today. Anyone who gets claustrophobic in large crowds might prefer the (more relaxed) jazz brunch at weekends to a night session.

▶ ⑯ **Café Carlyle**
781 Madison Ave.

Live musicians in the Village Vanguard

(near 76th St., in the Carlyle Hotel)
Tel. 212-744-1600
Woody Allen likes to play clarinet here on Mondays, accompanied by the Eddy Davis New Orleans Jazz Band.

▶ Cotton Club
656 W 125th Street / Broadway
The Harlem jazz club has hosted music greats like Duke Ellington; there is still a traditional pro-gramme with mainly African American guests. The jazz brunch at weekends is a favourite with tourists.

▶ ⑰ Iridium
1650 Broadway / 51st St.
Tel. 212-582-2121
Since opening in 1994 the club has brought some prominent jazz

players to the stage and developed into one of the best clubs of the city. New jazz trends are created here. Definitely worth a visit.

▶ ⑱ The Jazz Standard
116 E 27th St.
(between Park and Lexington Ave.)
Tel. 212-576-2232
The guest bands or musicians cover the whole jazz spectrum. There is also good food.

▶ Saint Nick's
773 Saint Nicolas Ave.
(between 148th and 149th St.)
Tel. 212-283-9728
This is what a bar must have looked like in the Roaring Twen-ties: cellar atmosphere, long bar, tiny stage. The traditional jazz is the very best.

▶ ⑲ Small's
183 W 10th St. / Seventh Ave.
Tel. 212-929-7565
As the name says: small – but nice. Here the hard-core jazz fans meet, but things don't really get rolling until the early morning hours. Show begins at 10pm.

▶ ⑳ Sweet Rhythm
88 Seventh Ave.
(between Grove and Bleecker St.)
Tel. 212-255-3626
Sweet Rhythm – the former Sweet Basil – is one of the honourable jazz domiciles in the West Village. What can be heard here should not shock or challenge – it is the best mainstream jazz. Also a »supper club« with a jazz brunch on Saturday and Sunday after-noon, a very pleasant establish-ment, not too loud and even quite reasonably priced.

▶ ㉑ **Village Vanguard**
178 Seventh Ave. South / Perry St.
Tel. 212-255-4037
Opened more than 50 years ago in
a cellar in Greenwich Village;
talents like Miles Davis and John
Coltrane appeared here. Today, the
best pieces and interpreters in
mainstream jazz can be heard
here. Not as exciting as in the
good old days, but still with
enough rhythm to get guests into
the mood. Very pleasant and still
very popular: be sure to make a
reservation in good time.

ROCK · FOLK · FUNK & DANCE

▶ ㉒ **Arlene Grocery**
95 Stanton St.
(between Ludlow and Orchard St.)
Tel. 212-358-1633
Rock, folk and funk fans from the
Lower East Side meet here.

▶ ㉓ **CBGB**
315 Bowery / Bleecker St.
Tel. 212-982-4052
The birthplace of American punk,
with a dark interior. The bands
that play here are mostly completely unknown, since the CBGB
is an open stage for new groups in
the punk and heavy metal scene.

▶ ㉔ **Cielo**
18 Little W 12th St.
(between 9th Ave. and Washington
St.) Tel. 212-645-5700
With world class DJs

▶ ㉕ **Irving Plaza**
17 Irving Place / 15th St.
Tel. 212-777-6800
The forum for independent bands
that have arrived, a New York
institution. Unfortunately the
drinks are pricey.

▶ ⑤ **Marquee**
289 Tenth Ave. (near 26th St.)
Tel. 646-473-0202
Techno remixes blast from the
speakers and a giant chandelier
changes colours constantly. The
bouncers only let people through
who are stylishly dressed.

▶ ⑪ **Secret Lounge**
525 West 29th St. (near Tenth
Ave.) Tel. 212-268-5580
Gays love this place. A chandelier
and many candelabras make for a
magical atmosphere. Music is
mainly European House. Vodka
and Red Bull is one of the
favourite drinks.

▶ ㉖ **The Living Room**
154 Ludlow St. (between Stanton
and Rivington St.)
Tel. 212-533-7235
Popular club

▶ ㉗ **The Knitting Factory**
74 Leonard St. (between Broadway
and Church St.)
Tel. 212-219-3006
Wide variety in a narrow
space – the best place for the new
trends in experimental jazz, rock
music and slam poetry.

▶ ㉘ **The Mercury Lounge**
217 E Houston St.
(between Essex and Ludlow St.)
Tel. 212-260-4700
Great view of the stage from all
sides of the lounge; the acoustics
are excellent too. The club is in the
firm grip of earthy rock and indie
bands.

▶ ㉙ **Roseland**
239 W 54th St. (between Eighth
Ave. and Broadway)
Tel. 212-245-5761

Originally a ballroom, today avant-garde rock bands and other unconventional artists appear here.

㉚ **The Supper Club**
240 W 47th St. (between Eighth Ave. and Broadway)
Tel. 212-921-1940
A carefully restored dance hall, ideal for rock and pop concerts. Such greats as Marianne Faithful have performed here, and cabaret is offered occasionally.

㉛ **S.O.B.'s**
204 Varick St. / Houston St.
Tel. 212-243-4940
The name stands for »sounds of Brazil«, but the repertoire has passed far beyond that. Today S.O.B.'s is the definitive world music club.

Vudu Lounge
1487 First Ave. (near 78th St.)
Tel. 212-249-9540
Latin Thursdays are the liveliest days and Latino couples twirl across the dance floor. Fridays are for HipHop and R&B, Saturdays mainstream and dance music. The dance floor with its giant crystal ball recalls the 1970s. Barely dressed go-go girls dance on stage. No admission charge.

CABARET

㉜ **Carolines On Broadway**
1626 Broadway
(between 49th and 50th St.)
Tel. 212-757-4100
Everyone starts small – like the famous satirist Jerry Seinfeld, for example, in Carolines, which many local people consider to be the best cabaret club in the city.

㉝ **Comic Strip Live**
1568 Second Ave.
(between 81st and 82nd St.)
Tel. 212-861-9386
A popular test stage for up-and-coming comedians, known as well as unknown. There are several shows at weekends.

Guests in front of CBGB the »Home of Underground«

Etiquette and Customs

Thanks to its many immigrants, almost no other city in the world is as cosmopolitan as New York. Visitors coming into contact with New Yorkers (which can happen quickly) soon notice that life in this city, at least for the middle and upper class, is marked much more strongly by **status symbols** than it is elsewhere. Conversations in New York – or more precisely Manhattan – naturally revolve around the most expensive shops like Takashimaya, the sinfully expensive food in one of Alain Ducasse's restaurants, and the name and address of employers: the higher the floor where the desk is, the lighter and larger the office, the better the job – and the better the pay, which the New Yorker who has arrived talks about openly. At the very top, naturally, are the bosses in suite-like luxury offices, and even the executive secretary or security personnel enjoy the view through the glass walls. At the bottom the rank and file work in mostly musty, tiny and often windowless cubicles.

Be it at an outdoor lunch in a Central Park restaurant, during the intermission in a musical theatre or in the best restaurant: the European will notice the **extreme noise level** – caused not by music, but by people talking so loud that it seems as if they haven't seen each other in years and need to make up for lost time in a cascade of conversation. But that's life here: New Yorkers love nothing more than to be the star of their own show – to talk about where they eat, where they shop or how their love life is shaping up.

In spite of the growing wealth of the last few years the crass **social disparity** is still visible. So do as the New Yorkers do: always keep a dollar bill in your pocket because it is considered an insult to give your spare change to a beggar. A folded, paper gift doesn't hurt anyone – and it certainly helps the one who's asking.

The **haste** of the Manhattanites is the stuff of modern legend. The expression »rush hour« doesn't come from New York for nothing, where the first subways went into service at the beginning of the 20th century. Particularly after 5pm, a hectic mass of people is set into motion all over the city – driven by the wish to get home as quickly as possible. Enjoy the hustle and bustle instead of cursing it: it's part of a dynamic city.

In New York, as in the rest of the USA and for that matter many places in the world, there are **clichéd expressions** and behaviours that shouldn't be taken too seriously: for example an invitation to »do lunch someday« is polite, but often not meant literally. Even if you get an address or telephone number, it will normally be the office number where there is no time for personal calls. An evening date is different however. The person who invites you out to dinner, an evening in the opera and a bar, or even to a party is serious, and accepting the invitation for a date equally so – in every respect, since 3.1 million singles live in New York.

The New Yorkers call it **hyping**: magazines, tour brochures, radio and TV adverts, self-appointed columnists or posters promise wonders – the best food, the cheapest tickets, biggest sale ever and so on. Even if it could all be true, it doesn't have to be. In the USA, above all in New York, advertising using comparatives (and superlatives) isn't taken as seriously as it is in Europe – so the best advice is to stay sceptical.

Last but not least there is **the call of nature** to take care of. In the USA, don't ask for the toilet: that's considered rude. Ask for the rest-room, bathroom or the ladies' or men's room. Tip: public restrooms are rare in New York City. Use the ones in one of the many fastfood restaurants.

Festivals, Holidays and Events

Holidays

New Year's Day (1 January)
Martin Luther King Day (the Monday closest to 15 January)
Washington's Birthday (on the Monday before the 22 February)
Easter Sunday
Memorial or Decoration Day (to remember the war dead; last Monday in May)
Independence Day (4 July)
Labor Day (first Monday in September)
Columbus Day (12 October or second Monday in October)
Veteran's Day or Armistice Day (11 November)
Thanksgiving Day (last Thursday in November)
Christmas Day (25 December)

Jewish holidays

Rosh Hashanah (ten days before Yom Kippur)
Yom Kippur (Day of Atonement, September or October)

Where and What New York Celebrates

Nobody comes to New York to rest; there's always something going on here. Anyone who has time to plan ahead should get a **free calendar of events** from the New York Visitors Bureau (▶Information). Information is also available online (**swww.nycvisit.com**). Beyond that the **daily newspapers** (▶ Media) carry most events; the Arts and Leisure section of the Friday issue of the *New York Times* is especially informative. The

! *Baedeker* TIP

Street parties

Visit one of the New York street festivals that take place throughout the summer in the various parts of the city. This is typical weekend entertainment with food booths, stages and goods of all kinds on sale. Information on dates and places: www.nyctourist.com.

More or less creepy costumes are shown off in the Halloween Parade

Village Voice appears on Thursday, and reports on all important dates. **Time Out** is also a good source of information. In addition bars have various what's-on guides and flyers listing events of a less official nature.

Theatre programmes by telephone

Hotlines give event tips around the clock:
Broadway and Off-Broadway Shows: http://ilovenytheater.com and 1-800-BROADWAY
Theater Direct: tel. 1-800-334-8457; park concerts: tel. 212-7360-2777; Jazz-Line: tel. 212-479-7888
TDF NYC/ON STAGE Hotline (theatre, dance and music events): tel. 212-768-1818
Sports: tel. 212-877-NYC.Sports

Reservations and remaining tickets ►Box offices

Tickets

▶ FESTIVAL CALENDAR

JANUARY

▶ **Chinese New Year**
Ten-day Chinese New Year festival, beginning on the first New Moon after 21 January; fireworks and giant dragons in Mott Street

FEBRUARY

▶ **Annual Empire State Building Run Up**
Who can run up the 1,576 steps from the lobby to the 86th floor the fastest?

MARCH

▶ **St Patrick's Day Parade and Greek Independence Day**
Festivals and parades of the Irish (17 March) and the Greeks (25 March) on Fifth Ave.

▶ **New Directors' Film Festival**
Film festival of new directors in the Museum of Modern Art

APRIL

▶ **Opening of the baseball season**
A classic: Yankees versus Mets

▶ **Easter Parade**
Easter Parade on Fifth Ave. near St Patrick's Cathedral

▶ **Ukrainian Festival**
On E 7th St., with various music and dance groups (second weekend after Easter)

MAY

▶ **Black World Championship Rodeo**
Rodeo championship in Harlem

▶ **Bike NY**
»Bike New York: the great five boro bike tour« runs 42 miles through the city.

▶ **Martin Luther King Parade**
On Fifth Avenue (around 20 May)

▶ **Brooklyn Bridge Day Parade**
Great hubbub with parade across the legendary bridge (middle of the month)

▶ **Ninth Avenue International Food Festival**
Large food fest (middle of the month)

JUNE

▶ **Puerto Rican Day Parade**
Exuberant music and dance of the Puerto Ricans on Fifth and Third Ave. (first Sunday in June)

▶ **Gay and Lesbian Pride Day**
Annual gay and lesbian parade from Columbus Circle via Fifth Avenue to Greenwich Village to remember the Stonewall Riot of 1969, when homosexuals for the first time resisted the police; Christopher Street Day (last Sunday of the month)

▶ **Mermaid Parade**
Mermaids and sea gods on the Coney Island Boardwalk, Brooklyn (Saturday after 21 June)

▶ **Free performances**
of the Metropolitan Opera in the parks of all parts of town

▶ **JuneFest**
Staten Island celebrates the beginning of summer with concerts and many art exhibits.

► Long Island Motorcycle Fair
Popular meeting place for bikers and their fans at Riverhead Raceway. Many stunt contests and shows. Concerts and open bars keep this event lively until late in the night

► 52nd Street Festival
Italian street festival in honour of St Antonius of Padua in Little Italy

► Shakespeare in the Park
Free theatre performances in the Delacorte Theater in Central Park (until August); generally very great demand

JULY

► Free
Shakespeare performances in Prospect Park in Brooklyn
Concerts on the South Street Seaport and in the summer garden of the Museum of Modern Art
Park concerts of the New York Philharmonic Orchestra in all parts of the city (until August)

► Music festival
On Washington Square

► Independence Day, 4 July
Celebrate American Independence Day in Battery Park; mostly with a parade of ships on the Hudson River and a large fireworks, which can best be seen from Riverside Park, West 80th to 105th St.

► American Indian Mid-Summer Pow Wow
Native American summer solstice festival in the County Farm Museum, Queens

AUGUST

► Harlem Week
Big street festival with many performers

► U.S. Open Tennis Championships
Open American tennis championships in Flushing Meadows, Queens

Thanksgiving in New York

► **Washington Square Art Show**
Art exhibition on Washington Square

► **New York Film Festival**
Famous and prestigious film festival

► **Festival San Gennaro**
Ten-day street festival on Mulberry Street in Little Italy; processions and Italian folklore (around 19 September)

► **Steuben Day Parade**
Traditional German-American parade to honour the German general von Steuben, a hero of the Revolutionary War; third weekend of the month

► **New York Giants**
Beginning of the football season

OCTOBER

► **Madison Square Garden**
The basketball season of the New York Knicks and the hockey season of the New York Rangers opens in Madison Square Garden.

? DID YOU KNOW ...?

■ The pilgrims of the Mayflower only survived their first winter in the new world in 1621 because the Algonquin people showed them how to grow and store corn (maize). The settlers then celebrated the »First Thanksgiving« with the Native Americans – which didn't alter the fact that the following generation fought each other. In 1898 Thanksgiving became an official holiday in order to help foster a »common national identity« which had been missing until then.

► **Columbus Day Parade**
Colourful parade on Fifth Ave. (around 12 October)

► **Halloween Parade**
In Greenwich Village the American spooky carnival is celebrated with great enthusiasm; the Village Halloween Parade takes place on Sixth Ave., the final party on Washington Square (31 October)

NOVEMBER

► **New York City Marathon**
Great marathon run through all five boroughs from Staten Island to the Tavern on the Green in Central Park.

► **Macy's Thanksgiving Day Parade**
A gigantic advertising event for children; the parade begins at 9am at the Museum of Natural History (West 77th Street / Central Park) and continues via Broadway to Macy's on Herald Square / 34th Street; the best place to watch is Duffy Square (from Seventh Ave., Broadway and 46th St.).

► **Veterans' Day Parade**
Parade to remember the end of the First World War, Fifth Ave.

DECEMBER

► **Lighting of giant Christmas tree**
Beginning of December: New York's largest Christmas tree is put up at the Rockefeller Center.

► **New Year's Eve**
Celebration at Times Square from 7pm and in Grand Central Terminal with a midnight marathon in Central Park

Food and Drink

New York is a gourmet's paradise. Well-known award-winning chefs from all over the world work in the top restaurants. Even the French chef-of-the-century Joel Rouchon can't get past New York anymore. Recipes from all over the world are united in the more than 18,000 resdtaurants. Many immigrants brought recipes from their home countries and were encouraged by the influence of their new neighbours to try new and in part daring creations. Nowhere is the selection more colourful or varied. A renowned French food critic would love to make New York the "capital of Europe."

The newest trend of the chefs is **fusion food**, a combination of often completely different cuisines of the world, for example Vietnamese

Various trends

Not only fast food is on offer in New York – the creations of world famous chefs can be enjoyed here as well

and Italian, French and Russian, Cuban and Argentinean (»Nuevo Latino«). The motto: creative, light, healthy and, above all, exotic. **Japanese food** has become a regular with its trendy sushi bars. The rice tidbits with raw fish overtook steaks and sandwiches in popularity long ago. The healthy trend has overflowed from Europe to America: **organic food**. Other restaurants offer more solid food. **Southern food**, pork chops with beans, spicy honey fried chicken with fiery barbecue sauce and pancakes, juicy, sizzling spare-ribs, is opulent and rich (also in calories). The food of the Texas ranchers and cowboys is one element of so-called **soul food**, a term primarily referring to the food traditionally eaten by the African Americans of the southern states, but which also includes regional dishes from white southern US cuisine. Currently it is combined with Caribbean spices and dishes – an interesting mixture that New York's scene is in the process of discovering, as with Mexican food some years ago. New York's often strange sounding dishes often come from **kosher cooking**, like knishes, fried pastry pockets with a mashed potato filling, pretzels made of yeast dough or **bagels**, round sourdough rolls with a hole in the middle, often eaten with smoked salmon or cream cheese. The name bagel is said to be derived from the German word (Steig-)Bügel, meaning stirrup. **Cheesecake** is also made according to a Jewish recipe – with cream cheese and cottage cheese.

Delis   Originally, deli or delicatessen was simply the name of the shops of Jewish immigrants in which kosher specialities were sold, for example blintzes, a type of crêpe with cream cheese filling, or fresh pastrami (corned beef) sandwiches, which served with sauerkraut is called a Reuben. In the meantime delis, which are open around the clock, also sell sushi, pizza, Chinese food and other international titbits.

Eating out in style   With more than 18,000 restaurants in the city, one thing is clear: New Yorkers like to eat out, and whoever isn't actually sitting in an expensive restaurant is talking about going to one. The most recent stock market boom has refilled the pockets and purses of many – and for some it can't be exclusive or expensive enough. Wherever a visit to a restaurant becomes a status symbol, the corresponding scene develops. Every Wednesday the *Times* food pages cover »Dining In, Dining Out«, reporting on culinary heaven or hell – anyone who wants to eat in restaurants that have just opened ought to read these pages. Ruth Reichl, the feared former food critic of the *Times*, was so well-known by the end of her career that she had to visit restaurants in disguise in order not to be recognized.

It can be done more cheaply, too – and still with style. The first **diners** were simple restaurants in old train cars or construction huts; and a bit of that old charm still exists today. A must seems to be the pastel colours, heavy plastic-covered benches and ochre coloured plastic or glittery chrome tables – and of course the typical Art Deco elements like the steel geometric trim that was considered chic in the 1930s. Simple, inexpensive meals are listed in the menus, often as a daily special served on a blue plate, the so-called »Blue Plate Special«. Incidentally: it is considered rude to sit at an already occupied table in diners, delis, fast-food restaurants or cafés in New York.

Better value, but still stylish

The love of good **coffee** only arrived in Manhattan at the end of the 20th century – but for that all the more intensely. In the meantime even chains like Starbucks or Seattle Coffee Roasters serve Arabicas or Robustos of the best quality, whether from Brazil, Kenya or the highlands of Jamaica. All sorts of **drinks** are mixed in the many bars of the city; cocktails from Brazil such as the caipirinha are of course especially popular, and a fresh, cool beer, maybe even from a local brewery like the **Heartland Brewery**, is just as popular in New York as elsewhere. The fruit of the vine, from all over the world, is currently especially popular; **wine bars** are sprouting like mushrooms.

Drinks

In better restaurants the patrons are shown to their tables by a member of the staff, the host or hostess at the entrance, who also checks the (almost always necessary) reservation. There may be a short wait – New Yorkers like to use this for a drink at the bar.

Smart dress is desirable at better restaurants (suit/evening dress). If there is no stated **dress code**, men always have a tie in the pocket of their jacket just in case, just like New York's experienced restaurant patrons. As for women: well, in New York there's no such thing as a woman who's not well-dressed in the evening!

Smokers, incidentally, suffer (▶ Smoking Ban) and at best can only indulge in the few remaining restaurants with a smoking area. One more thing: good times bring with them better manners. Nowadays requesting a doggy bag in a better restaurant is considered a *faux pas*.

> ! *Baedeker* TIP
>
> **Lunchtime bargains**
>
> Whoever doesn't want to pay the prices in the better restaurants or just wants a quick meal should either dine at midday or go for the more reasonable pre-theatre dinner before the big shows begin, between 6pm and 8pm. Prix fixe menus at midday or in the evening are also economical. One area where no savings should be made: the tip ▶Tipping.

The best known restaurant guide available in bookshops is called *Zagat New York City*. Tips and reviews are also available at www.zagat.com.

Restaurant guide

⏵ RECOMMENDED RESTAURANTS

▶ ① etc. ▶**Maps p. 104 – 107**
No number: not on map

▶ **Price categories**
Expensive: main course more than $30
Moderate: main course $20 to $30
Inexpensive: main course up to $20

EXPENSIVE

▶ ① **Alain Ducasse at
The St. Regis**
5 E 55th St./Fifth Ave.
Tel. 212-710-2277,
Subway: Fifth Ave./53rd St.
One of the best chefs in the world prepares (evenings only) the finest French cuisine here for stars and starlets and anyone else who can afford the prices (small prix fixe menu from $65, tasting menu $110).

▶ ② **Aureole**
34 E 61st St.
(between Madison and Park Ave.)
Tel. 212-319-1660
Subway: Lexington Ave.-63rd St. or Lexington Ave.-59th St.
Halibut filet on a bed of risotto with asparagus sabayon, soba noodles with tuna sashimi, triple crème brûlée – the Aureole, with branches in Las Vegas, Sonoma, Los Angeles and Washington, is a classic purveyor of fusion cuisine, which mixes food and spices from various parts of the world. The always fresh, extravagant flower decorations are great.

▶ ③ **Babbo**
110 Waverly Place (between Mac-Dougal St. and Sixth Ave.)

Tel. 212-777-0303
Subway: Grand St. or W 4th St.
Mario Batali is king of the kitchen here – and what he creates is simply heavenly, be it light gnocchi on oxtail Carpaccio, calamari à la minute or fritelle di ricotta with caramel bananas. Certainly one of the best Italian restaurants on the city.

▶ ④ **Le Bernardin**
155 W 51st St.
(between Sixth and Seventh Ave.)
Tel. 212-757-2390
Subway: Rockefeller Center
Master chef Eric Ripert gets his fresh seafood from fishermen under contract to him and only fillets them in his kitchen, of course. No wonder they call him »King of the Seas«.

▶ **Nobu**
105 Hudson St.
(near Franklin St., Tribeca)
Tel. 212-219-0500
Subway: Franklin St.
Can anything more be said about Robert De Niro's legendary restaurant? For years now, chef Nobuyuki Matsuhisa has served up the best sushi, sashimi and miso soups in the city along with tasty entrées like tuna fish tartare with beluga caviar, sprinkled with sake. The dining room is a mixture of bistro, cocktail bar and interior designer's dream. Very trendy, chic clientele; many celebrities can be seen here, too.

▶ **River Café**
1 Water St. / Old Fulton St.,
Dumbo (Brooklyn)

Tel. 718-522-5200
Subway: High St.
Not in a skyscraper but on a freighter: an elegant restaurant with exorbitant prices, offering a wonderful panoramic view of the skyline of Manhattan. Fish in particular is a speciality here.

▶ ⑦ **The View**
1535 Broadway
(between 45th and 46th St.)
Tel. 212-704-8900
Subway: 42nd St., 42nd St.-Times Square
One of the finest gastronomic establishments of the city: a fascinating restaurant with a fantastic view. Situated on the 48th floor of the Marriott Marquis Hotel near Broadway and Times Square, the restaurant rotates 360° in one hour.

▶ **Water's Edge**
East River / 44th Drive, Long Island City (Queens)
Tel. 718-482-0033
Subway: 23rd St.-Ely Ave.
This exclusive restaurant serving American cuisine is on the shore of Queens. The trip there is a pleasure, too: at 6pm Mon–Sat from the marina at 34th St. on the East River the restaurant's own water taxi transports guests.

▶ **Tribeca Grill**
375 Greenwich St. / Franklin St.
Tel. 212-941-3900
Subway: Franklin St.
American bistro cuisine, opened a few years ago by the movie stars Robert De Niro, Sean Penn, Bill Murray and Christopher Walken among others. Atmospheric, congenial, always crowded and loud.

▶ **Peter Luger**
178 Broadway / Driggs Ave.,Williamsburg (Brooklyn)
Tel. 718-387-7400
Subway: Marcy Ave.
Considered to be New York's best steakhouse. Big portions; beer garden atmosphere. Founded in 1887.

▶ ⑩ **Boathouse Café**
Central Park Lake, Park Drive North / East 72nd St.
Tel. 212-517-2233
Subway: 72nd St.
Very nice restaurant in Central Park on the lakeshore with a great terrace for dining. Fish dishes and American cuisine.

▶ ⑪ **Osteria del Circo**
120 W 55th St.
(between Seventh and Sixth Ave.)
Tel. 212-265-3636
Subway: 57th St.
One of the in-demand gourmet restaurants of New York, run by Mario, Marco and Mauro Maccioni. Tuscan cuisine – wonderful meals, both light and more substantial. Reservation necessary.

▶ ⑫ **Hatsuhana Sushi Restaurant**
17 E 48th St.
(between Fifth and Madison Ave.)
Tel. 212-355-3345
Subway: Fifth Ave.-53rd St.
Stylish restaurant that succeeds in combining Japanese tradition with the modern.

▶ ⑭ **Gotham Bar & Grill**
12 E 12th St.
(between Fifth Ave. and University Place)
Tel. 212-620-4020
Subway: 14th St.-Union Square-
Gourmet temple of Greenwich

The chefs in the Hatsuhana and the products of their labour

Village. American food, sophisticated preparation. The interior looks good, too.

MODERATE

▶ **Chart House**
Pier D-T, Lincoln Harbor, Weehawken (New Jersey)
Tel. 201-348-6628
The Chart House is on the other side of the Hudson River in New Jersey. It is in a two-storey frame house at the end of two piers. The typical American cuisine with big steaks and lots of salad at affordable prices is complemented by a fantastic view of the Manhattan skyline (get there by taxi through the Lincoln Tunnel).

▶ ⑥ **Darbar Grill**
157 E 55th St. (near Third Ave.)
Tel. 212-750-8170, subway: Lexington Ave./59th St.
At first glance a refined steakhouse, but chef Simon Gomes presents Indian cooking with an international touch.

▶ ⑧ **Mia Dona**
206 E 58th St. (corner Third Ave.)
Tel. 212-750-8170, subway: Lexington Ave./59th St.
Tiny restaurant that convinces with first-class Mediterranean cooking. The lamb spareribs are the best.

▶ ⑬ **Beyoglu**
1431 Third Ave.
(corner 81st St.)
Tel. 212-650-0850
Subway: 77th St.
Some critics call it the »best Turkish restaurant in town«. The döner kebab is made from top quality meat.

▶ ⑮ **Dallas BBQ**
261 8th Avenue/ 23rd St.
Tel. 212-462-0001
www.bbqnyc.com
Subway: 23rd St.
Fairly large restaurant in the middle of Chelsea with typical American food.

▶ ⑳ **Union Square Café**
21 E 16th St.
(between 5th Ave. and Union Square)
Tel. 212-243-4020
Subway: 14th St./Union Square
Since 1985 one of the most popular restaurants; it combines a first-class kitchen with a relaxed atmosphere. American cooking with a touch of Italy.

▶ ㊲ **Arturo's**
106 W. Houston St. (corner
Thompson St.)
Tel. 212-677-3820
Subway: Houston St.
Even native Italians swear by the
first-class wood-burning oven
pizza. The most delicious varieties
include shrimp marinara and veal
parmesan. Large selection of Indian dishes. The chicken is especially good.

▶ ⑯ **Oyster Bar & Restaurant**
Grand Central Terminal, 42nd St.
Tel. 212-490-6650
Subway: Grand Central-42nd St.
Excellent restaurant in the lower
floor of the railway station. Spe-
cialities: fish and oysters.

▶ ⑰ **Brasserie**
100 E 53rd St.
(between Park and Lexington
Ave.)
Tel. 212-751-4840
Subway: Lexington Ave.-53rd St.
French cuisine. Limited selection,
but not expensive. Always open.

▶ ⑱ **Boqueria**
53 W 19th St. (between 5th and
6th Ave.)
Tel. 212-255-4160
Subway: 23rd St./Fifth Ave.
Inspired by Boqueria Market in
barcelona, this hip restaurant offers the ultimate spanish cooking.
The tapas and raciones taste better
than in Catalonia.

▶ ㉑ **Prune**
54 E First St., tel. 212-677-6221
Subway: Bleeker St.
The sensational hamburger and
spaghetti carbonara are among the
highlights in this unique lunch
restaurant. The cocktail menu

Enjoy excellent fish and seafood at the Oyster Bar in Grand Central Terminal

includes twelve different kinds of
bloody marys.

▶ ㊳ **Angelo**
146 Mulberry St. (near Grand St.)
Tel. 212-966-1277
Traditional Neapolitan cooking,
especially good is the homemade
pasta.

▶ **Sylvia's**
328 Lenox Ave.
(between 126th and 127th St.)
Tel. 212-996-0660
Subway: 125th St.
Restaurant in Harlem, which
serves reasonably priced soul food,
the spicy dishes of the southern
African Americans. During Sunday brunch there is live gospel
music.

▸ ㉒ **Justin's**
31 W 21st St.
(between Fifth and Sixth Ave.)
Tel. 212-352-0599
Subway: 23rd St.
Yuppie venue for the Flatiron
district – the later it gets, the more
beautiful the guests! Maybe you'll
get lucky and sit next to P.
Diddy – one of the great New York
hip-hop stars. Speciality of the
house: fried chicken with fresh
waffles.

▸ ㉓ **Candle 79**
154 E 79th St. (between Third and
Lexington Ave.)
Tel. 212-537-7179
Very good vegetarian cooking.
Sunday brunch from noon until
4pm.

▸ ㉔ **Orsay**
1057 Lexington Ave. (corner 75th
St.), tel. 212-517-6400
Subway: Lexington Ave./77th St.
Looks like an authentic French
bistro. Mainly light dishes like
lobster salad to tempt the palate.

*Comfortable atmosphere
at Sylvia's*

▸ ㉜ **Primola**
1226 Second Ave. (near 64th St.)
Tel. 212-758-1775
Subway: 68th St.
One of the most popular Italian
restaurants on the Upper East
Side. The fish and clam dishes are
especially good. Atmosphere like
in a comfortable living room.

INEXPENSIVE

▸ ⑤ **Accademia di Vino**
1081 Third Ave. (near 64th St.)
Tel. 212-888-6333, subway: 68th
St.
Cozy Italian restaurant is known
especially for its great variety in
wines. Very good pizzas, salads
and antipasti.

▸ ⑨ **Pom Pom Diner**
610 Eleventh Ave. (near 45th St.)
Tel. 212-397-8395, subway: 42nd
St./Eighth Ave. Has served traditional American fast food like
cheeseburgers and club sandwiches since 1969.

▸ ⑲ **Cinema Café**
45 E 60th St. near madison Ave.
Tel. 212-750-7500, subway: Lexington Ave.
Unique sandwiches and wraps, the
crispy pizzas are good too. Legendary film posters and photos on
the walls support the café's name.

▸ ㊴ **Kefi**
222 W 79th St. (near Amsterdam
Ave.)
Subway: 72nd St., tel. 212-873-
0200
Good traditional Greek cooking
on the Upper West Side.

▸ **Lantern**
101 Montague St., Brooklyn
Tel. 718-237-2594

The staff at Jesus' Taco is always in a good mood

Thai cooking with quick, cheap business lunch in a pretty interior.

㉕ La Bonne Soupe
48 W 55th St.
(between Fifth and Sixth Ave.)
Tel. 212-586-7650.
The best soups in all of Manhattan are said to be served here. Congenial restaurant where diners have to queue up at lunchtime.

㉖ Hummus Place
305 Amsterdam Ave. (between 74th and 75th St.)
Subway: 72nd St., tel. 212-799-3335
www.hummusplace.com
A vegetarian menu majoring in hummus (chick peas) in a tiny Israeli-Neareastern restaurant with cheerful atmosphere.

Jesus' Taco
501 W 145th St./Amsterdam Ave.
Tel. 212-234-3330
Subway: 145th St.
Jeffry Chen and his crew offer the very best Tex Mex food around the clock. Only fresh ingredients are used.

Elaine's
1703 Second Ave.
(between 88th and 89th St.)
Tel. 212-534-8103
Subway: 86th St.
For three decades now (and because of that a bit out of fashion these days) this little restaurant on the Upper East Side has served excellent desserts. Scenes from the TV series *Sex in the City* were filmed here.

㉗ Madras Mahal
104 Lexington Ave.
(between 27th and 28th St.)
Tel. 212-684-4010
Subway: E 28th St.
This economical restaurant serving mainly vegetarian dishes is one of the best Indian restaurants in the city.

㉘ Carnegie Deli
854 Seventh Ave.
(between 54th and 55th St.)
Tel. 212-757-2245
Subway: Seventh Ave.
Eastern Jewish cuisine with huge portions.

㉙ Katz's

205 E Houston St./Ludlow St.
Tel. 212-254-2246
Subway: Lower East Side-Second
Ave.
The chairs wobble, the rattle of
dishes is constantly in the background, and it smells of meat,
fried food, sauerkraut and beer.
Politicians, film stars, sports heroes, Wall Street managers and
regular Joes alike enjoy dining in
the restaurant at Katz's Delicatessen, a New York institution since
1888. Specialities of the house are
the up to 14cm/5.5in-high pastrami sandwiches. Incidentally the
famous orgasm scene from the
movie *When Harry Met Sally* was
filmed here.

㉚ Ess-a-Bagel

359 1st Avenue/21st St.
Tel. 212-260-2252
Subway 6 to 23rd Street
The name is the programme:
perfect bagels with a light, crispy,
not too firm crust, a barely
existent hole in the middle and
with tasty schmear, that is filling – for less than $1.

㉛ Second Avenue Deli

156 Second Ave./10th St.
Tel. 212-677-0606
Subway: Astor Place
One of the last authentic Jewish
delis, there since 1954, offers
excellent matzo ball soups
– chicken soup with dumplings.

Jackson Diner

37-47 74th St.
(between Roosevelt &
37th Ave., Queens)
Tel. 718-672-1232
Subway: 74th St.-Broadway
The big Indian community that

lives in Queens swears by this very
authentic restaurant – is it because
of the large portions, the authentic
(that is really hot!) spices or
because the interior, despite being
kitschy, reminds them of home?

㉝ Rai Rai Ken

214 E 10th St. (near Second Ave.)
Tel. 212-477-7030
Subway: Astor Place
Soba, udon and ramen in all
shapes and forms of the menu in
this Japanese noodle-bar. A successful alternative to the many
sushi bars.

㉞ The Highliner

210 10th Ave./22nd Street
Tel. 212-206-6206
Typical diner as it is known from
fims and television: Try typical
diner cooking in a former trendy
club just a stone's throw from
Highline Park.

㊱ Zen Palate

663 Ninth Ave./46th St.
Tel. 212-582-1669
Subway: 42nd St.-Port Authority
Whether it's the spinach crepes
filled with beans or the shepherd's
pies, **vegetarians** feel like they're
in heaven here. There are branches
at 34 Union Square and 2170
Broadway, near 76th St.

COFFEE BARS · COFFEEHOUSES

▶ Bread Market Café

1290 Sixth Ave. (near 52nd St.)
Tel. 212-957-5677
Subway: 50th St.
This café swears by fresh ingredients in the sandwiches and
wraps. Organic a must. Hungry
customers order the Mexican
burritos.

▶ Café Lalo
201 W 83rd St.
(between Amsterdam Ave. and Broadway)
Tel. 212-496-6031
Subway: 79th St.
Very atmospheric café with European ambience, ideal for a late visit after the cinema or theatre. The espresso is divine.

▶ Cybercafé
250 W 49th St.
(between Seventhth and Eighth Ave.)
Tel. 212-333-4686
Subway: Rockefeller Center
Trendy venue for drinking strong espresso and playing computer games.

▶ Hard Rock Café
221 W 57th St.
(between Seventh Ave. and Broadway),
Tel. 212-489-6565
Subway: 57th St.
Hamburger and sandwiches with deafening rock music. All sorts of rock'n'roll memorabilia on the walls.

▶ Le Grainne Café
183 Ninth Ave., subway: 8th Ave./23rd St.
Very comfortable café, serves a broad spectrum of people with good food. Excellent French toast.

▶ Brown Cup
334 8th Ave
(between 26th and 27th St.)
Subway: 23rd St.
Caffeine kick and light refreshments.

▶ Café Gitane
242 Mott St.
(between Houston and Prince St.)
Tel. 212-334-9552
Subway: Prince St., Broadway-Lafayette St.
Bistro venue of the cool scene from the trendy new neighbourhood NoLita (North of Little Italy).

▶ Veniero's Pasticceria
342 E 11th St.
(near First Ave.)
Tel. 212-674-7264
Subway: Astor Place
This Italian café has been one of the best addresses for sweet tooths for over a century. Italian sweet dishes of the best quality taste good at any time. The best liqueurs are also on the menu.

▶ Limbo
47 Ave. A
(between 3rd and 4th St.)
Tel. 212-477-5271
Subway: Second Ave.
Authentic East Village atmosphere, venue for artists, literary types and young actors.

▶ MarieBelle
484 Broome St.
(between Broadway and Wooster St.), tel. 212-925-6999
Subway: Canal St.
The Cacao Bar is hidden behind the Chocolate Emporium and serves a very choice selection of hot chocolates and cocoas. Solid chocolate and pralines are available in the shop.

▶ Emack & Bolio's
389 Amsterdam Ave.
(between 78th and 79th St.)
Subway: 79th St.
Supposed to have the best ice-cream on the East Coast

Hotels and Restaurants Manhattan Midtown

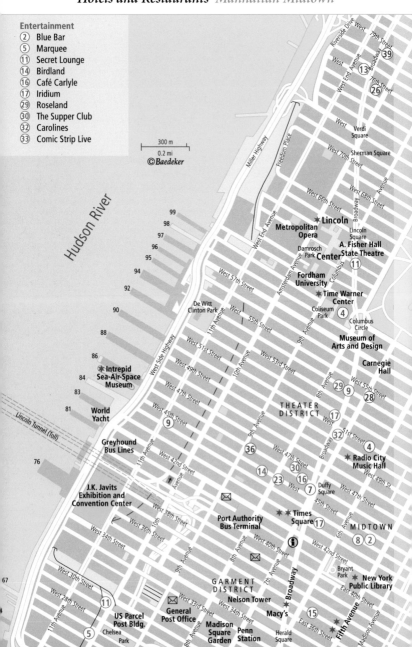

Entertainment
- ② Blue Bar
- ⑤ Marquee
- ⑪ Secret Lounge
- ⑭ Birdland
- ⑯ Café Carlyle
- ⑰ Iridium
- ㉙ Roseland
- ㉚ The Supper Club
- ㉜ Carolines
- ㉝ Comic Strip Live

300 m
0.2 mi
©Baedeker

Where to stay

1. Carlyle
2. Four Seasons
3. Pierre
4. Mandarin Oriental
5. St. Regis
6. Waldorf Astoria
8. Algonquin
9. Ameritania
10. Box-Tree
11. West Side YMCA
12. Lexington
13. Belleclaire
15. Metro
16. Paramount
17. Millennium Broadway
19. Salisbury Hotel
23. Milford Plaza
25. The Lucerne
26. Vanderbilt YMCA

Where to eat

1. Alain Ducasse at the St. Regis
2. Aureole
4. Le Bernardin
5. Accademia di Vino
6. Darbar Grill
7. The View Marriot Marquis
8. Mia Dona
9. Pom Pom Diner
10. Boathouse Café
11. Osteria del Circo
12. Hatsuhana Sushi Restaurant
13. Beyoglu
16. Oyster Bar & Restaurant
17. Brasserie
19. Cinema Cafe
23. Candle 79
24. Orsay
25. La Bonne Soupe
26. Hummus Place
28. Carnegie Deli
32. Primola
36. Zen Palate
39. Kefi

Hotels and Restaurants Manhattan Downtown

Entertainment
- ① Avalon
- ③ bOb
- ④ Bubble Lounge
- ⑥ 230 Fifth
- ⑦ Gramercy Tavern
- ⑧ Kaña
- ⑨ Momofuku
- ⑩ Mc Sorley's
- ⑫ Webster Hall
- ⑬ Zum Schneider
- ⑮ Blue Note
- ⑱ The Jazz Standard
- ⑲ Smalls
- ⑳ Sweet Rhythm
- ㉑ Village Vanguard
- ㉒ Arlene Grocery
- ㉓ CBGB
- ㉔ Cielo
- ㉕ Irving Plaza
- ㉖ The Living Room
- ㉗ The Knitting Factory
- ㉘ The Mercury Lounge
- ㉛ S.O.B.'s

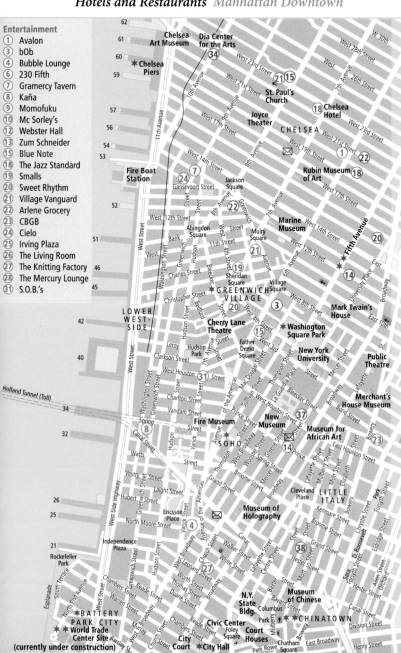

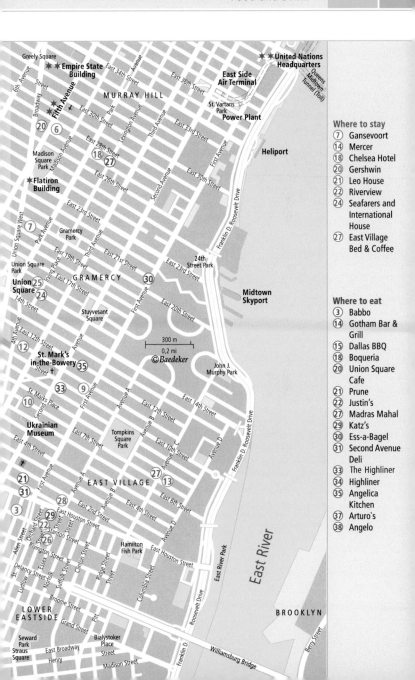

Greely Square

** Empire State Building

East 34th Street

East 36th Street

** United Nations Headquarters

East Side Air Terminal

Queens Midtown Tunnel (Toll)

MURRAY HILL

St. Vartans Park

Power Plant

East 33rd Street

Heliport

** Fifth Avenue

East 30th Street

East 30th Street

⑳ ⑥

East 28th Street

Madison Square Park

⑱

㉗

East 26th Street

* Flatiron Building

East 23rd Street

⑦

Gramercy Park

East 21st Street

East 19th Street

24th Street Park

㉚

East 23rd Street

Union Square Park

East 20th Street

Franklin D. Roosevelt Drive

Midtown Skyport

GRAMERCY

Union Square ㉕ ㉔

14th Street

East 17th Street

Stuyvesant Square

300 m
0,2 mi
©Baedeker

John J. Murphy Park

East 12th Street

⑫

St. Mark's in-the-Bowery

㉟

East 14th Street

㉝ ⑨

St. Marks place

⑩

Ukrainian Museum

East 7th Street

Tompkins Square Park

East 10th Street

East 14th Street

㉗

EAST VILLAGE ⑬

East 6th Street

East 4th Street

㉑

㉛

East Houston Street

⑶ ㉘

East 2nd Street

㉙

㉒

Stanton Street

㉖

Rivington Street

Hamilton Fish Park

East Houston Street

East River Park

East River

Franklin D. Roosevelt Drive

LOWER EASTSIDE

Grand Street

Seward Park Straus Square

Bialystoker Place

East Broadway

Henry

Madison Street

Broome Street

Delancy Street

Williamsburg Bridge

BROOKLYN

Roosevelt Drive

Health

Pharmacies   American **drug stores** or **pharmacies** cannot be compared with European pharmacies. Prescription medication is only a small part of the stock for most of them, and many look like small department stores. Drug stores are listed in the *Yellow Pages*. They are open daily from 9am–6pm, some until 9pm or midnight.

Hospitals   The city clinics are mostly overcrowded, the private hospitals expensive. There is a list of private hospitals in the blue pages of the telephone book. Information is also available from **Travelers' Aid**, a US organization for tourists headquartered in Washington DC (tel. 202-546-1127, www.travelersaid.org).

PHARMACY

▸ **Open 24 hours**
Rite Aid, 50th St. / Eighth Ave.
Tel. 212-247-8384
Duane Reade
244 57th St. / Broadway
Tel. 212-541-9708

AMBULANCE · POLICE

Tel. 911

HOSPITALS

Dial 411 to locate the closest private or public hospital with a hospital emergency room.
▸ **St Vincent's**
11th St. / Seventh Ave.
Tel. 212-604-7998

▸ **Columbia Presbyterian Medical Center**
622 W 168th St.
Tel. 212-305-2500

▸ **St Luke's Roosevelt**
58th St. / Tenth Ave.
Tel. 212-523-4000

▸ **Mount Sinai Medical Center**
100th St. / Fifth Ave.
Tel. 212-241-6500

▸ **New York Hospital**
525 E 68th St.
Tel. 212-746-5454

Information

▶ USEFUL ADDRESSES

IN USA – UK

▸ **New York City's Official Tourism Organization**
NYC and Company

810 Seventh Avenue, New York, NY 10019
Tel. 212-484-1200

NYC and Company (London Marketing Office)
Hills Balfour, Notcutt House, 36 Southwark Bridge Road, London, SE1 9EU
www.nycvisit.com
Information on accommodation, restaurants, events, shopping, business concerns
Tel. +44 (0) 207 202 6367

IN NEW YORK

▶ New York's Visitor Information Center
810 Seventh Ave. (between 52nd and 53rd St.)
Tel. 212-484-1200
Fax 212-246-6310
Mon–Fri 8.30–6pm, Sat, Sun 9am–6pm, www.nycvisit.com
Infos from hotels to sightseeing, City Pass etc.

▶ Times Square Visitor Center
1560 Broadway (between 46th and 47th St.)
Pick up a *NYC Travel Planner* here with all sorts of important information (including sightseeing, addresses, opening times and events).

▶ Additional tourist offices
The **Brooklyn** Tourism Council
30 Flatbush Ave.
Tel. 718-855-7882
www.brooklynx.org

Bronx Tourism Council
198 E 161st St.
Tel. 718-590-2766
www.ilovethebronx.com

Harlem Visitors & Convention Association
219 W 135th St.
Tel. 212-862-8497

Queens Tourism Council
Queens Borough Hall
Kew Gardens, tel. 718-263-0546
www.discoverqueens.info

Staten Island Tourism Council
1 Edgewater Plaza, Staten Island
Tel. 718-442-4356

▶ NY State Division of Tourism
www.nylovesu.com
www.iloveny.com

▶ Further Information
Weather report: tel. 1212
Time check: tel. 1616
Lost and found:
Taxi: tel. 212-639-9675
Subway and bus:
Tel. 212-712-4500

US EMBASSIES

▶ In UK
24 Grosvenor Square, London, W1A 1AE
Tel. (0)20 7499-9000
http://london.usembassy.gov
US Consulates General in Cardiff, Edinburgh and Belfast

▶ In Republic of Ireland
42 Elgin Road, Ballsbridge
Dublin 4
Tel. +353 1 668-8777
Fax +353 1 668-9946
http://dublin.usembassy.gov

▶ In Australia
Moonah Place, Yarralumla, ACT 2600
Tel. (02) 6214-5600, Fax (02) 6214-5970
http://canberra.usembassy.gov

▶ In Canada
490 Sussex Drive, Ottawa, Ontario K1N 1G8
Tel. 613-688-5335

Fax 613.688.3082
http://canada.usembassy.gov

CONSULATES IN
NEW YORK

▶ **British Consulate General**
845 Third Avenue
Tel. 212-745-0200
Fax 212-754-3062
www.britainusa.com/ny/

▶ **Consulate General of Ireland**
Ireland House, 345 Park Avenue,
17th Floor
Tel. 212 319-2555
Fax 212-980-9475
www.irelandemb.org

▶ **Australian Consulate General**
150 East 42nd Street, 34th Floor
Tel. 212-351-6500
Fax 212-351-6501
www.australianyc.org

▶ **Consulate General of Canada**
1251 Avenue of the Americas
Tel. 212-596-1628
Fax 212-596-1790
http://geo.international.gc.ca/
can-am/new_york

INTERNET

▶ **www.newyork.citysearch.com**
Information of all kinds, including
events, theatre, museums, shopping etc

▶ **www.nyc.gov**
The city's official website

▶ **www.timeoutny.com**
Website of the weekly city magazine with information on events,
restaurants, nightlife etc

▶ **www.villagevoice.com**
Website of the well-known city

Literature

Non-fiction   **Kenneth T. Jackson (ed.)**, *The Encyclopedia of New York City*, Yale University Press and The New York Historical Society, New Haven & London / New York 1995. Here is everything you ever wanted to know about New York, from A to Z.

Italo Rota, *Not Only Buildings*, Te Neues Publishing Company 2000. A kind of field guide on the buildings in Manhattan, in which all are depicted in the form of hand-coloured postcards from the first half of the 20th century.

Bill Harris, Jörg Brockmann, *1000 New York Buildings*, Black Dog & Leventhal Publishers 2005. Brockmann photographed New York's architecture, and Harris wrote the sober explanations.

Georges Perec, Robert Bober, *Ellis Island*, New Press 1995. A poetic volume about the history of emigration and an account of the millions of immigrants who passed through Ellis Island between 1862 and 1942.

There are countless books on New York — we'll tell you which ones are worth reading

Gil C. Alicea, Carmine DeSena, *The Air Down Here,* Chronicle Books 1995. A Hispanic American teenager reflects on life in the South Bronx.

Suzy Gershman, *Born to Shop New York: The Ultimate Guide for Travelers Who Love to Shop,* Frommer's 2006. A guide to shopping in Manhattan, including flea markets and factory outlets, as well as gift ideas and tips on hotels and restaurants (for more shopping guides see ►Shopping).

Time Out New York, Penguin Books. Annually updated New York guide with many important tips.

Beyond the above there are numerous novels that take place in New York. **Paul Auster** captured the character of the city especially well in *The New York Trilogy, Moon Palace, The Brooklyn Follies,* Henry Holt and Co. 2005.

Kevin Baker, *Paradise Alley,* Harper Perennial 2003. This exciting novel brings historical New York to life. It takes place on three days in July 1863, considered to be the three most awful days in the history of New York until 11 September 2001. The novel is part of a trilogy.

The following novels are also recommended:
Rita Mae Brown, *Rubyfruit Jungle,* 1973
Truman Capote, *Breakfast at Tiffany's,* 1958
Herbig Jerome Charyn, *Metropolis New York,* 1973
Max Frisch, *Montauk,* 1975
F. Scott Fitzgerald, *The Great Gatsby,* 1925 – a morality tale from old Long Island
Tama Janowitz, *Cannibal in Manhattan,* 1987
Toni Morrison, *Jazz,* 1992
John Dos Passos, *Manhattan Transfer,* 1925
Joseph Roth, *Job: The Story of a Simple Man,* 1930

Hubert Selby, *Last Exit to Brooklyn*, 1951
Lynne Tillman, *No Lease on Life*, 1998
Tom Wolfe, *Bonfire of the Vanities*, 1987
Paul Auster, Joachim A. Frank, *City of Glass*, 2004
Candace Bushnell, *Sex and the City*, 2001

New York in Film ▶Baedeker Special p.42

Media

Newspapers In spite of its size New York has only three daily newspapers: The *New York Times* is the most respected newspaper in America. The weekday editions are 72 to 124 pages long, the Sunday edition 300 to 500. The boulevard papers *Daily News* and *New York Post* are quite sensationalistic. The quickest source of information is the nationwide publication *USA Today*.

UK and Irish Newsstands sell papers from the UK and Republic of Ireland, but
newspapers they are normally a day old. Some publications, such as the UK newspaper the *Times*, are available in a US edition the same day.

Money

The US monetary unit is the **dollar** (US$), colloquially called the »buck«. Apart from notes, or bills, worth $1, 2, 5, 10, 20, 50 and 100 (there are also larger notes for bank business), there are coins worth 1 (penny), 5 (nickel), 10 (dime), 25 (quarter) cents, and more rarely

▶ ALL ABOUT MONEY

EXCHANGE RATE

1 US$ = 0.61 GBP
1 GBP = 1.63 US$
1 US$ = 0.70 €
1 € = 1.43 US$

Rates from May 2011
Current exchange rates:
www.oanda.com

LOST CREDIT CARD
▶ **Telephone numbers**
There is a number on the back of
every credit card which should be called in the case of the card being lost or stolen – it's a good idea to make a note of this number as well as those given by your bank.

For visa cards, the Visa Global Card Assistance Service will arrange for lost cards to be cancelled. In the USA, the number for this free and multi-lingual service is 1-800-847-2911.

50 cents (half-dollar) and 1 dollar in circulation. It is better to exchange money in your home country – part of it into traveller's cheques, which are accepted almost everywhere. Up to $10,000 may be brought in to or taken out of the country freely. Larger amounts must be declared in the customs declaration form which non-residents are required to complete in the aeroplane.

Traveller's cheques and major foreign currencies can be exchanged without difficulty in banks or in branches of Thomas Cook or American Express. **Opening times of banks:** Mon–Thu 9am–3.30pm, Fri until 4.30pm

Traveller's cheques and foreign currency

The most common method of payment is the **credit card**; Euro/MasterCard and Visa are the most common. When renting a car a credit card is required for the deposit; most hotels require them as well.
ATMs (automatic teller machines) are available at many locations around the clock. **UK bank cards** Most UK bank cards will enable you to withdraw money from ATMs in New York, though there will probably be a charge incurred and the exchange rate is likely to be less advantageous than offered by banks and bureaux de change at home. Of course, the PIN number is necessary for withdrawals.

Credit cards

◄ debit cards

Museums and Galleries

The museums in New York are privately owned and run, but many are subsidized. In a few museums there is no set entry fee; visitors pay what they can (»Pay what you wish«).
On the »Museum Mile«, Fifth Ave. between 79th and 103rd Street there is no admission charge at certain times (mostly Tue from 5pm). More information on reduced prices and discounts can be found in the chapter ► Prices and Discounts. The museums marked with an arrow (►) are described in detail in the section ► Sights from A to Z.

There are around 500 art galleries in New York. Contemporary art can be found above all in ► SoHo and ► Chelsea, established modern and older art on the ► Upper East Side. An **overview** is provided by the monthly *Art Now Gallery Guide* and the website www.galleryguide.org. The guide can be bought in galleries, bookshops and at newsstands.

✔ DON'T MISS

- American Museum of Natural History p.172
- Frick Collection p.245
- Guggenheim Museum p.254
- Metropolitan Museum p.271
- Museum of Modern Art p.280
- Dia: Beacon p.168
- Intrepid Sea, Air & Space Museum p.119
- Whitney Museum of Art p.322

▶ NEW YORK'S MUSEUMS AND GALLERIES

ART · CULTURE · ARCHITECTURE

▶ **American Folk Art Museum**
45 W 53rd St. (between Fifth and Sixth Ave.), tel. 212-265-1040
www.folkartmuseum.org
Subway: 59th St.
Tue–Sun 10.30am–5.30pm
Fri until 7.30pm
Folk and applied art from America and other countries. Not limited to traditional techniques and subjects. Many exhibits have a strong relationship to the contemporary art scene. The new building by architect Tod Williams and Billie Tsien (opposite Eero Saarinen's CBS headquarters) captivates above all with its dark shimmering metal façade with 63 bronze panels (the irregular texture comes from a special casting process: the molten metal was poured onto a bed of coarse sand). There is a branch of the museum at the ►Lincoln Center of the Performing Arts.

▶ **American Numismatic Society**
►Harlem, Audubon Terrace

▶ **Asia Society and Museum**
725 Park Ave./70th St.
Tel. 212-288-6400
www.asiasociety.org
Subway: 68th St.-Hunter College
Tue–Thu, Sat, Sun 11am–6pm
Fri until 9pm
John D. Rockefeller III (1906 to 1978), the oldest son of the great patron, founded the Asia Society in 1956 in order to further America's relationship with the Far East. One of the galleries shows his private collection, sculptures, bronzes, ceramics and pictures from China, Japan, India and Southeast Asia. In addition temporary exhibits, dance shows, lectures, concerts and film viewings are offered. There is also a well stocked bookshop. The seven-storey building in reddish granite and sandstone was built in 1981 according to plans by Edward Larrabee Barnes.

▶ **Bronx Museum of Arts**
1040 Grand Concourse/165th St. (Bronx)
Tel. 718-681-6000
www.bronxmuseum.org
Subway: 161st St.
Tue, Sat, Sun 10am–6pm
Fri until 8pm
Art exhibits, especially New York artists

▶ **The Cloisters**
►The Cloisters

▶ **Cooper-Hewitt National Design Museum**
Fifth Ave./91st St., tel. 212-849-8341, subway: 96th St.
Mon–Fri 10am–5pm, Sat until 6pm, Sun noon until 6pm
www.cooperhewitt.org
New York's design museum most worth seeing belongs to the semi-private Smithsonian Institution, which has the world's largest collection of design and applied art, shown here in rotating exhibits. The basis of the collection was compiled by the sisters Sarah, Eleanor and Amy Hewitt, the granddaughters of the steel magnate Andrew Cooper. The building itself is the somewhat extravagant town villa of the steel magnate Andrew Carnegie, built in 1901 in

the neo-renaissance style, where his family lived until 1946. The city also has him to thank for Carnegie Hall.

▶ **Dahesh Museum**
580 Madison Ave.
(between 56th and 57th St.)
Tel. 212-759-0606
www.daheshmuseum.org
Subway: Lexington Ave.-53rd St.
Tue–Sun 11am–6pm
First Thu of the month until 9pm
Sculptures, paintings and prints by academic artists of the 19th century from France and England.

▶ **Dia Art Foundation**
www.diacenter.org
Tel. 212-989-5566
The Dia Art Foundation has an art museum in beacon with art from the 1960s onwards (▶p.168).

▶ **Fashion Institute of Technology – Museum at FIT**
Seventh Ave. / 27th St.
Tel. 212-217-5800
www.fitnyc.edu
Subway: 28th St.
Tue–Fri noon–8pm, Sat 10am–5pm
Rotating exhibits on the subject of fashion and textiles.

▶ **Forbes Magazine Galleries**
62 Fifth Ave.
Tel. 212-206-5548
Subway: 14th St.
Tue, Wed, Fri, Sat 10am–4pm
Private collection of the deceased multimillionaire Malcolm Forbes.

▶ **Frick Collection**
▶Frick Collection

▶ **Guggenheim Museum**
▶Guggenheim Museum

▶ **Hispanic Society of America**
▶Harlem, Audubon Terrace

▶ **Isamu Noguchi Museum**
▶Queens

▶ **Metropolitan Museum of Art**
▶Metropolitan Museum of Art

▶ **Morgan Library and Museum**
▶Morgan Library

▶ **Museo del Barrio**
1230 Fifth Ave. / 104th St.
Tel. 212-831-7272
Subway: 103rd St.
Wed–Sun 11am–5pm
Mainly Puerto Ricans and other Spanish-speaking ethnic groups from the Caribbean, Central and South America live east of Fifth Ave., between 103rd and 125th Street. The museum shows Puerto Rican and Latin American art, folklore and historical crafts. Among the main attractions are the carved sacred figures called the Santos de Palo (saints of wood). There is also pre-Colombian art.

▶ **Museum of Arts and Design**
2 Columbus Circle
Tel. 212-299-7777
www.americandraftmuseum.org
Subway: Columbus Circle
Tue, Wed, Fri–Sat 10am–6pm Thu until 9pm, Sun 10am–6pm
The Museum of Arts and Design is located in an office building by the architects Kevin Roche/John Dinkeloo opposite the ▶Museum of Modern Art. Along with temporary exhibits there are crafts made of ceramics, textiles, glass, wood, paper, silver and metal, quilts and furniture dating from 1900 to the present day on display. The museum is moving to a new, larger

Museum of Arts and Design

building on Columbus Circle: opening is planned for 2008.

▶ **Museum of African Art**
until Fall 2011: 36-01 43rd Ave. (Queens), subway: 33rd St.; then 1280 Fifth Ave./East 110th St.
www.africanart.org
The Museum of African Art (architect: Robert A.M. Stern) displays historic and modern African art; lectures and events.

▶ **Museum of Modern Art MoMA**
▶Museum of Modern Art – MoMA

▶ **Museum of the Performing Arts**
▶Lincoln Center for the Performing Arts

▶ **Staten Island Museum**
75 Stuyvesant Place (Staten Island)
Tel. 718-727-1135
www.statenislandmuseum.org
Ship: Staten Island Ferry, from Battery Park
Open: Mon–Fri noon–5pm, Sat from 10am, Sun from noon
Exhibitions on natural history and fine arts.

▶ **National Academy of Design**
1083 Fifth Ave. / 89th St.

Tel. 212-369-4880
www.nationalacademy.org
Subway: 86th St.
Wed, Thu noon–5pm
Fri–Sun noon–5pm
American and European design, architecture, art.

▶ **Neue Galerie**
▶Neue Galerie

▶ **Newhouse Center for Contemporary Art**
▶Staten Island

▶ **New Museum of Contemporary Art**
556 W 22nd St.
www.newmuseum.org
Wed 11am–6pm, Thu until 9pm, Fri, Sat, Sun until 6pm
The New Museum of Contemporary Art is a mixture of art museum and gallery. The newest art movements are shown in changing exhibits. Along with the presentation of internationally known stars the young scene is supposed to be promoted here – as also in P. S. 1 (▶Queens) – and helped on towards a breakthrough. The New Museum of Contemporary Art is presently housed in the Chelsea Art Museum (▶Chelsea). In late 2007 it will move into a new building downtown (235 Bowery / Prince St.).

▶ **Pierpont Morgan Library**
▶ Morgan Library

▶ **P. S. 1 Contemporary Art Center**
▶Queens

▶ **Queens Museum of Art**
▶Queens

▶ Rubin Museum of Art
150 W 17th St. / Seventh Ave.
Tel. 212-620-5000
www.rmanyc.org
Subway: 18th St.
Mon, Thu 11am–5pm, Wed until 7pm, Fri until 10pm, Sun until 6pm
Painting from Tibet and the Himalayas.

▶ Schomburg Center for Research in Black Culture
▶Harlem

▶ Skyscraper Museum
39 Battery Place
Tel. 212-968-1961
www.skycraper.org
Subway: South Ferry, Bowling Green
Wed–Sun noon–6pm
Lots of valuable information about New York's high rise architecture.

▶ Studio Museum in Harlem
▶Harlem

▶ Tibetan Museum
▶Staten Island, Jacques Marchais Center of Tibetan Art

▶ Whitney Museum of American Art
▶Whitney Museum of American Art

PHOTOGRAPHY

▶ International Center of Photography – ICP
1133 Sixth Ave. / 43rd St.
Tel. 212-857-0000
www.icp.org
Subway: 42nd St.
Tue–Thu 10am–5pm
Fri until 8pm
Sat, Sun 10am–6pm
The only museum in New York solely devoted to photography was founded in 1974 by Cornell Capa, the brother of the famous photojournalist Robert Capa. The collection includes photographs by Werner Bischof, Robert Capa, David Seymour and Dan Weiner, who were all killed while photographing, as well as works by Ansel Adams or Henri Cartier-Bresson, shown in rotating exhibitions.

▶ Alice Austen House Museum
▶Staten Island

▶ Aperture Foundation Gallery
547 West 27th St., 4th floor (between 10th and 11th Ave.)
Subway: 23rd St., tel. 212-505-5555, www.aperture.org
Tue–Sat 10am–6pm
The exhibition in an historical brownstone house gives an overview of artistic photography in the 20th century.

FILM · TELEVISION

▶ American Museum of the Moving Image
▶Queens

▶ Museum of Television and Radio (MT&R)
25 W 52nd St.
(between Fifth and Sixth Ave.)
www.mtr.org
Subway: 47-50th St.-Rockefeller Center
Thu–Thu 10am–6pm, Tue until 8pm
This museum was built by Philip Johnson and John Burgee and is dedicated to the history of radio and television. The imposing entrance hall leads to the Steven Spielberg Gallery, devoted to temporary exhibitions. The two cine-

mas and smaller viewing rooms show, in rotation, films from the museum's archive, which contains more than 100,000 TV and radio programmes and commercials. In the third floor visitors can put together their own viewing programme at one of the computers using the museum catalogue.

MUSEUMS FOR CHILDREN

▶ **Brooklyn Children's Museum**
  ▶Brooklyn

▶ **Children's Museum of Manhattan**
  ▶Children in New York

▶ **Staten Island Children's Museum**
  ▶Staten Island, Snug Harbor Cultural Center

HISTORY · CULTURAL HISTORY

▶ **Museum of Bronx History Valentine-Varian House**
  3266 Bainbridge Ave. / E 208th St.
  Tel. 718-889-8900
  www.bronxhistoricalsociety.org
  Subway: 205th St.
  Sat 10am–4pm, Sun 1pm–5pm
  The history of the Bronx is exhibited in a farmhouse from the year 1758.

▶ **Mount Vernon Hotel Museum and Garden**
  421 E 61st St.
  (between 1st and York Ave.)
  Tel. 212-838-6878
  Subway: Lexington Ave.-59th St.
  Tue–Sun 11am–4pm
  Colonial style house with garden from the year 1799.

▶ **Bowne House**
  ▶Queens

▶ **Brooklyn Historic Museum**
  ▶Brooklyn

▶ **Chinatown History**
  ▶Chinatown

▶ **Dyckman Farmhouse Museum**
  Broadway / 204th St.
  Subway: 207th St.-Dyckman Street
  www.dyckmanfarmhouse.org
  Wed–Sat 11am–4pm,
  Sun noon–4pm
  The only remaining farmhouse in Manhattan in the so-called colonial style from 1783. The furniture is from the 18th century; in the garden is one of the cherry trees for which the Dyckman Farm was famous years ago.

▶ **Ellis Island Immigrant's Museum**
  ▶Ellis Island

▶ **Fraunces' Tavern Museum**
  ▶Financial District

▶ **Hall of Fame for Great Americans**
  ▶Bronx

▶ **Historic Richmond Town**
  ▶Staten Island

▶ **Lower East Side Tenement Museum**
  ▶Lower East Side

▶ **Merchant's House Museum**
  ▶East Village

▶ **Morris-Jumel Mansion**
  ▶Harlem

▶ **Museum for American Financial History**
  ▶Financial District

▶ Museum of the City of New York

1220 Fifth Ave. / 103rd St.
www.mcny.org
Wed–Sun 10am–5pm
With over 500,000 objects the 300-year history of the city of New York is displayed, from the discovery of the island by Verrazano, on to the settlement Nieuw Amsterdam, through the colonial period and the American Revolution, and up to the present day. The theatre collection is famous, and the collection of doll's houses and toys from days gone by is especially popular.

▶ New York Historical Society

170 Central Park West/77th St.
Tel. 212-873-3400
www.nyhistory.org
Subway: 81st St.-American Museum of Natural History
Tue–Sat 10am–6pm,
Sun 11am–5.45pm
The New York Historical Society, founded in 1809, is one of the oldest scientific institutions of the city. The museum, the oldest in New York State, has been in the same building since 1908, often renovated and expanded, next to the ▶American Museum of Natural History. The society organizes rotating exhibits all year on the city's history and has a comprehensive library on the history of the city and country. The museum's treasures include lamps from the workshop of Louis Comfort Tiffany (1848–1933) and aquarelles by the bird painter John James Audubon (1785-1851).

▶ NYC Fire Museum

258 Spring St. (between Hudson and Varick St.), tel. 212-691-1303
www.nycfiremuseum.org
Subway: Spring St. or Houston St.
Tue–Sat 10am–5pm
Sun until 4pm
History of the New York City Fire Department.

▶ Queens County Farm Museum

73?50 Little Neck Parkway, Floral Park (Queens)
Tel. 718-347-3276
www.queensfarm.org
Subway: Kew Gardens, then Bus Q 46 to Little Neck Parkway
daily 9am–5pm (only outside), Sat, Sun 10am–5pm
History of agriculture in New York, presented in an old farm.

▶ Snug Harbor Cultural Center
▶Staten Island

▶ Staten Island Historical Museum
▶Staten Island

▶ Theodore Roosevelt Birthplace
▶Flatiron District

▶ Van Cortlandt House Museum
▶Bronx

NATURE · TECHNOLOGY

▶ American Museum of Natural History
▶American Museum of Natural History

▶ Intrepid Sea, Air & Space Museum

Pier 86 Hudson River
Tel. 212-245-0072
Subway: 42nd St.-Port Authority, then Bus 42 to Twelfth Ave.
www.intrepidmuseum.org
Apr–Sept Mon–Fri 10am–5pm, Sat, Sun 10am–6pm Oct–March Tue–Sun 10am–5pm

A Concorde can also be viewed

Tel. 212-249-8950
www.americas-society.org
Subway: 68th St.
Wed–Sat noon–6pm
Exhibitions on Central and South America, Canada and the Caribbean.

▶ **Japan Society Gallery**
333 E 47th St.
Tel. 212-832-1155
www.japansociety.org
Subway: Lexington Ave. / 53rd St.
Tue–Fri 11am–6pm
Sat, Sun until 5pm
The Japan Society, situated somewhat northwest of the ▶United Nations Headquarters, was founded in 1907 to promote understanding between the USA and Japan. The black building was built in 1971 according to the plans of Junzo Yoshimura and George Shimamoto in Japanese style. Rotating exhibits of Japanese crafts are shown here. In addition there is a Japanese garden, a lecture hall in which Japanese films and theatre productions are shown as well as lectures held, a language centre and a library.

This impressive naval museum tells you all you need to know on the subject of the US Navy. The main attraction is the *Intrepid*, which served in the Pacific during the Second World War. The aircraft carrier was bombed seven times, five Kamikaze pilots dived at her and a torpedo broke through her side. Along with viewing historical and modern aeroplanes including a Concorde, a submarine, a destroyer and other ships as well as air, sea and space technology can be seen. As well as trying a flight simulator that places would-be pilots into the cockpit of an F/A 18 fighter jet, visitors can test their stomachs in a g-force simulator. (Neither attraction is included in the entry fee.) Right now the Intrepid is not at its pier: for restoration and refurbishment the ship is on a mission once more and will return in fall 2008.

▶ **New York Aquarium**
▶Brooklyn, Coney Island

▶ **New York Hall of Science**
▶Queens

▶ **New York Transit Museum**
▶Brooklyn

▶ **South Street Seaport Museum**
▶South Street Seaport

ETHNOLOGY

▶ **Americas Society**
680 Park Ave.

▶ **Jewish Museum**
▶Jewish Museum

▶ **Museum of the American Indian**
▶Museum of the American Indian

▶ **Museum of Jewish Heritage**
▶Battery Park

▶ **Ukrainian Museum**
▶East Village

OTHER MUSEUMS

▶ **Edgar Allan Poe Cottage**
▶Bronx

▶ Madame Tussaud's New York

234 W 42nd St. (between Seventh and Eighth Ave.)
Tel. 800-246-8872
www.madame-tussauds.com
Subway: 42nd St.-Times Square
Sun–Thu 10am–8pm, Fri, Sat until 10pm;
Along with famous names in world history, local greats like actors Woody Allen, Whoopi Goldberg, Barbra Streisand, Brad Pitt, former mayor Rudolph Giuliani and the real estate magnate Donald Trump have been eternalized in wax.

▶ Museum of Sex

233 Fifth Ave. / 27th St.
Tel. 212-689-6337
www.museumofsex.com
Subway: 28th St.
Sun–Thu 10am–8pm, Fri, Sat until 9pm
Find out about various aspects of human sexuality, from the murder of the prostitute Helen Jewett in 1830 to the great clean-up under former mayor Giuliani, in the rotating exhibitions at the »MoSex«.

▶ Museum of Comic and Cartoon Art (MoCCA)

594 Broadway, Suite 401
(between Houston and Prince)
Tel. 212-254-3511
www.moccany.com
Tue–Sun noon–5pm

▶ American Craft Museum

40 W 53rd St., tel. 212-956-3535
www.americancraftmuseum.com
Mon–Wed, Sat, Sun 10am–6pm, Thu until 8pm
Interesting overview of American crafts, especially from the last two centuries.

▶ Aquavella

18 E 79th Street, tel. 212-734-6300
Impressionist and post-impressionist French masters.

▶ Mary Boone

745 Fifth Ave. and 541 W 24th St.
Tel. 212-752-2929
She assisted Julian Schnabel, Eric Fischl and David Salle among others to achieve their breakthroughs.

▶ Barbara Mathes

22 E 80th St.
Tel. 212-570-4190
Modern paintings and sculptures by young artists in a setting full of atmosphere.

▶ Leo Castelli Gallery

18 E 77th St., tel. 212-249-4470
American artists like Jasper Johns, Claes Oldenburg and James Rosenquist.

▶ Paula Cooper Gallery

534 W 21st St.
Tel. 212-255-1105
Works by Carl Andre and Robert Wilson, among others.

▶ Larry Gagosian

980 Madison / Fifth Ave.
Tel. 212-744-2313
Presently probably the internationally most prominent dealer in modern and contemporary art.

▶ Barbara Gladstone

515 W 24th St.
Tel. 212-206-9300
Promotes new artists.

▶ Marian Goodman Gallery

24 W 57th St.
Tel. 212-977-7160

Considered to be one of the best establishments in the field of installations.

▶ Guggenheim
575 Broadway, tel. 212-423-3500
Exhibitions and museum shop of the Guggenheim Museum.

▶ Marlborough
40 W 57th St., tel. 212-541-4900
Works by artists such as Bacon, Botero etc.

▶ Mathew Marks
523 W 24th St.
Tel. 212-243-0200
Ellsworth Kelly, Bryce Marden, as well as American newcomers.

▶ John McEnroe
42 Greene St.
Tel. 212-219-0395
The former tennis champion now serves up modern art, above all figurative painting.

▶ Metro Pictures
519 W 24th St.
Tel. 212-206-7100
Contemporary art.

▶ Pierogi
167 N 9th St., Williamsburg
Tel. 212-599-2144
Traditional gallery in Brooklyn.

▶ Andrea Rosen
525 W 24th St., tel. 212-627-6000
One of the best noses for new talent.

▶ Tony Shafrazi Gallery
544 W 26th St.
Tel. 212-274-9300
He made Keith Haring and his stick figures famous, among others.

▶ Sonnabend Gallery
536 W 22nd St., tel. 212-627-1018
Modern classics, young artists – pop art, minimal art, conceptual art, including Gilbert & George.

▶ Michael Werner
4 E 77th St., tel. 212-988-1623
Works by the »Jungen Wilden« Baselitz, Immendorff, Kirkeby and Sigmar Polke from the gallery of the former patron from Cologne.

▶ The Pace Gallery
534 W 25th St., tel. 212-929-7000
and
545 W 22nd St., tel. 212-989-4258
Old masters and French Impressionists.

▶ David Zwirner
525 W 19th St., tel. 212-727-2070
Contemporary art.

PHOTO GALLERIES

▶ Janet Borden
560 Broadway
Tel. 212-431-0166
Includes pictures by Martin Parr of England's money aristocracy.

▶ Pace/McGill
32 E 57th St., tel. 212-759-7999
Photos that imitate paintings by old masters and classical works.

▶ Staley-Wise
560 Broadway, tel. 212-966-6223
Fashion photos in particular are shown here.

▶ Witkin Gallery
900 West End Ave.
Tel. 212-280-0303
The Witkin Gallery is the city's oldest photo gallery and offers exhibitions on almost all subjects of photography.

Post and Communications

Post and telephone services are separate in the USA. The post offices are open weekdays 8am–6pm, Fri until 7pm and Sat until 1pm; the **main post office** (General Post Office, 421 Eighth Ave. / 33rd St.) is open around the clock.

Post

Postage for letters within the United States is currently 44 cents for up to 3.5 ounces (98g, ▶ Weights, Measures, Temperatures); postcards cost 28 cents. Postage for letters and postcards to Europe is 98 cents.

Postal rates

The zip code is placed after the two-letter abbreviation for the state (for example New York, NY 10017; variable four-number additions for different parts of the city).

zip code

The telephone service in the USA is privately operated. The operator, who can be reached free of charge by dialling 0, will answer any questions. Calls using a **telephone card** (a prepaid card for $5, 10, 20 or 50), which can be bought at newsstands, are reasonably priced and easy. Dial the number of the provider first (providers are listed on the card), enter the PIN number and telephone worldwide.
Mobile phones (cell phones) will work if the provider has an international roaming agreement. Telephone numbers often have **letter combinations**, for example »USA-WIND«. These correspond to the letters on the telephone keys.
There are also toll-free telephone numbers for hotels, airlines etc, which mostly begin with 1-800 or 1-888.

Telephone

◀ Card phone

◀ Toll-free numbers

In New York the **area code** (Manhattan 212 or 646, Bronx, Brooklyn, Queens and Staten Island 718 and 347) is part of the telephone and fax numbers. When calling within New York always dial 1 + area code + 7-digit telephone number.

Area code

COUNTRY CODES

▶ **Calls from New York**
to UK: 0 11 44
to Republic of Ireland: 0 11 353
to Australia: 0 11 61
to Canada: 1 (North American Numbering Plan)

▶ **Calls to New York**
from UK and
Republic of Ireland: 00 1
from Australia: 0011 1
from Canada: 1

INFORMATION

Tel. 411
and www.411.com

Prices and Discounts

Admission
Students and senior citizens (often starting at the age of 58) get numerous discounts, for example for museum admissions. Children (almost) always pay less.

City Pass, New York Pass
The **City Pass** ($79) includes admission to the six biggest attractions, the **New York Pass** ($75–$190, for 1, 2, 3, 7 days) includes about the same discounts for about 50 attractions (almost all of the city's main attractions); both include a tour on the Circle Line. The passes are available online (www.citypass.com, www.newyorkpass.com) as well as at all participating attractions and the Visitor Information Center (►Information).

 WHAT DOES IT COST?

Ticket
$ 2.25

Double room
from $ 180

Simple meal
from $ 10

Shopping

New York is a shopping paradise. Not only clothes and CDs, but also hi-fi and camera equipment is cheaper here than at home. The selection is huge – from exclusive fashion and jewellery shops on Fifth Avenue (► Sights from A to Z, Fifth Avenue) to exotic items from Asia (► Sights from A to Z, Chinatown), to trashy goods on 42nd Street. The city also offers shopping opportunities for the most unique tastes. Countless shops are concentrated in malls, markets and centers.

Sales tax
Price tags usually show pre-tax prices. Except for books, periodicals and groceries as well as clothing and shoes under $110 (starting April 2012), a so-called **sales tax** is charged on all items, currently set at 8.875%.

Opening hours
Opening hours are not set by law. Some shops, including supermarkets, are open seven days a week, 24 hours a day; the large department stores from 9.45am–6.45pm, Mon and Thu until 9pm (before

Christmas every evening), Sun 11am / noon–5pm. Many small shops, especially those close to department stores, have the same opening hours.

Gerry Frank's book *Where to Find It, Buy it, Eat It*, which is revised every year, lists all department stores and shops. Current sales and bargains are listed in the magazine *Sales and Bargains*, which appears monthly and is available from: The S&B Report, 108 E 38th St., Suite 2000, New York. Finally there is the *New York City Shopping* guide by Zagat (www.zagat.com), in which the evaluations come from 7,200 buyers; expert shopping tours are offered by *A Friend in New York*, tel. 201-656-7282, www.friendny.com; see also Suzy Gershman's *Born to Shop New York* ►Literature.

Guide to the shopping paradise

 SHOPPING

MARKETS

► **Chelsea Market**
75 Ninth Ave. (between 15th/16th St.)
City block with numerous shops and small restaurants including the excellent Fat Witch Bakery and Hale and Hearty Soups.

► **Farmers' Markets**
There are more than 20 farmers' markets in the city. The best known takes place at Union Square, between 16th and 17th St.
Mon, Wed, Fri, Sat 8am–6pm
Cheese from small producers, flowers, herbs, honey, fruit and vegetables

► **Chinese Market**
Canal St., Saturdays
Fruit, vegetables and all sorts of odds and ends

FLEA MARKETS

► **Annex Flea Market**
West 39th/Ninth Ave.
Sat, Sun from sunrise to sunset
Largest and most frequented flea market in the city; right next door:
Indoor Antiques Fair

(122 W 26th St.)

► **PS 44 Flea Market**
Columbus Ave. / 77th St.
Sun 10am–5pm
All sorts of bric-a-brac of greatly varying quality

► **The Garage**
112 W 25th St.
Sat, Sun 7am–5pm
Indoor flea market – ideal for a visit on rainy weekends, affordable antiques.

DEPARTMENT STORES

► **Barney's**
660 Madison Ave. / 61st St. and Seventh Ave. / 17th St.(branch)
One of the most exclusive department stores in the city and the largest men's store in the world

► **Bergdorf Goodman**
754 Fifth Ave. / 58th St.

? DID YOU KNOW ...?

■ More than 4,000g/141fl oz of perfume are sprayed from tester bottles every day at Bloomingdale's.

Macy's self-promotion

Very formal, very expensive; exquisite fashion by various couturiers

▶ **Bloomingdale's**
Lexington Ave. / 59th St.
»Bloomies« is one of the leading department stores in the city; designer fashion, cosmetics etc, fashionable, elegant and yet affordable.

▶ **Lord & Taylor**
4245 Fifth Ave./38th St.
Classic, conservative style with a casual note at affordable prices

▶ **Macy's**
Broadway / 34th St.
A New York institution, also because of the annual Thanksgiving Day Parade. Almost anything is available here; the gourmet department in the basement is definitely worth a visit.

▶ **Saks Fifth Avenue**
611 Fifth Ave. / 50th St.
Typical American fashion, exclusive perfume department, accessories

▶ **Takashimaya**
693 Fifth Ave.
Branch of the largest Japanese department store, a Mecca of good taste

SHOPPING CENTRES MALLS

▶ **South Street Seaport and Pier 17**
Boutiques, bookshops and galleries ▶Sights from A to Z, South Street Seaport

▶ **Rockefeller Center**
▶Rockefeller Center

▶ **Trump Tower**
▶Fifth Avenue

▶ **Manhattan Mall**
Sixth Ave. / 33rd St.
Pleasant, covered shopping street with good restaurants

ELECTRONICS

▶ **Apple Store**
767 Fifth Ave.
Open almost around the clock.
I-Macs, I-Pads, I-Pods and more

► B&H Photo – Video-Pro Audio Superstore
420 Ninth Ave.
This camera department store carries everything that the photographer's heart desires at attractive prices.

► J & R Music & Computer World
9176 Park Row and Broadway (opposite City Hall)
Supermarket for cameras, computers and CDs

► Nintendo World Store
24 West 48th St.
Interactive paradise

MUSIC AND BOOKS

► Bleeker Music Inc. Store
239 Bleeker St.
Overwhelming selection of old phonograph records and rare CDs, informed staff

► Westsider Records
233 W 72nd St.
Classical and jazz records and CDs, some of which are long since »out of print.«

► Jazz Record Center
236 W 26th St., 8th floor
Tue–Sat
Jazz specialist

► Barnes & Noble
1972 Broadway
Huge »book department store« with not just bestsellers. Book prices are reduced just a few weeks after coming on the market. A café allows relaxed browsing in books and periodicals. Numerous branches.

► St. Mark's Comics
148 Montague St.
Inexhaustible selection of comics, also plastic figures, t-shirts, jackets and bags with comicbook figures.

► Strand Book Store
828 Broadway / corner 12th St.
The largest book shop in the world with over 2 million used books. Unfortunately individual titles are sometimes difficult to find.

► Rizzoli
31 W 57th St.; 454 W Broadway; 250 Vesey St.
A most elegant bookshop

► Bluestockings
172 Allen St.
Bookshop for all sorts of alternative subjects like women, black power, globalization etc., with organic coffee and events

GIFTS

► Museum shops
New York museum shops are famous. The nicest are in the Metropolitan Museum of Art, Fifth Ave. / 82nd St.;
Museum of Modern Art, 11 W 53rd St.: MoMA has branches directly opposite the museum, 44 W 53rd St., and in SoHo, 81 Spring St.;
Guggenheim Museum, 1071 Fifth Ave. / 88th St.;
Neue Galerie, 1048 Fifth Avenue / 86th St.

CLOTHING · ACCESSORIES

► Eddie Bauer
578 Broadway/Prince St.
Reasonably priced outdoor clothing

► Brooks Brothers
346 Madison Avenue / 44th St., 666 Fifth Ave.

! *Baedeker* TIP

Urban Outfitters

This successful chain store has trendy clothing at affordable prices. Designer jeans by Diesel and True Religion, dresses and blouses by their own Free People label and t-shirts with unusual texts (628 Broadway, between Houston and Bleeker St.)

The leading store for classic men's and women's clothing

▶ **Anna Sui**
113 Greene St.
In-boutique in SoHo with rock'n'roll clothes from the 1970s and cool glamour from the gangster era

▶ **Century 21**
22 Cortlandt St. (between Broadway and Church St., at Ground Zero)
Designer clothing and much more at reasonable prices

▶ **Forever 21**
1540 Broadway/Times Square
Until 2009 the largest Virgin Megastore, now an even larger store with inexpensive clothing for young people

▶ **The Gap**
527 Madison Ave. / 54th St.
Very good jeans at low prices

▶ **The Original Levi's Store**
750 Lexington Ave.
The whole Levi's palette at reasonable prices

▶ **Manolo Blahnik**
15 W 55th St.
Since *Sex and the City* the most famous shoe store in New York

▶ **Marc Jacobs**
163 Mercer St., SoHo
The current star of the New York fashion scene; the more affordable line is at 403/404 Bleecker St.

▶ **NBA Store**
666 Fifth Ave. / 52nd St.
Shirts, jackets, caps and jewellery with club emblems of the National Basketball Association

▶ **Niketown**
6 E 57th St.
Prestige shop of the famous sporting goods producer

▶ **Prada**
575 Broadway
Rem Koolhaas has converted the former Guggenheim SoHo to a flagship store of a different kind; along with the current collections there are also models from past Prada epochs.

▶ **Stella McCartney**
429 W 14th St.,
Meatpacking District
For four years she was the head of the fashion house Chloé, in 2001 the designer started her own label. Exclusive clothing and accessories

▶ **Barneys New York**
660 Madison Ave.
The designer fashion temple in one of the most expensive parts of the East Side doesn't scrimp with exclusive selections or with prices.

▶ **Artbag**
1130 Madison Ave.
For more than 60 years, a large selection of imaginative handbags, wallets and other leather goods

Atmos
203 W 125th St.
Running shoes in bright colours, crazy t-shirts and unusual accessories

Crocs
270 Columbus Ave.
Huge, colourful selection of the trendy plastic shoes

JEWELLERS

Bulgari
730 Fifth Ave. / 61st St.
Branch of the family-owned business from Rome

Cartier
653 Fifth Ave. – Classical jewellery, watches and accessories by the well-known designer

Tiffany & Co.
727 Fifth Ave.
Jewellers made famous by the film *Breakfast at Tiffany's* with Audrey Hepburn in the leading role. But there are also affordable gifts.

FOOD

Zabar's
2245 Broadway / 80th St.
An institution: gigantic deli selection and kitchen utensils

Best Cellars
1291 Lexington Ave. (near 86th St.) – The wooden shelves hold only excellent, but surprisingly reasonable wines (none over $15). Even beginners have no trouble finding their way around.

Dean & DeLuca
560 Broadway / Prince St.
Gourmet food from throughout the world with a popular espresso bar

Whole Foods
230 Seventh Ave./24th St.
Supermarket for organic foods and fresh products

La Maison du Chocolat
1018 Madison Ave.
Top quality in a branch of the well-known French chocolate boutique. Excellent pralines, own production

DISCOUNT · SECOND-HAND · OUTLETS

Tokio 7
64 E 7th St.
One of the best and hippest second-hand shops in Manhattan

Woodbury Commons
498 Red Apple Court
Central Valley
Tel. 845-928-4000
www.premiumoutlets.com
Daily 10am–9pm (shuttle bus: Shortline New York from Port Authority, 42nd St. / Eighth Ave.; schedules: www.njtransit.com;)
Designer outlet with over 220 shops, including clothing – from Armani to Tommy Hilfiger to Puma – shoes, sporting goods, gifts and household items

Jersey Gardens
New Jersey, Exit 13A of NJ Turnpike
Tel. 908-354-5900
www.jerseygardens.com
Mon–Sat 10am–9pm, Sun 11am–7pm (shuttle bus from Newark International Airport as well as from New York Port Authority, address ►above)
200 shops under one roof, only 30min from Manhattan.

TOYS

► F. A. O. Schwarz
787 Fifth Ave. (near 58th St.)
A paradise (not only) for children.
Overwhelming selection of toys,
also handmade collector's items.
The store windows are especially
worth seeing around Christmas.

► The Sharper Image
Pier 17, South Street Seaport,
4 West 57th St.
Unusual technical toys

► American Girl Place
609 Fifth Ave./49th St.
»Girls' headquarters USA«: the
whole selection of the American
Girl dolls on four floors

► Toys 'R' US
1293 Broadway / 33rd St.
The largest toy chain in the world
has a store on Times Square. There
is a Ferris wheel inside.

AUCTION HOUSES

► Auctioneers
Auctionsof works of art, carpets,
jewellery and craft items take place
almost daily; the large auctions at
Sotheby's and Christie's are also
social events, worth a visit even if
you don't buy anything. The
objects to be auctioned can be
viewed beforehand. The **Arts and
Leisure** section in the Friday edition of the *New York Times* gives
information on auctions.

► Christie's
20 Rockefeller Plaza
Tel. 212-636-2000
www.christies.com

► Sotheby's
1334 York Ave. / 72nd St.
Tel. 212-606-7000
www.sothebys.com

Smoking Ban

*In most places, smoking is only
allowed outdoors*

Smoking is prohibited in all public
places (including parks, beaches,
buildings), on public transport (including taxis and inside ferries), in
railway stations, and in restaurants,
pubs, clubs and bars (a tip for those
who can't resist a postprandial ciga-
rette: the *Zagat New York City* restaurant guide lists about 400 restaurants where smoking is allowed.)

Smoking is also prohibited in rental
cars, many hotel rooms, and on all
domestic flights. There are small
smoking areas in airports and in some restaurants.

Sport and Outdoors

New York is a paradise for sports fans. Fishing and golf is available in the Bronx, Brooklyn, Queens and Staten Island (►Information). But the centre of sporting activity is ► **Central Park** in the heart of Manhattan. Here you can roller skate, ice skate, ride horses, play tennis, row or bike. There are also any number of fitness centres in the city as well as a large number of public and private tennis courts.

DID YOU KNOW …?

- …that 55,000 tennis balls are used every year in the U.S. Open? Or that 28,000 runners take part in the NYC Marathon?

Many hotels have a fitness room, some even an indoor pool. New York also has several public pools. Chelsea Piers (►Baedeker Special p.208) are also popular.

 ## SPORTS VENUES

PRO SPORTS

There are professional teams in basketball, baseball, American football, hockey and soccer. Tickets are available at the following **ticket agencies**:
ABC Tickets, tel. 1-800-355-5555 and Prestige Entertainment Tel. 800-243-8849; tickets for playoff games especially are difficult to get and expensive.

► **American Football**
American football is especially popular, but its complicated rules are not easy for the uninitiated to understand. It developed from rugby and has nothing to do with European football, which is always referred to as soccer in the USA. New York has two pro teams, the **New York Giants** and the **New York Jets**. They play Sept–Dec in the new Meadowlands Stadium in East Rutherford, New Jersey, tel. 877-694-2010, www.giants.com (Giants) or tel. 800-469-JETS,

www.newyorkjets.com
(for the Jets).
Directions: NJ Transit Meadowlands Sports Complex Bus from Port Authority Bus Terminal, Eighth Ave./42nd St.

► **Baseball**
Baseball, which developed from cricket, is *the* American sport (►Baedeker Special p.184). In New York there are even two pro teams: the Yankees and the Mets. The baseball season starts in April and ends in October. Both teams play in new stadiums: the **Mets** in Citi Field in Queens, tel. 718-507-8499, www.mets.com; subway: Mets Willets Point-Station.
Yankee Stadium is on River Ave. in the Bronx, tel. 718-293-6000, www.yankees.com; subway: 161st St.-Yankee Stadium.

► **Basketball**
New York's professional basketball team is the Knickerbockers

(Knicks). They play from October until June.

New York Knicks, Madison Square Garden, Seventh Ave., between 31st and 33rd St., tel. 212-465-6073, www.nba.com/knicks; subway: 34th St.-Penn Station

New Jersey Nets, Continental Airlines Arena, East Rutherford, New Jersey; tel. 201-935-883900, www.nba.com/nets; directions: NJ Transit Meadowlands Sports Complex Bus from Port Authority Bus Terminal, 42nd St.

▸ Soccer

The only professional soccer team is the **Red Bulls**. They play in Red Bull Arena, 600 Cape May St., Harrison, New Jersey, tel. 877-RB-SOCCER.

▸ Ice hockey

New Jersey Devils, Continental Airlines Arena, East Rutherford (▸above), tel. 973-757-6200, www.newjerseydevils.com

New York Rangers, Madison Square Garden, Seventh Ave., between 31st and 33rd St., tel. 212-465-6000, www.newyorkrangers.com
Subway: 34th St.-Penn Station

▸ Horse racing

Aqueduct Race Track, 110th St./Rockaway Blvd., Ozone Park (Queens); tel. 718-641-4700, www.nyra.com

Belmont Park, 2150 Hempstead Turnpike, Elmont (Long Island); tel. 718-641-4700, www.nyra.com/belmont

Meadowlands Racetrack, East Rutherford, Meadowlands (New Jersey); tel. 201-843-2446, www.thebigm.com

NBA live: The New Jersey Nets play the Toronto Raptors

► Tennis – U.S. Open

USTA National Tennis Center, Flushing Meadows-Corona Park (Queens); tel. 718-760-6200, www.usopen.org (August/September; subway: Shea Stadium/Willets Point)

SPORTS ACTIVITIES

► New York Marathon

Since 1970, the world's largest marathon has taken place on the first Sunday in November. The organizer is the New York Road Runners Club. The 42.2km/26.2mi course starts on the Verrazano Narrows Bridge (Staten Island), goes through Brooklyn, Williamsburg, across the Pulaski Bridge to Queens, across the Queensboro Bridge to Manhattan, up to Harlem and finishes in Central Park (information: New York Road Runners Club, 9 E 89th St. Tel. 212-860-4455).

► Ice skating

Lasker Rink, Central Park (between 106th and 108th St.) Nov–March daily
Rockefeller Center Ice Rink, Rockefeller Plaza – the most famous skating rink in the world. The nicest time to skate is in the Christmas season. Oct–Apr daily
Sky Rink, Chelsea Piers, ►Baedeker Special p.208
Wollman Rink, Central Park, 62nd St.; end of Oct–March daily

► Cycling

Bike rentals, Gotham Bike Shop, 112 West Broadway, between Duane and Reade St.
Tel. 212-732-2453
www.togabikes.com
Onion Apple Bike Tours, 315 Berry St., tel. 718-388-2633, www.onionapplebiketours.org

Sightseeing and exercise in one: Biker on the Brooklyn Bridge

Theatre, Music and Ballet

Theatre
With more than 250 theatres, two opera houses, numerous orchestras, ballet and dance groups as well as an event calendar that's filled to bursting point, New York is one of the world capitals of entertainment. It is a programme whose variety is boundless. There are almost 40 Broadway, 20 Off-Broadway and more than 200 Off-Off-Broadway theatres. While the elaborate musicals dominate the theatres on Broadway between 41st and 53rd Street, the Off and Off-Off-Broadway stages are more likely to be in Midtown or the Village.

Opera
Grand Opera is at home in the Metropolitan Opera. It is part of Lincoln Center (▶ Sights from A to Z, Lincoln Center for the Performing Arts). In addition there is a number of smaller opera companies that perform only occasionally.

Ballet
Ballet fans can chose from a unique selection in New York. The centre of the scene is the **Lincoln Center**, where from November until February and from the end of April until the beginning of June the New York City Ballet performs in the New York State Theater and the American Ballet Theater in the Metropolitan Opera House. Alongside the city ensembles there are regular guest appearances by companies from all over the United States and the rest of the world.

Concerts
In the main season (Oct–Apr) about 150 musical events take place in New York every week. Along with the (Tue, Thu, Fri, Sat) concerts of the New York Philharmonic Orchestra four times a week in Avery Fisher Hall (▶Sights from A to Z, Lincoln Center for the Performing Arts) there are guest appearances by American and foreign orchestras, choir concerts, chamber music, vocal music, jazz and rock

Sacred music ▶
concerts. Sacred music concerts take place in many New York churches, especially in the Christmas and Easter seasons (but by no means only then). They are listed in the Saturday edition of the *New

Concerts in the
parks ▶
York Times*. Free concerts and opera performances are held in the summer months by the New York Philharmonic Orchestra and the Metropolitan Opera in Central Park as well as in parks of the other four boroughs of New York (information: Tel. 212-360-3456).

Ticket sales
▶Advance ticket sales

Late Show
David Letterman is one of the best known hosts of US talk shows. In his *Late Show* (Mon–Thu) prominent people from show business, sport and politics meet at the door. Tickets for live shows are available, up to two tickets per request. (Tel. 212-247-6497, www.cbs.com/lateshow, Mon–Fri 9.30am–12.30pm, Sat, Sun 10am–6pm, West 1697 Broadway, between 53rd and 54th St.; stand-by-tickets are also available on the day of recording at around 11am.)

⏵ INFORMATION AND ADDRESSES

WHAT'S ON ·
THEATRE PROGRAMMES

Local information is available in the *New York Times* as well as various scene pages (see p.81 and p.88) and at the following telephone numbers or internet sites:
Jazz Line:
tel. 212-479-7888

Concert Hotline:
tel. 212-777-1224
www.broadwayonline.com
www.broadway.org
www.broadway.com and
www.nytheatre.com

OPERA · CONCERTS

► Metropolitan Opera House (Met)

Lincoln Center, 65th St./ Columbus Ave.
Tel. 212-362-6000
www.metopera.org
Subway: 66th St.-Lincoln Center
The season of the Met, one of the most famous operahouses in the world, runs from the end of September until April.

► New York City Opera

Lincoln Center
(► above)
Tel. 212-870-5570
www.nycopera.com
Season: July–Nov.
This establishment, founded in 1943 as a kind of common folk opera, aims to promote the music of contemporary, predominantly American composers, along with its conventional repertoire. Admission is less than in the Met, but there are rarely famous names amongst the performers.

► Alice Tully Hall

Lincoln Center (► above)
Tel. 212-671-4050
www.chambermusicsociety.org
Seat of the chamber orchestra of Lincoln Center; concerts and song recitals.

► Avery Fisher Hall

Lincoln Center (► above)
Tel. 212-875-5030
www.nyphilharmonic.org
The rehearsals of the New York Philharmonic on Thursday mornings are open to the public and cost much less than a concert.

► Brooklyn Academy of Music (BAM)

30 Lafayette Ave. (Brooklyn)
Tel. 718-636-4100
www.bam.org
Subway: Atlantic Ave., Pacific or Fulton St.
The Brooklyn Academy of Music BAM, founded in 1859, has for years been the focal point in New York of international theatre and music experimentation.

► Carnegie Hall

154 W 57th St. / Seventh Ave.
Tel. 212-247-7800
www.carnegiehall.org
Subway: Seventh Ave. or 57th St.
Classical music as well as pop and rock concerts

► 92nd Street Y

1395 Lexington Ave. /
92nd St.
Tel. 212-415-5500
www.92y.org
Subway: 96th St.
Literature and music events

BALLET

▶ New York City Ballet

Lincoln Center (▶ above)
Tel. 212-870-5570
www.nycballet.com
Season: May–beginning of July,
Nov–Feb
The traditional dance company in
the New York State Theater in the
Lincoln Center is famous for its
classical ballet.

▶ Alvin Ailey American Dance Theater

405 W 55th St. / Ninth Ave.
Tel. 212-767-0590
www.alvinailey.org
Subway-Station: 57th St.
Season: first half of May and
second half of November
The Alvin Ailey shows African
American dance theatre in its
perfect form. The theatre is the
Mecca of modern dance and ex-
perimental performances.

▶ Joyce Theater

175 Eighth Ave. / 19th St.
Tel. 212-242-0800
www.joyce.org
Subway: 14th St., 18th St.
In this renovated cinema in Chelsea, expressive modern dance
from all over the world is performed.

JAZZ

▶ Jazz at Lincoln Center

33 W 60th St. / Broadway
Tel. 212-258-9800
www.jazzatlincolncenter.org
The Lincoln Center has offered the
best classical jazz for decades.
Frederick P. Rose Hall in the newly
built Warner Center now offers
the perfect surroundings. Tip:
there is a good view over Central
Park from the Allen Room.

▶ Jazz clubs

▶Entertainment

ROCK

▶ Madison Square Garden

Seventh Ave. (between 31st and
33rd St.)
Tel. 212-465-6741
www.thegarden.com
Subway: 34th St.-Penn Station
Bob Dylan, Bruce Springsteen and
Madonna, among others, have
performed in the gigantic sports
arena.

THEATRE

▶ Shubert Theatre

225 W 44th St.
Tel. 212-239-6200
The traditional house was built in
1913 and named after one of the
three Shubert brothers, who
financed some of the most famous
Broadway theatres.

▶ Imperial Theatre

249 W 45th St.
Tel. 212-239-6200
This has been one of the best
known musical theatres of the city
since 1923. *Annie Get Your Gun*
and *Les Miserables* were performed
here.

▶ Majestic Theatre

247 W 44th St.
Tel. 212-239-6200
This theatre has existed since 1927
and is also profiting from the
musical revival.

▶ Marquis Theatre

1535 Broadway
Tel. 212-307-4100
The modern theatre is in the
building complex of the Marriott
Marquis Hotel.

► **Biltmore Theatre**
261 W 47th St.
Tel. 212-239-6200
First opened in 1925, in the 1950s and 1960s this theatre was used as a CBS television studio.

► **Neil Simon Theatre**
250 W 52nd St.
Tel. 212-307-4100
This old playhouse presents comedies in the tradition of the writer Neil Simon.

► **Gershwin Theatre**
222 W 51st St.
Tel. 212-307-4100
One of the big names on Broadway.

► **Ambassador Theatre**
219 W 49th St.
Tel. 212-239-6200
This theatre is one of the most respected stages in the city.

► **Cadillac Winter Garden Theatre**
1634 Broadway
Tel. 212-239-6200
Between 1982 and 2000 *Cats* played here 7,485 times.

► **Manhattan Theatre Club**
City Center, 131 W 55th St.
Tel. 212-581-1212
www.manhattantheatreclub.com
»The Club« is one of the most sophisticated theatre ensembles in New York.

► **Booth Theatre**
222 W 45th St.
Tel. 212.239-6200
This theatre, which was built in 1913, shows mostly dramas, sometimes with known Hollywood stars.

Tickets

In general, tickets can always be purchased in person at the venue. Another possibility is to ask the hotel concierge who will try to obtain tickets, for a 20% surcharge.

Since popular performances and shows are often sold out months in advance, order your tickets ahead of time by telephone, either at a travel agency, from the theatre itself or – for a fee – from a ticket agency. This only applies to credit card purchases, and the number and expiration date must of course be provided. This is however not exactly the cheapest way to get tickets.

It is much cheaper to call the theatre directly on the day of the performance (though this is not advisable during the Christmas season or at weekends). Tickets for matinees and previews will be cheaper than those for regular evening performances.   **Same day tickets**

There are often reduced same day tickets available on the day of the performance – payable only in cash or with a traveller's cheque. But   **TKTS**

these can be the most expensive tickets for the show which the theatre isn't able to sell and therefore turns over to TKTS offices, so a bargain isn't always guaranteed.

Programmes For information on programmes and events, see ► Entertainment, p.79, ► Festivals, Holidays and Events, p.88 and ► Children in New York, p.77.

TICKET AGENCIES – BOOKING OFFICES

► **Broadway Bucks & Group Sales**
Tel. 1-800-223-7565,
www.bestofbroadway.com
Largest theatre ticket agency

► **Broadway.com**
Tel. 1-800-BROADWAY,
www.broadway.com
Tickets for Broadway and Off-Broadway shows

► **Keith Prowse**
Tel. 212-398-4175,
www.keithprowse.com
Tickets for Broadway and Off-Broadway shows, opera etc.

► **New York Show Tickets**
www.nytix.com
Broadway tickets at reduced prices, tickets for TV shows etc.

► **Telecharge**
Tel. 800-432-7250 and 212-239-6200, www.telecharge.com

► **Ticket Central**
Tel. 212-279-4200
www.ticketcentral.com

► **Ticketmaster**
Tel. 800-653-8000
www.ticketmaster.com
Tickets for theatre, concerts and sports events; 4 locations in Manhatten including Macy's and the NBA Store

► **TKTS**
Tel. 212-221-0885
www.tdf.org
Times Square) (W 47th St./Broadway); Theatre Centre in South Street Seaport, corner Front/John St.; Downtown Brooklyn, 1 MetroTech Center, Jay St./Myrtle Ave. Promenade
Times Square: for evening shows on the same day: Mon, Wed, Fri, Sat 3pm–8pm, Tue 2pm–8pm, Sun 3pm until one half hour before the show starts
Matinee tickets: Wed, Sat, 10am–2pm, Sun 11am–3pm
South Street: for evening shows on the same day and matinees on the next morning: Mon–Sat 11am–6pm, Sun 3pm–3.30pm
For a generous fee some agencies are able to get good tickets for sold-out performances:

► **Prestige Entertainment**
Tel. 800-243-8849
www.prestigeentertainment.com

► **Tixx.com**
Tel. 800-688-4000
www.tixx.com

► **TicketCity**
Tel. 800-880-8886,
www.ticketcity.com

Time

From the last Sunday in October until the first Saturday in April **Eastern Standard Time** is in effect; in the remaining months **Eastern Daylight Saving Time**.

New York's time zone is five hours behind Greenwich Mean Time/British Summer Time. Depending on when the clocks are changed the time difference in April can be seven hours, in October five hours. Time check: tel. 212-976-1616

Tipping

Since restaurant prices (generally) don't include a service charge and the staff's hourly wage is (often) quite low, waiters get a 15 to 20% tip. To save having to work this out in your head, do as the New Yorkers do and simply double the sales tax (8.63%) written on the bill. Then either have the tip added to the credit card bill or leave it in cash on the table. Meanwhile, some waiters write the tip on the bill themselves: check the bill and if you're uncertain and ask if the tip is included.

Tipping in restaurants

It is normal to give the cloakroom attendant $1 when he or she returns your coat, and porters generally receive $1 per   piece of luggage. The chambermaid will expect to find $2–5 in the room after several days' stay, and the doorman $1–2 for calling a   taxi. Taxi drivers get 15% of the amount on the meter – up to 20% for short distances.

Tipping others

Tours and Guides

There are many companies in New York that offer a variety of guided tours ranging from the usual bus tours, to private tours in limousines and on to organized shopping tours.

A tour often includes a visit to a restaurant, a show or the like. A list of **organizers** can be obtained in the New York Visitors and Convention Bureau and in the *Big Apple Visitors Guide* (▶Information).

Along with the classic bus and ship tours, helicopter tours and excursions outside New York can be arranged at www.sightseeing-world.com. For those who prefer to do it slowly, there are personally organized walking tours as well.

⏵ ORGANIZERS

! *Baedeker* TIP

Brooklyn up close

Cindy VandenBosch at Urban Oyster surprises with unusual tours: »Brewed in Brooklyn« visits historic breweries, most of which were started by German immigrants. The »Food Cart Walking Tour« visits the city's movable restaurants – with samples. And the »Craft Beer Crawl« introduces interesting bars and beers. Highly recommended: tel. 347-599-1842, www.urbanoyster.com.

▶ **Gray Line New York Tours**
777 Eighth Ave.
(between 47th and 48th St.)
Tel. 212-397-2600
www.graylinenewyork.com
The buses go to all the famous attractions. These multi-lingual two-to-four hour tours are good for a first overview. The ride begins at Central Park South on the west side of Fifth Ave.; passengers can also join the tour en route.

▶ **Big Apple Greeter**
1 Center Street, tel. 212-669-8159
www.bigapplegreeter.org
Committed New Yorkers conduct multi-lingual tours through the city. The route and highlights should be agreed upon at least three weeks in advance.

▶ **NYC Discovery Walking Tours**
1120 6th Ave., tel. 212-465-3331
only Sat, Sun by appointment
Six different tours including American History, Biography (from George Washington to John Lennon), Culture (from art to baseball), Neighbourhood

(Brooklyn Bridge Area to Central Park) and Tasting & Tavern

▶ **Big Onion Walking Tours**
1317 3rd Ave., tel. 212-439-1090
www.bigonion.com
Wide selection of guided tours through the city

▶ **New York City Cultural Walking Tours**
Tel. 212-979-2388
www.nycwalk.com
Guided tours through Manhattan's architectural and cultural history

▶ **Municipal Art Society Tours**
457 Madison Ave.
Tel. 212-935-3960
www.mas.org
Architectural tours

▶ **Harlem Heritage Tours**
104 Malcolm X Blvd.
Tel. 212-280-7888
www.harlemheritage.com
Harlem Heritage dedicates itself by bus or on foot to the Harlem Renaissance, the soul of Harlem and Harlem's nightlife.

▶ **Harlem Spiritual Inc.**
690 Eighth Ave.
(between 43rd and 44th Street)
Tel. 212-391-0900
www.harlemspirituals.com
A variety of tours through Harlem with gospel concerts in churches; various languages

▶ **On Location Tours**
Tel. 212-683-2027
www.screentours.com
In the footsteps of famous TV series and cinema films

▶ Inside/Out
Tel. 718-644-8205
www.insideouttours.com
Unique tours, for example behind
the scenes of the New York fashion
industry

▶ By horse drawn carriage
A tour through Central Park in a
horse drawn carriage. Starting
point is the former Plaza Hotel on
Fifth Ave./59th St.

▶ Bike the Big Apple
Tel. 201-837-1133
www.bikethebigapple.com
If you want to take a long look at
the Manhattan skyline and still be
on the move, try a bike ride from
Harlem, via Manhattan and
Queens to Coney Island.

▶ Central Park Bike Tours
Bite of the Apple Tours
Tel. 212-541-8759
www.centralparkbiketour.com
Two hours by bike through Cen-
tral Park, starting at the New York
Visitors Bureau, 2 Columbus
Circle, corner of West 59th Street/
Broadway.

▶ Circle Line Cruises
Pier 83 / 42nd St., or Pier 16 on
South StreetSeaport
Tel. 212-563-3200
www.circleline42.com
The half-hour to three hour boat
tours go around the southern
point or the whole of Manhattan
and are great for photographing
the skyline.

▶ NY Waterway
Pier 78, 38th St. / West Side
Highway; tel. 800-533-3779
www.nywaterway.com
Boat tours around the southern
point or circumnavigating the
whole of Manhattan.

▶ Travelling in a limo
Erol's New York
Tel. 212-696-6445
www.erolsnewyork.com
Discover Manhattan like a VIP in
a stretch limo: Erol Inanc, who has
been working as a city guide in
New York for ten years, can
arrange this.

▶ Liberty Helicopter Tours
VIP Heliport
West Side Highway/30th St. and
Pier 6 (between Broad Stand Old
Slip)
Tel. 212-967-6464, 800-542-9933
www.libertyhelicopters.com
Breathtaking views; flights up to
20 minutes, as well as charter
flights and flights to the airport are
available.

*Many tours also include the chance
to view works of art*

Transport

Public Transport

Thanks to the street grid introduced in 1811, getting around in New York is no problem. **Avenues** run north–south, **streets** run east–west. Fifth Ave. divides Manhattan into the East Side and West Side, that is the street numbers east of Fifth Ave. have an E for East, those west with a W for West. Broadway is the only important exception. The streets north of Washington Square are numbered continuously. Most avenues have numbers from 1 in the east to 12 in the west, but in between and east of First Ave. there are some with names and even letters of the alphabet (in the lower part of the city).

By ship, harbours

Thanks to its location New York has always been an important port city. Manhattan was surrounded by a border of piers up to about 100th Street. The restored historic core of the old harbour, the **South Street Seaport**, is reminiscent of bygone days. Only a few piers are used today for passenger transport, such as the Passenger Ship Terminal between 48th and 52nd Street. Most of this traffic consists of cruise ships that stop here on the way to the Caribbean; only one shipping line still travels between Europe and New York. The large container ships dock mostly on the side of New York Bay that belongs to New Jersey.

By ferry

Staten Island Ferry, from Manhattan to Staten Island
Departure: Battery Park, subway: South Ferry, Bowling Green
daily every 30 min, from 21.30pm to 5.30am every hour
Information: www.siferry.com
The cheapest (free) entertainment in New York with the nicest view of the Manhattan skyline. The ferry goes to Staten Island and back, past the Statue of Liberty and Ellis Island.

Circle Line, to the Statue of Liberty and Ellis Island
Departure: Battery Park, subway: South Ferry, Bowling Green
Information: tel. 866-977-6998, www.circlelinedowntown.com

Hoboken Ferry, from Manhattan to Hoboken (New Jersey)
Departure: from the pier below the World Financial Center across the Hudson River to Hoboken. Get off here – then back on again to return to Manhattan. Information: tel. 800-53-FERRY

The boats of the **New York Water Taxi** run from May until October. They stop at various landings and are an alternative in getting around town. **Fulton Ferry**, from Manhattan to Brooklyn

← *Whether on foot or by bus – there's lots to discover in New York*

Departure: Pier 11, south of South Street Seaport, to Brooklyn passing directly under the Brooklyn Bridge. Tel. 212-742-1969, www.ny-watertaxi.com.

By bus or coach | Long distance and local buses from the **bus terminal**, the Port Authority Bus Terminal at the intersection of 42nd Street and Eighth Avenue.

Local transport is covered by countless bus routes, almost 40 of which are found in Manhattan alone. Buses run on all avenues and along the most important streets. All bus stops are request stops; people who want to get off have to ring the bell. Passengers must have the fare ready when they get on. The MetroCard (▶below) can also be used on the bus. Regular buses stop on every street corner, limited stop buses only at every third or fourth corner, and express buses (increased fare) go directly to the suburbs. Bus stops can be recognized by the yellow curb stones and blue signs.

Information | Information: Metropolitan Transportation Authority (tel. 718-330-4847 – for non-English speaking customers – and 212-330-1234; www.mta.info)

Subway | The underground railway system, known as the **subway**, connects all parts of the city except for Staten Island. It runs around the clock, during rush hour usually every 2 to 5 minutes, during the day every 10 to 12 minutes, between midnight and 5am about every 20 minutes. Those wishing to know more about the subway will find out in the New York Transit Museum (▶Brooklyn) and in the ▶Baedeker Special p.145. Most of the lines run between Uptown (North) and Downtown (South). **Express** trains only stop at the most important stations; **locals** at all stations. Generally speaking, express trains run on the outer tracks, locals on the inner tracks.

Information | There is a **subway map** on the large city map included with this guide. Free schedules are available at the ticket windows of the New York City Transit Authority in subway stations or in the New York Convention & Visitors Bureau (▶Information). Further information: MTA ▶above, By bus.

! | *Baedeker* TIP

Cheaper fares in New York

The credit card sized MetroCard is valid on all New York subways and buses. There is no cheaper (or more comfortable) way the explore the city. It is available at subway stations, newsstands, in the New York Convention & Visitors Bureau (810 Seventh Ave./53rd St.) and in many hotels.

100 YEARS OF SUBWAY SERVICE

The subway in New York was opened with great pomp over 100 years ago: church bells pealed, ferries blew their horns and people celebrated in the streets. During the course of the first day, 150,000 people made use of the new means of transportation.

The first section – opened on 27 October 1904 – of the largest subway system in the world ran from the business district on Wall Street up to 145th Street and was 14.5km/9mi long. Meanwhile the network has grown to about 1,100km/683mi. 6,464 cars transport about 4.5 million people, around the clock and seven days a week.

In 1905 the Bronx, in 1908 Brooklyn and in 1915 Queens were connected to the subway. The building costs in the populous city with a geologically adverse location were immense. Two competing private companies went broke, and finally the government had to step in, and ever since the conflict between affordable tickets and the holes in the city budget caused by the government subsidy of the subway are part of local politics. In the 1980s the subway was a dangerous place to be. Anyone travelling late at night risked being attacked and mugged. It was only when the mayor at that time Rudolph Giuliani ordered police to patrol the subways that travel became safer.

Underground Artists

But the subway is more than just cheap transport, it also offers attractions above and below ground. Artists perform in many stations with the official support of the programme »Music under New York«. In some stations artists display their work. A ride on the A line in Queens is recommended: the route goes through the Jamaica Bay Reserve, a nature reserve with many rare animals and plants. More information and routes can be found at www.mta.info as well as help in planning your own trip via public transportation.

Travel New York by land, sea or air – whichever you prefer

Fares

The fare for one trip (bus and subway) is currently $2. The **Metro-Card**, valid for a certain number of trips, is recommended. There are also Unlimited Ride MetroCards for unlimited rides on one, seven or thirty days. In addition there is a Fun Pass for unlimited rides on one or seven days. Children under three years ride free.

Lost and found

The lost property office of the New York City Metropolitan Transit Authority (MTA) for questions about all items lost on a bus or sub-way can be contacted at tel. 212-712-4500.

Taxis

There are about 11,800 of the typical yellow New York **taxis** in the city. A taxi ride can be an entertaining, amusing and eventful experience, or vexing and frustrating – depending on the traffic and the driver. A good tip is to give the closest cross street with the address: this can save you and the often uninformed driver costly detours.

The **yellow cabs** get their licence from the New York City Taxi and Limousine Commission, which is where to call about lost property or to complain (tel. 212-302-8294). Always remember the licence number of the taxi. Getting a taxi within Manhattan is no problem, apart from in the rush hours or the rain: just stand on the street curb and wave at an approaching taxi. If the lighted sign on the roof says »off duty« or »on radio call«, it won't stop. There are no taxi ranks apart from at airports, railway stations, the Port Authority Bus Terminal and large hotels.

No mountains in New York, but there is a cable car nonetheless

The taxi fare is printed on the doors of the taxi. The minimum fare is currently $2.50, and each additional fifth of a mile costs an additional 40 cents. During rush hour (4pm until 8pm on weekdays) there is a $1 surcharge; night-time trips between 8pm and 6am incur a surcharge of 50 cents. Bridge and tunnel tolls are paid by the passenger, and it is normal to tip (15%; at least $1). There is no extra charge for baggage.

Those who would like to be driven around Manhattan for longer periods, or would like to get to know other parts of the city or the neighbouring New Jersey can order a limo with chauffeur from the doorman. Limousines have no meters, and the price must be agreed upon in advance.

A limo with room for up to four passengers can be rented starting at $30. Even a so-called stretch limousine, in which any Joe Shmoe will feel like a VIP and which has room for up to nine people, is available starting at $50 an hour.

Cars with drivers are available at:

Arrow Transportation, tel. 718-392-4060,

BLS Limousine Service, tel. 718-956-6267

Carmel Car & Limousine Service, tel. 212-666-3646
www.carmellimo.com.

Golden Touch Transportation, tel. 718-886-5204
www.goldentouchtransportation.com

LimoRes, tel. 212-527-7461, www.limores.net

Cable car An unusual means of transportation is the cable car, which goes from Second Ave., corner of 58th Street, every quarter of an hour to Roosevelt Island. It was built in 1976 and was supposed to disappear after Roosevelt Island was connected to the subway system in 1989, but was kept in service because of its popularity (▶Sights from A to Z, Bridges in New York).

Car Rental

In New York it doesn't make sense to drive your own or a rented car because of the heavy traffic and the lack of (or costly) parking spaces, especially since public transport and taxis work so smoothly. But for travellers for whom New York is the starting point of a longer trip, or those who want to explore the area around the city (▶ Tours p.168), a car is indispensable. Generally it is much cheaper to book a hire car from home before the trip.

Those wishing to rent a car must be at least 21 years old (and in some cases 25). A driving licence and – don't forget! – a credit card are required.

▶ CAR RENTAL

▶ **Avis**
Reservations in UK:
Tel. 0844 581 0147
Reservations in New York:
Tel. 800-331-1212
www.avis.com

▶ **Alamo**
Reservations in New York:
Tel. 877-462-9075
www.alamo.com

▶ **Budget**
Reservations in UK:
Tel. 0844 581 9998
Reservations in New York:
Tel. 800-527-0700
www.budget.com

▶ **Sixt/Holiday Car**
Reservations in UK:
Tel. 08701 567 567
Reservations from New York:
Tel. 1-888-SIXTCAR

or 1-888 749 8227
www.e-sixt.co.uk

▶ **Dollar**
Reservations in New York:
Tel. 1-800-800-3665
www.dollar.com

▶ **Hertz**
Reservations in UK:
Tel. 08708 44 88 44
Reservations in New York:
Tel. 1-800-654-3131
www.hertz.com

▶ **National Car**
Reservations in New York:
Tel. 877-222-9058
www.nationalcar.com

▶ **Thrifty**
Reservations in New York:
Tel. 1-800-847-4389
www.thrifty.com

Boating Excursions

Departure: Pier 83, 42nd Street/West Side Highway, on the Hudson, and Pier 16, South Street Seaport, between Burling Slip and Fulton St. on the East River; information: tel. 212-563-3200, www.circleline42.com

A three-hour tour goes down the Hudson and into New York Bay to the ► Statue of Liberty, up the East River and around Manhattan, and back to the departure point. A guide describes the sights – this is a classic among the guided tours and especially recommended for short visits. There is also a two-hour trip down the Hudson, up the East River to the UN Building and back.

Circle Line Statue of Liberty and Ellis Island Ferry ► p.143/144.

Departure: Pier 78, W 38th Street/West Side Highway, on the Hudson, and Pier A, W 38th St., Battery Place; information: tel. 212-742-1969, www.nywaterway.com

Various tours, among them an all-day tour up the Hudson to the »Rockefeller Castle«, the home of the famous family.

Full steam ahead – a round trip around Manhattan is well worth it

Shearwater Sailing Departure: Hudson River, between Liberty and Vesey St.; information: tel. 212-619-0907, www.manhattanbysail.com. From April to October various tours are available on a yacht built in 1929.

Further information Staten Island and Hoboken Ferry ▸By ferry, p. 143

Travellers with Disabilities

Many public buildings, museums, theatres and hotels in New York are accessible to the disabled. Sidewalks have ramps at the corners so that wheelchair users can cross streets easily. Buses have special lifts for wheelchairs, and the hard of hearing can rent headphones and the like in theatres. In Avery Fisher Hall, concert programmes are available in large print.

The brochure *A Guide to Accessible Travel in NYC* is available free of charge from New York Mayor's Office (100 Gold St., between Frankfort and Spruce St., tel. 212-788-2830; Subway: Chambers Stand Brooklyn Bridge-City Hall). *Access for All* is also very informative. The brochure published by Hospital Audiences Inc. (548 Broadway, tel. 212-575-7660, www.hospaud.org) provides information on the accessibility of buildings. An Access Guide can be downloaded at www.nycgo.com.

Information for the **deaf and hard of hearing**: New York Society for the Deaf (161 Williams St., between Ann and Beekman St., tel. 212-777-3900, www.nysd.org).

Information and literature in Braille for the **blind**: Lighthouse International (111 E 59th St., between Park and Lexington Ave., tel. 800-829-0500, www.lighthouse.org).

Weights, Measures, Temperatures

Linear measures

1 inch (in;) = 2.54 cm	1 mm = 0.03937 in
1 foot (ft;) = 12 in = 30.48 cm	1 cm = 0.033 ft
1 yard (yd;) = 3 ft = 91.44 cm	1 m = 1.09 yd
1 mile (mi;) = 1.61 km	1 km = 0.62 mi

Square measures

1 square inch (in²) = 6.45 cm²	1 cm² = 0.155 in²
1 square foot (ft²) = 9.288 dm²	1 dm² = 0.108 ft²
1 square yard (yd²) = 0.836 m²	1 m² = 1.196 yd²
1 square mile (mi²) = 2.589 km²	1 km² = 0.386 mi²
1 acre = 0.405 ha	1 ha = 2.471 acres

Sailing into New York →

Cubic measures	1 cubic inch (in³) = 16.386 cm³	1 cm³ = 0.061 in³
	1 cubic foot (ft³) = 28.32 dm³	1 dm³ = 0.035 ft³
	1 cubic yard (yd³) = 0.765 m³	1 m³ = 1.308 yd³

Liquid measure	1 gill = 0.118 l	1 l = 8.747 gills
	1 pint (pt) = 4 gills = 0.473 l	1 l = 2.114 pt
	1 quart (qt) = 2 pt = 0.946 l	1 l = 1.057 qt
	1 gallon (gal) = 4 qt = 3.787 l	1 l = 0.264 gal

Weights	1 ounce (oz;) = 28.365 g	100 g = 2.527 oz
	1 pound (lb;) = 453.59 g	1 kg = 2.206 lb
	1 cental (cwt;.) = 45.359 kg	100 kg = 2.205 cwt

Temperature

Fahrenheit: 0   10 20 32 50 68 89 95
Celsius: -18 -12 -6.5 0 10 20 30 35

Conversion:
Fahrenheit = 1.8 x Celsius + 32 $Celsius = \dfrac{5(Fahrenheit - 32)}{9}$

Clothing sizes

Men's clothing
For men's suits, coats and shirts measurements are identical in the UK and the USA.

Men's shoes:

UK	7	8	9	10	11
US	8	9	10	11	12

Women's clothing:

UK	8	10	12	14	16	18
US	6	8	10	12	14	16

Women's shoes:

	3	4	5	6	7	8
	5.5	6.5	7.5	8.5	9.5	10.5

Children's sizes:

UK	3-4 yrs	4-5 yrs	5-6 yrs	6-7 yrs	7-8 yrs
US	3	4	5	6	6X

When to Go

New York City lies at the same latitude as **Naples**. In general the weather is good in New York (250 to 300 sunny days per year), since low pressure zones generally pass quickly and high pressure zones are stable.

The best time to visit New York is May as well as from 15 September until the beginning of December. The summer months should be avoided: even though most buildings are air conditioned the high humidity out of doors can be oppressive.

The **average temperatures** vary between 28°C/83°F in June (average 10 hours of sun, 7 days with precipitation) and 4°C/39°F in January (average 4 hours of sun, 3 days with precipitation). There is rarely snow before January. The highest summer temperature ever measured in New York was 41°C/106°F, the lowest winter temperature minus 24°C/minus 11°F. The general rule: if it turns cold, then it gets really cold. Blizzards that swoop in from Canada often bring the traffic to a halt; in these circumstances snowfall of over 50cm/19.7in in one night is not unusual.

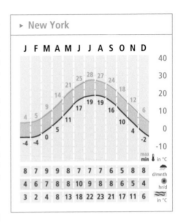

▶ New York

Weather reports are made regularly in almost all news programmes on TV and radio.

Weather reports are also available by telephone, tel. 212-976-1212, as well as on the internet at www.weather.com.

Tours

IF YOU'RE NOT SURE YET
WHERE TO GO IN
NEW YORK, TRY FOLLOWING SOME OF
THE INTERESTING AND ATTRACTIVE ROUTES
SUGGESTED HERE.

TOURS THROUGH NEW YORK

Five walks – for those fleet of foot, they can be completed in no time. But there's no hurry, and you'll find it pays to linger. By the way, the same applies to the destinations just outside New York described in the chapter entitled »Excursions«.

Sun worshipper in Central Park

Getting Around in New York

It's very simple to get around in this huge city. Avenues (numbered or with names) always run north to south, and the numbered streets always run east to west. Above Washington Square Park, 5th (also Fifth) Avenue divides the streets into »east« and »est«. The following rule of thumb applies for the nicest (albeit the most strenuous) way to get around in New York – on foot: in Manhattan one mile (c1.6km) corresponds to ten blocks. At a brisk pace it will take one minute to walk one north-south block, about five minutes to walk one block crosstown (in an east-west direction), and from avenue to avenue five to eight minutes.

The beginning or the end of a stay in New York should be marked by a visit to the **✷ ✷ Empire State Building**, whose observation platform gives the nicest view of the city. Those in New York for the first time or for only a brief stay can get their first overview in an organized **city tour** (►Practicalities, p.140). Walking is the best way to get around in the centre (do as the New Yorkers do: wear comfortable walking shoes!), while more distant destinations can easily be reached by subway. The bus network is well developed, too; the buses run either downtown or uptown (from north to south and back) or crosstown, east to west and back.

New to New York?
A few tips

> **!** *Baedeker* TIP
>
> **The best lookout points**
> The observation platform of the Empire State Building on the 86th floor
> Terrace of the River Cafe in Brooklyn
> Bar on the roof of the Peninsula Hotel (700 Fifth Ave./55th St.)
> Bar of the Rainbow Room in Rockefeller Center
> Sculpture Garden on the roof of the Metropolitan Museum
> Lawns in Central Park
> Roosevelt Island Tram
> Brooklyn Bridge
> Chart House Restaurant in New Jersey
> Water's Edge Restaurant in Queens

Tour 1 Midtown, the heart of the city

Start and finish: Grand Central Terminal

Duration: 4 hours

This tour goes through Midtown. Here in the heart of Manhattan the city is exactly as people imagine it to be: gigantic skyscrapers made of steel, concrete and glass, hustling people, blinking lights. To get a first impression at a safe distance, go first of all to the observation platform on the Empire State Building.

The tour starts and finishes at the ❶✳✳ **Grand Central Terminal**. An artificial sky and magnificent chandelier transform the imposing Beaux Arts style building into a work of art. Leaving the station and heading towards 42nd Street, on the left hand side you see the ❷✳✳ **Chrysler Building,** reaching to the sky with its stainless steel point. Walk west along 42nd Street to Fifth Avenue to the ❸✳ **New York Public Library**, the second largest library in the USA. In good weather the stairs to the entrance are a popular place for lunch with the people who work in the surrounding offices. The most opulent street, ✳✳ **Fifth Avenue**, gets its nickname »Boulevard of Golden Credit Cards« from the luxury shops like Tiffany and Cartier, all of which are between 49th and 59th Street. Eight blocks to the south at 34th Street/Fifth Avenue, what is probably the most beautiful sky-scraper in the world rises into the heavens: the ❹✳✳ **Empire State Building**. It was built from 1929 until 1931 and its observatories on the 86th and 102nd floors are among the quietest places in midtown Manhattan. Follow 34th Street west for one block to reach **Herald**

42nd St., Times Square and Broadway are the »Bermuda Triangle« of entertainment

Square, and turn onto ✴ **Broadway**, the famous entertainment district. Eight blocks to the north is ❺ ✴✴ **Times Square**, which pulsates with life both day and night. A visit is particularly worthwhile at dusk when the electric advertising brings a touch of Las Vegas to the heart of Manhattan.

It slowly gets quieter further north on Broadway up to **Columbus Circle**, where the new ✴ **Time Warner Center** towers with its luxury shops, hotels and restaurants, and where there is an entrance to ❻ ✴✴ **Central Park**, Manhattan's

? DID YOU KNOW ...?

■ The most expensive billboard in the USA is on Times Square. The monthly rent for 2,813 sq m/ 3,364 sq yd is more than $150,000. The average lifespan of a neon light here is, incidentally, 2.5 years.

»green oasis«. Head east across the park, which is a nature reserve, in a route of your own choosing. On ❼ ✳ **Grand Army Plaza** the Pulitzer Fountain and horse-drawn carriages, which offer a relaxed ride through Central Park, attract the attention. Opposite is the Plaza Hotel, built in 1907 in French chateau style.

Walk back along Fifth Avenue, this time south, past the black ❽ **Trump Tower**, where a spectacular atrium houses a two-storey shopping mall, to ❾ ✳ **St. Patrick's Cathedral**, the seat of the archbishop of New York. Directly opposite the cathedral is the ❿ ✳✳ **Rockefeller Center**, a city within a city with its 19 interleaved high rises. In the winter, when a Christmas tree with around 30,000 coloured electrical lights illuminates Rockefeller Plaza, a famous skating rink attracts thousands of ice skaters. Follow Fifth Avenue now to 42nd Street and turn left to get back to the start and finish of the tour, **Grand Central Terminal**. Here, the lower floor restaurants and bars are an inviting place to take a well-earned break.

Tour 2 Downtown: where it all began

Start and finish: Civic Center – South Street Seaport

Duration: 4 hours

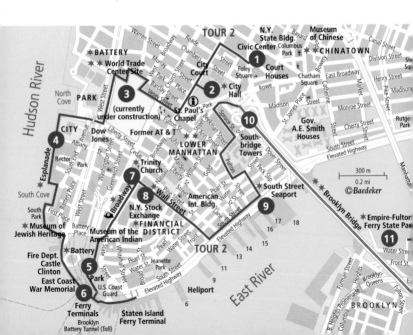

Bronze bull at the Custom House is the symbol of Wall Street

The rise from a Native American village to a the world-famous metropolis began in southern Manhattan. The Statue of Liberty, the Brooklyn Bridge and the largest stock exchange in the world are visible signs of the unbending will that made the city into one of the most important centres of the Western world. But Ground Zero is here too, evidence of the largest terrorist attack in the United States of America.

The tour's starting point is the ❶ **Civic Center**, a city in the city, where over 300,000 employees of various city offices and departments work. Walk south along ✳ **Broadway** to reach the seat of the mayor and the city council, ❷✳ **City Hall**. Opposite is the ✳ ✳ **Woolworth Building**, built in 1913; with its copper dome it was the tallest build-ing in the world for 17 years and began the era of the skyscrapers. A little further along Broadway is Park Row; turn right here into **Vesey Street**, on which the site of the ❸ ✳ ✳ **World Trade Center** with **Ground Zero** is located. Compared to the noise in the rest of the city, there is a strange quiet at the place where, on 11 September 2001, the greatest catastrophe in the history of the USA took place. Follow West Street south and make a detour to ✳ **Battery Park City**. The high rises were built in the 1980s on ground artificially created from the material excavated during construction of the World Trade Center. 30% of south Manhattan stands on reclaimed land.

World Financial Center on the Hudson

Take a stroll on the ❹ ✳ **Esplanade** along the **Hudson River** and enjoy the spacious green areas. At the end is ❺ ✳ **Battery Park** with **Castle Clinton**, the **East Coast War Memorial**, dedicated to the missing soldiers of the Second World War, and the ❻ **ferry terminals**. Tickets for the ferry to ✳ **Ellis Island** are available here as well as to the ✳✳ **Statue of Liberty**, though the stairs to the crown are accessible with a special »crown ticket«, which has to be reserved ahead of time (www.statecruises.com). Just as good (almost) and above all cheaper – in fact it's free – is a ride on the **Staten Island Ferry**. The route passes relatively close to the Statue of Liberty and offers a beautiful view of the skyline of downtown Manhattan.

Leaving the park and heading north leads to the beginning of ✳ **Broadway**, and it is a short walk up to ❼ ✳ **Trinity Church**. The church with New York's oldest cemetery provides a strong contrast to the »filthy lucre« that otherwise predominates here in the world of bankers and brokers. ✳ **Wall Street**, the legendary financial street, begins directly opposite the church. Where once a massive wall protected Dutch Nieuw Amsterdam from the Native Americans and the English now stands the largest and most important stock exchange in the world today, the ❽ **New York Stock Exchange** (NYSE). At the end of Wall Street are the docks on the **East River**; follow the river north to the ❾ ✳ **South Street Seaport** at the end, a popular meeting place after work with its shopping mall, restaurants and bars. Walkers who still have the energy will find the entrance to the ❿ ✳✳ **Brooklyn Bridge** in Park Row near the Civic Center – the starting point of this tour. For those with less energy there is a subway station here to Brooklyn. The ⓫ ✳ **Empire-Fulton Ferry State Park** invites people to relax, especially in the evening. It lies at the foot of the Brooklyn Bridge and offers a wonderful view of Manhattan.

Tour 3 From west to east –
a cable car in New York

Start and finish: 72nd St./Central Park   **Duration:** 2 hours
– United Nations

Cable cars are not only found in the Alps: New York has one too. It
doesn't go up mountains but it does take passengers across the
East River and delivers them on Roosevelt Island – with dry feet.

Strawberry Fields, memorial to John Lennon

Before getting into the cable car, why not take a walk along
✷ ✷ **Central Park**. Enter the park from 72nd Street West and go into
❶ **Strawberry Fields**, a garden with a mosaic which John Lennon's
widow Yoko Ono had created in memory of the Beatles' singer. Take
whatever route you wish across the park but it is well worthwhile to
make a detour to ❷ **Bethesda Fountain** on **The Lake** – with its boats
in the summer – and to ❸ **The Mall**, an avenue of elm trees with
sculp-tures by various artists. Leave the park at ❹ ✷ **Grand Army
Plaza** to get to ✷ ✷ **Fifth Avenue**. Follow 59th Street further east past
the   towering 215m/705ft-high ❺ **General Motors Building** on the
right, which cannot be said to be one of the most beautiful buildings
in New York. Further up 59th Street on the corner of Lexington Avenue is ❻ **Bloomingdale's**, one of the city's famous shrines to consumerism.

Two blocks further, on the corner of 60th Street/Second Avenue, is
the entrance to the ❼ **aerial tramway** to ❽ **Roosevelt Island**. In good
weather there is a very pleasant and somewhat alternative view of
Manhattan from the cable car (the trip costs as much as a subway
ticket: $2.25). There is not much to see on the former hospital island
so decide for yourself whether to take the cable car or the subway
back. Walking further along First Avenue, which runs parallel to the
East River, leads to neutral ground 15 blocks to the south: neither
the USA nor the City of New York call the shots here, as this is the
headquarters of the ❾ ✷ ✷ **United Nations** – and the end of this
tour. Numerous works of art and the UN souvenir shop are found in
the entrance hall, which is open to the public.

Tour 4 Museum Mile: »culture tour«

Start and finish: Radio City Music Hall – American Museum of Natural History   **Duration:** varies

World famous museums like the MoMA, Guggenheim or MET lure art lovers from all over the world to the city on the Hudson. It takes days just to get a rough overview – making the right choices is an art form in itself.

Guggenheim Museum

At the start of the »culture tour« it's worth taking a look inside **① ✳ Radio City Music Hall** with the largest theatre auditorium in the world. Only three blocks to the north on **② 53rd Street**, between Fifth Avenue and the Avenue of the Americas, there are two notable museums, the **Museum of American Folk Art** and the **✳ ✳ Museum of Modern Art (MoMA)**. Now follow **③ ✳ ✳ Fifth Avenue** north to reach 70th Street between Fifth and Madison Avenue and the former home of the industrialist Frick with the **④ ✳ ✳ Frick Collection**, which he accumulated himself. It contains masterpieces by Rembrandt, Titian and Goya among others. Five blocks to the north on the corner of Madison Avenue/75th Street is the **⑤ ✳ ✳ Whitney Museum of American Art**, which specializes in American art of the 20th and 21st centuries.

The **⑥ ✳ ✳ Metropolitan Museum of Art (MET)**, on Fifth Avenue/82nd Street, the probably best known art museum in the world surprises with constantly changing exhibitions and a unique art collection. Directly opposite, hardly noticed by tourists, is the **✳ Goethe Institute New York/German Cultural Center**, the venue for many German cultural events. It also has an interesting library. Not far away, on 86th Street between Fifth and Madison Avenue, Café Sabarsky in the **⑦ ✳ Neue Galerie New York** offers Austrian specialities. After this well-earned refreshment, visitors can take a look at the carefully restored palais with German and Austrian art from the early 20th century.

On Fifth Avenue, between 88th and 89th Street, the unusual exterior of the **⑧ ✳ ✳ Guggenheim Museum** attracts all the attention. The great collection contains paintings by Picasso, Kandinsky and Klee. New York's only design museum, the **⑨ ✳ Cooper-Hewitt Design Museum**, is only two blocks further north. The corner of Fifth Avenue/92nd Street with the **⑩ Jewish Museum**, devoted to over 4,000 years of Jewish history, is at the end of the walk along Fifth Avenue. Those who can still take anything in may enjoy the walk through the upper part of Central Park to the first class **⑪ ✳ ✳ American Museum of Natural History**, where the 15 billion year history of evolution is on display – marking the end of the »culture tour«.

Tour 5 Chelsea: neighbourhood on the upswing

Start and finish: Madison Square
Garden – Chelsea Piers

Duration: approx. 2 hours

Chelsea in New York and Chelsea in London actually don't have anything to do with each other, but there are some parallels. Just as in London New York's Chelsea developed from a ghetto to become a »place to be«, as in the last years more and more artists and gallery owners as well as unusual shops have moved here.

❶**Madison Square Garden**, the starting point of the walk and home of the Knicks and the New York Rangers, holds more than 20,000 people. A tour through the concrete bowl is worthwhile for sports fans, and on days when no event is taking place visitors can even go into the arena's holy of holies, the teams' locker rooms. The transformation from the Rangers' ice hockey rink to the Knicks' basketball court is interesting. Across from the »Garden« on Eighth Avenue is the ❷**General Post Office** with its Corinthian pillars. Since the old Penn Station was torn down in 1963 the building seems to be a bit out of proportion. On 34th Street going west between Seventh Avenue and the Avenue of the Americas is the largest department store in the world, ❸**Macy's**, while a little to the east looms New York's tallest building, the ❹ ✴ ✴ **Empire State Building**.

Follow ✴ ✴ **Fifth Avenue** south, and the surroundings become a bit more dismal. But it is precisely here, on the intersection of Broadway, Fifth Avenue and 23rd Street, that New York's first steel skeleton skyscraper stands, known as the ❺ ✴ **Flatiron Building** because of its

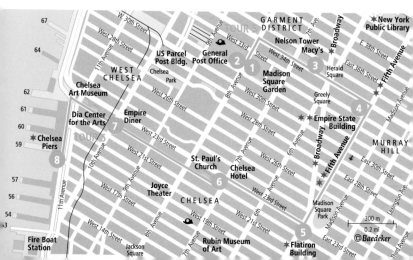

triangular shape. The famous ❻**Chelsea Hotel** on 23rd Street, between Seventh and Eighth Avenue, was once the favourite hotel of the beat and rock scene. Jack Kerouac wrote his cult novel *On the Road* here, and Thomas Wolfe and Dylan Thomas were regulars. **West Chelsea** lies west of Ninth Avenue; the former industrial area is one of the trendiest neighbourhoods in New York. Here, particularly between West 22nd and West 29th Street in so-called Gallery Row, countless young artists and gallerists have set up shop. Follow 22nd Street, stopping off for refreshments at the ❼**Empire Diner** on 22nd Street, on the corner of Tenth Avenue, or noting its location for a late-night visit, when you will be joined by a clientele of local celebrities, artists and drag queens. Continue on to the Hudson, reaching the recreation area known as ❽✳ **Chelsea Piers**. The site where ocean liners and freighters once docked has been converted into one of the largest sports facilities in the world with golf courses, trains, walking and jogging paths (►Baedeker Special p.208). For those not interested in sport, the piers also offer attractive bars and restaurants, and are a nice finish to the tour.

Excursions

The graceful landscape of the Hudson River with pretty villages, art galleries and imposing country homes awaits the visitor outside the gates of New York, as well as Long Island, a charming summer refuge. Some destinations can be reached with public transport, but a hire car is necessary for those who want to explore further.

✳✳
Hudson Valley

A few miles upriver from New York the Hudson becomes a mighty river. The graceful countryside of the Hudson Valley stretches from both banks with villages such as **Sleepy Hollow** and art colonies like **Sugarloaf**. Located in **West Point** on the west bank of the Hudson is the most famous military academy of the USA (Visitor Center, Highland Falls, tel. 845-938-2638, daily 9am–4.45pm; guided bus tours only possible with passport or driving licence). The **Storm King Art Center**, where sculptures by Alexander Calder, Henry Moore and Louise Nevelson enliven the lawns, achieves an accomplished connection between art and nature (Old Pleasant Hill Road, Mountainville, tel. 845-534-3115, www.stormking.org, Wed until Sun 10am–5.30pm).

Beacon

The town Beacon on the east bank of the Hudson has a spectacular museum for contemporary art, known as **Dia:Beacon**. In the halls of a former paper factory, as large as football fields, works by 24 artists including Judd, Heizer, Serra, Darboven, Warhol and Palermo are exhibited (3 Beekman St., Beacon, tel. 845-440-0100, www.diaart.org; open: summer Thur–Mon 11am–6pm, winter until 4pm; directions: Metro-North Railroad from Grand Central Terminal to Poughkeepsie, 90 min travel time; ten minutes walk from Beacon station).

The **Home of Franklin Roosevelt**, the four-times US president's man-   **Historic sites** sion, rises like a European castle from the graceful landscape of Hyde Park on the east bank of the Hudson (4097 Albany Post Road, Hyde Park, tel. 845-486-1966, www.nps. gov/hofr; open daily 9am–5pm). The **Eleanor Roosevelt National Historic Site**, the country home of the First Lady where she lived after her husband's death, is also worth a visit (address ►above).
Further proof of the almost inconceivable wealth of private individuals is the **Vanderbilt Mansion National Historic Site**: the castle-like country home unites Greek, Roman and Baroque style elements and is crammed with valuable art treasures (4097 Albany Post Road, Hyde Park, tel. 845-229-7770, www.nps.gov/vama; open daily 9am–5pm).

> ## ! _Baedeker_ TIP
>
> ### Bear Mountain State Park
> The recreational area was named after Bear Mountain, which from a distance looks like a reclining bear. The open woods and the large lake are very popular among New Yorkers. Sing-Sing Prison was supposed to be built here (Palisades Parkway/Route 9W).

Long Island, the island 180km/111mi in length on whose western tip   **✶✶** lie Queens and Brooklyn, can be reached from Manhattan via va-   **Long Island** rious tunnels and bridges. Pretty villages and broad beaches are reminiscent of New England. From as early as the year 1800 members of the upper class and famous people settled here, and today the island is a popular destination for a day trip for New Yorkers. **Jones Beach** is generally overcrowded at weekends, while **Shelter Island** further offshore is quieter.
The Hamptons, former whaling villages which give the area its name, are a refuge of the rich and famous. Steven Spielberg, Tom Wolfe, Calvin Klein and others have a villa here. White wine is grown on **North Fork**, to the east of the northern point. Most vineyards are found along Route 25 (information: Long Island Wine Council, 104 Edwards Avenue, Calverton, www.liwines.com). In **Sag Harbor**, one of the oldest villages on Long Island, there is a small whaling museum (open: May–Oct Mon–Sat 10am–5pm, Sun 1pm–5pm). **Montauk**, which lies at the northernmost end of the island, is one of the best surfing areas on the east coast. Go to the island using the Long Island Rail Road from Penn Station (Manhattan), Flatbush Avenue (Brooklyn) or Long Island City (Queens; information: tel. 718-330-1234, www.lirr.org). The Hampton Jitney Bus (tel. 212-362-8400, www.hamptonjitney.com) runs between Manhattan and the Hamptons. Those who want to get to know the island better are well advised to rent a car.

Sights from A to Z

NEW YORK: CAPITAL OF ART AND ENTERTAINMENT, SHOPPING PARADISE, NON-STOP RUSH-HOUR, INFECTIOUS RHYTHMS, COLOURFUL AND TRENDY NEIGHBOURHOODS – AND FOUR MULTIFACETED BOROUGHS IN ADDITION TO MANHATTAN

★★ American Museum of Natural History

E 8

Location: Central Park West, 79th St.　　**Subway:** 81st Street

Founded in 1869, this is the oldest museum in New York. With more than 35 million exhibits it is the largest museum of natural history in the world.

⊙
Opening hours:
daily 10am–5.45pm
www.amnh.org

The museum is housed in a building complex built in 1874–1899 by Calvert Vaux and J. Wrey Mould in the monumental Roman triumphal style; its façade, which faces Central Park, is by John Russel Pope. Guided tours to the main attractions take place daily at 10.15am, 11.15am, 12.15pm, 1.15pm, 2.15pm and 3.15pm; the meeting point is in the second floor between the Theodore Roosevelt Memorial Hall and the Hall of African Mammals.

Since the end of the 1990s the separate departments have been gradually transformed away from the dusty charm of the late 19th century and brought up to the latest standards. Especially recommended are the **Hall of Biodiversity** with its life-size diorama of a rainforest, the **Hall of Planet Earth**, which is concerned among other things with the interior of the earth, the recently converted **Hall of Ocean Life** and the **Dinosaur department** – in the foyer the **Barosaurus lentus**, the tallest dinosaur in the world, amazes visitors. The Rose Center for Earth and Space is connected to the museum (▶ p.175).

? DID YOU KNOW …?

■ A good rule of thumb for getting around in Manhattan is: one minute for the north-south blocks between Uptown and Downtown, five minutes for the cross-town blocks going east to west.

First floor　The collection is primarily dedicated to human and animal biology and the natural history of the North American continent. Along with flora and fauna, the life of the American Indians of the Pacific Northwest and the Eskimos is documented. Every department features numerous life-size models; the model of the blue whale in the **Hall of Ocean Life** is especially impressive. The significant collection of precious stones and minerals includes the »Star of India«, the largest cut sapphire at 63 carats, and a 100 carat ruby along with various replicas. Since 1985, the museum has been in possession of the largest cut gem stone in the world, the »Brazilian Princess«, a light blue topaz which weighs 21,327 carats (4.3kg/9.5lb) donated by an anonymous patron. Meteorites are on display in the next room, among them Ahnighito, the largest meteorite ever to fall on Earth, which was discovered in 1897.

American Natural History Museum *Floor plan*

Third Floor

1 Pacific peoples
2 Eastern woodlands and plains Indians
3 Primates
4 North American birds
5 New York State mammals
6 New York City birds
7 African mammals
8 Hayden Planetarium Space Theater
9 Reptiles and Amphibians

Fourth Floor

1 Vertebrate origins
2,3 Dinosaurs, special exhibition gallery
4 Advanced mammals
5 Primitive mammals

First Floor

1 Meteorites
2 Gemstones and Minerals
3 Human origins
4 Environment in New York State
5 North American forests
6 Northwest coast Indians
7 Ocean life
8 Biodiversity
9 Small mammals
10 North American mammals
11 Rose Center for Earth and Space
a Rose Gallery
b Planet Earth

Second Floor

1 South American peoples
2 Mexico and Central America
3 Birds of the world
4 African peoples
5 Asian peoples
6 Asian mammals
7 African mammals
8 Rose Center for Earth and Space
a Cosmic pathway
b Big bang
c Scales of universe
9 Butterfly conservatory

Impressive reception in the American Museum of Natural History

Second floor Exhibits on ethnic groups and animals of Africa, Asia, Central and South America and the world of birds are the main attractions on the second floor.

Third floor The third floor shows exhibits on the history and life of North American Indians in the forests of the East Coast and the Great Plains as well as the Native American nations of the Pacific region. Further departments cover the birds of North America, mammals of New York State, African mammals, reptiles, amphibians and primates.

Fourth floor The rooms here have exhibits on natural history, early and late mammals, the world-famous dinosaur collection of the early and late periods with skeletons and reconstructions, as well as a collection of fossilized fish.

Other activities More than 200 scientists work behind the scenes at the museum, which has its own research laboratories. The museum also sends scientists on expeditions all over the world. New finds are constantly added to the museum's collection. Scientific films and multimedia shows are often shown on a giant screen.

✶ Rose Center for Earth and Space

The new Rose Center for Earth and Space, which also contains the Hayden Planetarium, explores the origins of the universe based on the latest scientific discoveries with the help of the most modern technology: from the big bang to the entire evolutionary process. Special attractions are the 15.5-ton »Williamette« meteorite, the **»Cosmic Collisions«** show in the Space Theater, narrated by Robert Redford, in which visitors are taken on a journey through the universe and through time, and the **»Sonic Vision«** show which makes music visible by means of computer animation.

> **!** *Baedeker* TIP
>
> **Halloween Parade**
> On the last Sunday in October the Avenue of the Americas is transformed into »Magical Sixth Avenue«. Already in early evening costumed New Yorkers mingle with artists, clowns, jugglers and bands on the broad avenue between Spring and 15th Street. Anyone wearing a costume may join in! The Halloween Parade has a different motto every year. For more information, see the website: www.halloween-nyc.com.

✶ Battery Park

A 19

Location: Southern tip of Manhattan   **Subway:** South Ferry, Bowling Green

The park on the southern tip of Manhattan is named after the battery of guns that used to defend the harbour. It offers a great view of Liberty Island with the Statue of Liberty (► Statue of Liberty), ►Ellis Island, Governor Island, the harbour with the docks and the Verrazano Bridge. Ships going to the Statue of Liberty and Ellis Island leave from here. At the southern end of the park is the Staten Island Ferry Terminal, with its round-the-clock ferries to Staten Island.

There are numerous sculptures and monuments in the park. At the entrance a monument commemorates Giovanni da Verrazano, who discovered New York Bay in 1524 (Ettore Ximenes, 1909). In front of Castle Clinton *The Immigrants*, a monument by Luis Sanguino, portrays the ethnic and social diversity of New York. Another monument honours Emma Lazarus (1849–1887), from whose poem *The New Colossus* the lines at the base of the Statue of Liberty come. At the nearby ferry dock the East Coast War Memorial (Albino Manca,

Sculptures and monuments in Battery Park

In the Museum of Jewish Heritage

1963) bears the names of the Navy troops lost in the Atlantic during the Second World War. **The Sphere** (Fritz König) originally stood on the plaza between the Twin Towers of the World Trade Center and now commemorates the victims of the terrorist attack of 11 September 2001. Behind the memorial – outside the park – towers the striking semicircular glass office building 17 State Street (Emery Roth & Sons, 1989), built on what was originally the site of the birthplace of Herman Melville, author of the novel *Moby Dick*. In the bar of the posh restaurant **Battery Gardens** (in the park, near 17 State St.) there is a nice view of the Hudson River (daily 11.30am–10pm, Sun only until 4pm, Tel. 212-809-5508).

Tip:
Battery Gardens ▶

Castle Clinton Castle Clinton was built in 1811 about 90m/98yd from the coast, but only used for a short time for military purposes. As early as 1824 the city opened an entertainment centre in the fortress, and 20 years later it was covered and converted into a concert hall. In 1850 the »Swedish nightingale« Jenny Lind performed here before 6,000 people. From 1855 the building served as a port of immigration and from 1896 on as a popular aquarium, which was moved to Coney Island in 1941. Today the history of New York is displayed here in dioramas; the tickets for the ferry to ▶Statue of Liberty and to ▶Ellis Island are sold here.

There is a beautiful promenade along the bank of the Hudson north-wards to Battery Park City. It passes the fire station at Pier A which reaches far out into the water; it was built in 1886 and is the former headquarters of the New York harbour police.

Fire station

Behind it is the striking building of the Museum of Jewish Heritage, A Living Memorial to the Holocaust: a three-storey, six-sided granite building with a six-step roof pyramid (architect: Kevin Roche). The number six refers to the six points of the Star of David and the six million murdered Jews; but six times three equals 18 – and this number stands for the Hebrew word »chaim« = life. The core exhibition focuses on three themes: »Jewish Life a Century Ago«, »The War Against the Jews« and »Jewish Renewal«. The tour of the museum ends – symbolically – in a room flooded with light with a view of the Statue of Liberty (open: Sun–Tue, Thu 10am–5.45pm, Wed until 8pm, Fri until 3pm, in summer until 5pm, www.mjhnyc.org). The arrestingly displayed documents, exhibit items from many survivors of the Holocaust, video films and computer games give a living impression of Jewish history and present day life. In 2003 the museum was expanded, and recently the »Garden of Stones« was opened. The 18 stone blocks, which the London land art artist **Andy Goldsworthy** collected from various regions in the north-eastern United States, and on which short varieties of oak trees grow, symbolize hope, transformation and survival in adverse conditions.

✱
Museum of Jewish Heritage

Ferries leave around the clock for Staten Island from the Staten Island Ferry Terminal at the southern end of Whitehall Street, one of the few free tourist attractions in New York. A one-way trip takes 30 minutes, and the view of the Manhattan skyline and the Statue of Liberty is unique. A tip: passengers can only go on deck on the »old« boats.

Staten Island Ferry Terminal

✱ Battery Park City

A 17–19

Location: South-western tip of Manhattan

Subway: Cortland St., Rector St., Chambers St., World Trade Center

The most important construction project of the 1980s in New York City was Battery Park City. It is located on reclaimed land – from the excavation of the ►World Trade Center (WTC), which was destroyed in a terrorist attack in 2001 – in the waters of the Hudson in Lower Manhattan, between West Street and the Hudson River.

The head architect was the Argentinean Cesar Pelli. The office and residential area for 60,000 people is composed of more than 30 buildings, among them the World Financial Center, and the generous

Battery Park City Plan

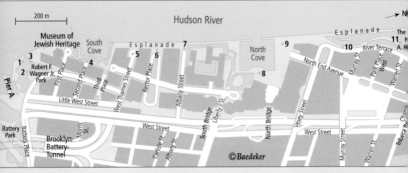

Robert F. Wagner Jr. Park
1 Louise Bourgeois
   The Welcoming Hands
2 Tony Cragg
   Resonating Bodies
3 Jim Dine
   Ape & Cat
   At The Dance

South Cove
4 Mary Miss, Stanton Eckstut
   & Susan Child
   South Cove

Esplanade
5 Richard Artschwager
   Sitting/ Stance
6 R.M. Fischer
   Rector Gate
7 Ned Smyth
   The Upper Room

North Cove
8 Siah Armajani, Scott Burton,
   Cesar Pelli, M. Paul Friedberg
   World Financial Plaza
9 Martin Puryear
   Pylons

The Governor Nelson
A. Rockefeller Park
10 Inscribed Writings
    The Lily Pool
11 Demetri Porphyrios
    The Pavilion
12 Tom Otterness
    The Real World
13 Kristin Jones & Andrew Ginze
    Mnemonics
14 Michelle Stuart
    Tabula
15 Inscribed Writings
    Stuyvesant Plaza

plaza with cafés, a yacht harbour, adjoining parks and a beautiful riverbank promenade – a popular and lively venue.

World Financial Center (WFC)
The heart and commercial centre of Battery Park City are the four glass and granite towers of the World Financial Center, cleverly staggered and of different heights, their roofs decorated with stylized domes and pyramids. The headquarters of American Express, the publishing house Dow Jones and Merrill Lynch, the largest dealers in stocks in the world, are located here. Between the towers Pelli constructed a **winter garden**, a 38m/123.5ft-high and 61m/66.7yd-long roofed inner courtyard the size of Grand Central Terminal, in which giant palm trees grow. It is the reception area of the WFC, a kind of piazza with restaurants and shops, where concerts and other events take place here. Stairs, corridors and lifts access the various office towers from here.

✳ Esplanade
A 2 km/1.3mi-long promenade runs along the bank of the Hudson River, from Chambers Street in the north to the small Robert F. Wagner Jr. Park at the southern tip of Manhattan. From here the

Statue of Liberty (► Statue of Liberty) is visible as well as the Colgate-Palmolive clock erected on the opposite bank in New Jersey in 1924. All in all 50% of Battery Park City is open space with numerous lawns, sports areas and playgrounds, something very untypical of older Manhattan; families with dogs and children, joggers, roller skaters and bikers come here. The park is decorated with the sculptures of contemporary artists, among others the New Yorker Tom Otterness in the North Park. His sculpture garden *Real World* deals with the subject of money, whose key role in the Financial District cannot be overlooked. Next to the sculpture garden, near Chambers Street, the newly built Stuyvesant High School can be seen. There are plans to extend the Esplanade from Chambers St. up to 57th St.

> **! Baedeker TIP**
>
> **New Yorkers on the waterfront**
> The New Yorkers have rediscovered their shoreline. Particularly in the summer at midday, smartly dressed office workers populate the steps of the plaza, families picnic with children, tourists doze in the benches on the esplanade with a view of the Hudson and the Statue of Liberty, and the athletic jog and skate along the promenade.

Bowery

C 16–18

Location: Between Chinatown and Greenwich Village

The 1.6km/1mi-long Bowery is New York's second oldest street after Broadway. It starts at Catham Square in ► Chinatown and runs northwards to Cooper Square (►Greenwich Village).

A Native American trail ran along here originally. In the 17th century the Dutch called the path »Bouwerie« (= farmer), since it ran through farmland. In 1651 the last Dutch governor Peter Stuyvesant bought the land; the Bouwerie became the access road to his estate. Until 1800 the Bowery lay outside the city limits, forming part of the main road to Boston. As the city expanded the Bowery developed in the 19th century to become a preferred residential area of rich New Yorkers, and both the railway magnate and philanthropist Peter Cooper and the fur dealer Jacob Astor had their residences built here. In 1826 the Great Bowery Theater opened, and other places of entertainment and restaurants followed. But at the end of the Civil War the district began to decline. Slowly but surely the Bowery lost the entertainment businesses to Broadway and the shops to Fifth Ave. Those who could afford it moved away and establishments offering cheap entertainment moved in. After the First World War the Bowery was a street with one of the worst reputations in the city.

Even today it has the most soup kitchens and flophouses. At the same time the Bowery is known for its shops selling electrical appliances and restaurant supplies.

New Museum of Contemporary Art Currently a new building is being built for the New Museum of Contemporary Art (235 Bowery, www.newmuseum.org;architects: Kazuyo Sejima and Ryue Nishizawa, SANAA, Tokyo). Until its completion the most recent trends in art are shown in the Chelsea Art Museum (▶Chelsea).

Bridges in New York

The geographical location on the East and Hudson Rivers makes New York a city of bridges, of which there are officially 2,027; 76 of them cross bodies of water – 18 connect Manhattan with the remaining boroughs and with New Jersey.
The first bridge was King's Bridge, built in 1693 between Manhattan and Spuyten Duyvil Creek (today Bronx); it was torn down in 1917. The oldest remaining bridge is High Bridge (▶below).

Brooklyn Bridge ▶ Brooklyn Bridge

George Washington Bridge This suspension bridge, which was completed in 1931 according to plans by Cass Gilbert and Othmar A. Amman as the Hudson River Bridge (West 179th St.), is carried by two piers each 194m/212yd high. With a total length of 2,650m/2898yd (largest span 1,065m/1165yd) and with one pedestrian walkway and roadways on two levels (14 lanes) – the lower one was added 1959–1962 – it connects Manhattan's west side with Fort Lee in New Jersey. The bridge, which is simply called GWB, offers an especially nice view of Manhattan at dusk.

Hell Gate Bridge The iron arched bridge from the year 1917 stretches from Queens to Ward's Island in the East River.

High Bridge Built in 1837–1848 to span the Croton Aqueduct, this construction with 13 arches over the Harlem River is the oldest Manhattan bridge. Today it is reserved for pedestrians (West 174th/175th St.).

Manhattan Bridge Gustav Lindenthal designed the bridge, which was opened in 1909 and connects Manhattan (Confucius Plaza) and the new up-and-coming area DUMBO in ▶ Brooklyn. Since 2001, pedestrians have been able to cross the bridge again.

Queensboro Bridge This bridge was also completed in 1909 (length 2,271m/2484yd) and in a broad arch spans the long and narrow Roosevelt Island (Second

! *Baedeker* TIP

Cable car in New York
It has appeared in countless films: the Roosevelt Island Tram between Manhattan and Roosevelt Island. The tram leaves Manhattan at the intersection 60th Street/Second Ave. and floats the 956m/1045yd across to the island at a height of 43m/141ft above the East River. The cable car offers a spectacular view of the Manhattan skyline (information: tel. 212-832-4543, www.rioc.com).

Avenue/East 60th St.). The view from the bridge inspired F. Scott Fitzgerald. In *The Great Gatsby* he has Nick Carraway rhapsodize: »The city seen from the Queensboro Bridge is always the city seen for the first time, in its first wild promise of all the mystery and the beauty in the world.« The bridge itself is rather ugly; »It looks like a scrapheap,« the architect is supposed to have groaned when it was done.

On the 3km/1.8mi-long and only 250m/273yd-wide Roosevelt Island ◄ Roosevelt Island
there was a prison and several hospitals until the mid 1950s. At the end of the 1970s a residential quarter (architects: Philip Johnson, John Burgee) for about 10,000 people was built.

Over Randall's Island or Ward's Island the broad, sweeping, multi- **Triborough**
section construction (1936; total length 5km/3mi, with access roads **Bridge**
and ramps 23km/14.2mi) connects Manhattan (Harlem; Franklin D. Roosevelt Drive/East 125th St.) with Queens and the Bronx. There is an especially good view of the bridge from Carl Schurz Park (East End Avenue; ►Gracie Mansion).

The bridge was completed in 1964 according to plans by Othmar A. **★**
Amman from Switzerland and connects Brooklyn and Staten Island. **Verrazano**
It crosses the Narrows, the strait that marks the entrance to New **Narrows Bridge,**
York's natural harbour. Giovanni da Verrazano, the first European to **Brooklyn Gowa-**
enter New York Bay, dropped anchor here in 1524. With an entire **nus Expressway**
length of 4,176m/4567yd (largest span 1,298m/1417yd) it is one of the longest suspension bridges in the world. The monument at the bridgehead consists of stones from Verrazano Castle in Tuscany as well as from the beach at the French city of Dieppe, from where Verrazano set sail.

This suspension bridge was built in 1903; its largest span is 488m/ **Williamsburg**
533.7yd; it connects Manhattan's Lower East Side (Delancey St.) with **Bridge**
Williamsburg in Brooklyn.

＊ Broadway

A 19–H 1

Location: Runs from the Battery in the south through the Bronx northwards

The streets and avenues of Manhattan are laid out in a grid pattern. Broadway is the only exception.

It begins at the Battery in the south, meanders north-west through all of Manhattan (about 20km/12.4mi) and the Bronx (another 6km/3.7mi), then it leaves New York and continues north past Yonkers, Westchester County and Albany. Broadway was originally a Native American trail which was also used as a trading route from early on and then developed into an important connecting road between the harbour and the hinterland.

Broadway, in the theatre district

It has completely different faces on its long course: at first with Wall Street it represents the heart of the ▶ Financial District, later the art trade and the new shops in ▶ SoHo. It is most often referred to in connection with the theatre district. Around 1730 one of the first theatres of the city did indeed open on Broadway, between Beaver St. and Exchange. Later hundreds of theatres, musical and opera houses followed, as well as cinemas. In the 1920s they moved to the area north of ▶ Times Square, where with the exception of London's West End there is the highest concentration of stages in the world today.

Bronx

Location: North of Manhattan

The 106 sq km/40.9 sq mi Bronx is the northernmost part of New York. It is separated from Manhattan by the Harlem River and is

the only part of New York that lies on the mainland. About 1.2 million people live here: one third are African American, the rest are primarily Puerto Rican and white. Belmont, the neighbourhood near the ►Bronx Zoo, is a large Italian community and there are more Italian restaurants and grocery shops on and around Arthur Ave. than in Little Italy.

Above all the South Bronx used to be considered to be the epitome of urban neglect. That was not always the case. »The invisible hand of the almighty Father must have guided me here, in this land full of untouched forests and unlimited possibilities,« wrote the Swedish seafarer Johan Bronck in 1639, the first European to settle on the peninsula named after him. Even when the Bronx was connected to the subway network in 1904 it retained its reputation as a preferred residential area. Beautiful brick homes with pretty front gardens, wide avenues, the Grand Concourse as the main boulevard with New York's most impressive ensemble of Art Deco houses, the famous Bronx Zoo and the Botanical Garden were built. The decline began in the 1930s. In the 1950s white people in particular left the area and went north while slum clearing in Manhattan forced the African Americans and the Puerto Ricans into the Bronx. At the same time New York lost over 600,000 jobs in industry. Unemployment and poverty changed the social climate and the »beautiful Bronx« decayed. At the end of the 1980s the vision of the new Bronx was born. Thanks to an energetic city government thousands of affordable flats were built, old houses restored and the unemployment rate reduced. Thus the situation in the once notorious South Bronx has become stable and the northern Bronx has even become a tourist destination.

Sightseeing in the Bronx

There are other attractions in the north Bronx in addition to the two main sights, the ►New York Botanical Garden and the ►Bronx Zoo. Get there either by taxi, hire car or subway, which emerges from underground in the South Bronx and becomes an elevated train.

Immediately east of the Harlem River is Yankee Stadium, home of the New York Yankees baseball team (►Baedeker Special p.184). The stadium was built in 1923 and holds 54,000 people. Two of the greatest players of all times played here, the legendary Babe Ruth, which is why the stadium is also known as »the house that Babe Ruth built«, and Joe DiMaggio, who was married to Marilyn Monroe (161st St./River Ave.; subway: B, D, 4 to 161st St.; information and tickets: tel. 718-293-6000, www.yankees.com).   **Yankee Stadium**

From Yankee Stadium the approx. 6.5km/4mi-long boulevard built in the 1920s runs north.   **Grand Concourse**

BASEBALL – A MAN'S WORLD

»Baseball is America« and America is baseball. As the great American poet Walt Whitman (1819–1892) put it: »I see great things in baseball. It's our game – the American game. It will take our people out-of-doors, fill them with oxygen, give them a larger physical stoicism. Tend to relieve us from being a nervous, dyspeptic set. Repair these losses, and be a blessing to us.« But what would baseball be without New York?

Opinions are divided on how, when and where baseball came to be. We can assume that the game developed from English cricket and German-Austrian »Schlagball« or »Kaiserball«. At any rate, New York had the first baseball team: the »Knickerbocker Club of New York« founded by Alexander Cartwright in 1845. It was also Cartwright who set the first rules for the **New York game** in 1846, which are still valid today, with the exception of a few changes. On 19 June 1846 in Hoboken, New Jersey the first official baseball match was held: between the »Knickerbockers«, and the »New York Nine«. In the following 15 years 60 baseball clubs were started in and around New York. When Cartwright followed the gold rush of 1849 to

California, he introduced San Francisco to baseball, too. The soldiers of the American Civil War (1861 until 1865) spread the game after the war through the whole country. Soon baseball was the most popular sport in the USA.

Trailblazer New York

And New York was the trailblazer. In 1876 the »National League of Professional Baseball Clubs« was founded here; and it was here that fans sang for the first time the official **baseball song** *Take Me Out to the Ballgame* (1908), composed by two New Yorkers. New York has the best baseball team in the New York Yankees, and the two baseball legends **Babe Ruth** and **Joe DiMaggio** played here. The

national popularity of baseball was of course also caused by the media: television, which broadcast a match for the first time in 1939 – from New York, naturally – and the press, which always had its headquarters in this city. A pitcher in the baseball film *Bull Durham* describes surely the most American of sports like this: »Baseball is a very simple game: you throw the ball, you catch the ball, you hit the ball. Sometimes you win, sometimes you lose. Sometimes it rains.«

The rules

Baseball is a game that differs from every other sport in one way: It is not the position of the ball which decides whether points are awarded, but the players completion of a circuit around the course of bases. In baseball the player runs in a circle from base to base. Two teams of nine players play against each other. The field has an area of 175 x 125m (194 x 136yd) at the most; balls, bats and leather gloves are the required equipment. The ball has a diameter of 7.3cm/2.84in and weighs 149g/5.25oz; it is made of cork or synthetic material wrapped in a thin layer of string and covered with white leather, which is sewn together. The club-shaped bat is made of wood or lightweight metal and may be no longer than 107cm/42in and have a diameter of no more than 7cm/2.8in. The team at bat is the offensive team, and the team in the field is the defensive team. A baseball match generally runs for **nine innings**. In each one the teams are each once in the defensive and once in the offensive position. Only the batting team can make points.

Scoring points

The **batter** stands between the **pitcher** and the **catcher** of the opposing team and must try to hit the ball, delivered by the pitcher, into the field in such a way that the defensive players in the field cannot easily catch it and he can run unhindered around the course of four bases – three running bases and **home plate** – touching each of them. If he succeeds, the team gets a point. The goal of the team in the field is to get the batter out of the game. A batting player is out when a fielder catches the ball without it bouncing, throws the ball to a base before the runner reaches it, or, holding the ball, touches a base before the runner reaches it. The batter is only safe when he is touching a base. If he gets on base, the next batter from the offensive team goes in to bat. If he in turn runs, the previous runner must advance so that the base is free, since only one runner can be on any one base at a time. The defensive team tries to get three offensive players out in this way in order to come up to bat itself. Errors by the batter can also lead to an out: if the batter swings at three balls and misses, he goes back to the bench. The team with the highest number of completed runs by batters around the field to home plate wins. There are no ties, innings are added until one team has more points than the other.

Dangerous game

Baseball can be dangerous. The batter doesn't wear a helmet without reason, the catcher wears a face mask, and stomach, knee and shin protectors. The ball thrown by the pitcher reaches speeds over 100 km/h

(60mph). It can **break bones** when it hits unprotected parts of the body. Clearly, baseball is seen as a real man's sport. In 1931 there was a woman professional player, but in 1952 women were banned from the sport: baseball is indeed a man's game. But the game is not dangerous for the spectator: fans of opposing teams sit together in the grandstands of baseball stadiums. There is rarely even quarrelling, let alone the riots which occur in European football stadiums. Tickets for a two to three hour game are not expensive, even though the professional players are highly paid.

Fair weather sport

If it begins to rain, the head umpire decides whether the game should be stopped or not. Rain quickly soaks into the balls and leather mitts. If a game is stopped or rescheduled because of rain the watchers get a »rain check«, a ticket for the continuation of the interrupted game or the repeat game. In New York there are two professional clubs, the Mets and the Yankees (► Sport and Outdoors, p.131).

Bronx *Plan*

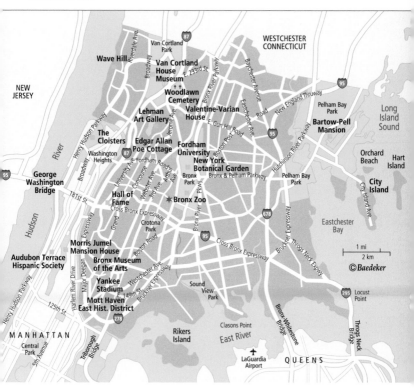

The simple farmhouse built in 1812 is the last home of the first American poet to become world famous. Poe, who was not comfortable in the overcrowded Manhattan, rented the house in 1846 in the (former) village of Fordham for $100 per year. The notorious alcoholic died in Baltimore on his way home from a lecture tour in 1849. The rooms in which he wrote some of his best known poems, like *Annabel Lee*, *Ulalume* and *Eureka*, are furnished as they were during his lifetime (2640 Grand Concourse/192nd St.; subway: B, D, 4 to Kingsbridge Rd.; open: Sat 10am–4pm, Sun 1pm–5pm; tel. 718-881-8900). The house is administered by the Bronx County Historical society, which also offers guided tours.

Edgar Allan Poe Cottage

Around 1900 the architects McKim, Mead & White built a branch of New York University (today Bronx Community College; 441 East Fordham Rd.) on a hill above the Harlem River. Part of this site is the American **Hall of Fame**, a colonnade designed by Stanford White,

Fordham University

Fordham Rd., the Bronx

in which the busts of about 100 famous Americans are displayed
⏱ (181st St., Morris Heights, subway: 183rd St. open: daily
10am–5pm).

Van Cortlandt In the north-west Bronx lies Van Cortlandt Park, where cricket, golf,
House Museum tennis and other sports are played. The colonial style country estate
of Frederick Van Cortlandt, built in 1748, is also located here. The
house is furnished with original furniture and gives a picture of the
life of its former occupants. The dining room is supposed to have
been George Washington's headquarters during the Revolutionary
⏱ War (subway: 242nd St., Van Cortlandt Park; open: Tue–Fri
10am–3pm, Sat, Sun 11am–4pm).

Woodlawn Many prominent and wealthy New Yorkers are buried in the 130-
Cemetery year-old cemetery, among them F. W. Woolworth, who rests in a kind
of Egyptian palace; Herman Armour, a meat dealer; Fiorello LaGuardia, mayor of New York (1932–1944); Roland Macy, founder of the
department store of the same name; the writer Herman Melville;
and the jazz musician Duke Ellington. A map of the cemetery show-

ing the most interesting graves is available from the cemetery office (Jerome and Banbridge Ave.; subway: Woodlawn; open: daily 8.30am until 4.30pm; tel. 212-920-0500).

Wave Hill in Riverdale

The English style manor house, built in 1843 and extended several times, lies directly on the banks of the Hudson in Riverdale in the north-west Bronx, probably the most exclusive rural part of New York. The 11ha/27.2ac, beautifully designed garden is especially attractive, and offers a grand view of **The Palisades**, the cliffs on the opposite bank of the Hudson in New Jersey. The original owner William Lewis Morris lived here, as well as Theodore Roosevelt, Mark Twain, Arturo Toscanini, George Perkins and others. The house and garden are open to the public and a venue for concerts, film viewings, lectures and art exhibits. The concerts mostly take place in Armor Hall, built in 1928 (West 249th St./Independence Ave., Riverdale; subway: 1 to 231st St. or 9 to 231st St., transfer to buses 7 or 10 to 252nd St.; tel. 718-549-3200. Open: Tue–Sun 9am–5.30pm, mid Oct. until mid May only until 4.30pm; free admission Tue and Sat until noon).

Pelham Bay Park

Pelham Bay is a small peninsula in the extreme north-east of the Bronx. In the park you can play golf, bike, ride horses, play ball and fish (subway: 6 to Pelham Bay Park, transfer to buses 12 to Orchard Beach or 29 to City Island). **Bartow-Pell Mansion**, which was built in 1842, is located in the park, today an historical museum (open: Wed, Sat, Sun noon–4pm). **Orchard Beach**, which is most popular on weekends, lies on the mainland directly before City Island. A bridge connects Pelham with City Island, a scant 2.5km/1.5mi long and only 800m/875yd wide. Today the former fishing village is a popular venue for New Yorkers, with numerous sailing boats in the harbour and excellent fish restaurants. The North Wind Undersea Institute Museum has an interesting exhibit on the history of whaling (open: Mon–Fri 10am–5pm, Sat, Sun noon–5pm).

◄ City Island

★ Bronx Zoo

Location: Fordham Rd., between Southern Boulevard and 185th St. (Bronx) **Subway:** Pelham Parkway, East 180th St.

Those needing a change from the concrete jungle of Manhattan should try a visit to the Bronx Zoo. With 107ha/264ac it is the largest of New York's five zoological gardens (the others are Central Park in Manhattan, Prospect Park in Brooklyn, Flushing Meadows in Queens and Barrett Park on Staten Island).
The zoo was built in the year 1899 and is, like the ►New York Botanical Garden, part of the Bronx Park. In a landscape of forests,

Opening hours:
Mon–Fri
10am–5pm
Sat, Sun, holidays
until 5.30pm
Nov–Mar only until
4.30pm

streams and parks live more than 4,000 animals mostly in generous open-air enclosures; there are also modern houses for birds, monkeys, large animals, aquatic birds, reptiles, penguins and gorillas. Look out for **Jungle World**, a newly built house for the animal world of tropical Asia, the architecturally interesting bird house **World of Birds**, the house for nocturnal animals **World of Darkness**, where you can see nocturnal animals during the daytime, and **Wild Asia**, where the Bengali Express, a small train, runs through the Asiatic forests and meadows. For the best overview, take the 25-minute ride on the Skyfari cable car. Children will enjoy a visit to the children's zoo).

Brooklyn

C–K 15–19

Location: South-east of Manhattan, on the western tip of Long Island

Until the boroughs were incorporated into New York in 1898, Brooklyn was the fourth largest city in the USA. It was named after the Dutch community Breuckelen. There is a fantastic view of Manhattan from here, as well as the Brooklyn Museum, the second largest museum in New York.

With 210 sq km/81 sq mi and 2.4 million residents Brooklyn is the largest New York borough and like Manhattan, Queens and Staten Island it lies on an island. Together with Queens it forms the south-west end of Long Island. Brooklyn is truly cosmopolitan: in 1997, 93 different ethnic groups with residents from 150 countries were counted here. Until 1898 Brooklyn developed independently of the neighbouring New York; its incorporation came after a minimal ma-jority of 277 votes.

The ► Brooklyn Bridge, completed in 1883, was the first concrete connection to Manhattan. In 1905 Brooklyn was joined to the sub-way network of Manhattan. The borough grew until the 1960s but when the economic decline began countless large industries closed their doors. The **Brooklynites** are proud of the boom of the 1970s, also called the Brooklyn Renaissance. Today Brooklyn has not only the most residents, but is also the first stop for many immigrants in the search for the American dream. In its neighbourhoods immi-grants run small shops and restaurants, and hear their own music and language – it almost feels like home. Ethnic variety is typical for Brooklyn: China and Arabia, Africa and Mexico, Italy, the West In-dies and Russia are often only a few streets apart.

The approximately 15km/9.3mi-long **Flatbush Avenue** roughly di-vides Brooklyn into halves: north-east and north of the avenue is Bedford-Stuyvesant, where more African Americans live than in Har-lem, Brownsville and Bushwick. **Brooklyn Heights** and **Park Slope**, both southwest of the avenue, are the two most historic and upper class areas. Since the 1990s Williamsburg, which is reached via the bridge of the same name from Manhattan and was once known for its large Jewish community, is an area on the upswing. Since the for-mer Bohemian areas like SoHo or East Village have become unaf-fordable an increasing number of painters, sculptors, filmmakers and performers have moved here and created their own infrastructure. However in the meantime the rents have almost reached Manhattan levels. The centre of Williamsburg is Bedford Avenue with many shops, restaurants and cafés.

On both sides of Flatbush Avenue

Baedeker TIP

Diner

The diner in Williamsburg, serving the best French fries in Brooklyn, has been standing firmly at the foot of the Williamsburg Bridge since the 1940s. The menu changes daily and offers a wide variety of dishes (85 Broadway/Berry St., tel. 718-486-3077).

Brooklyn Plan

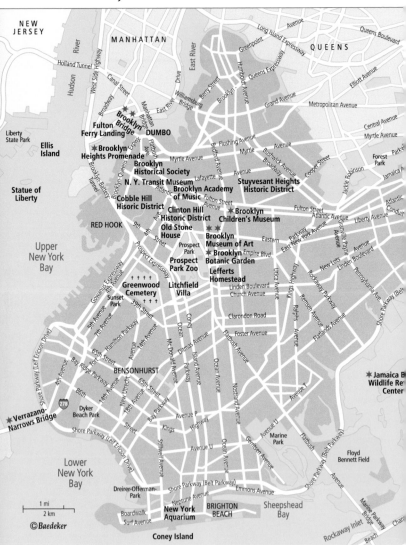

Flatbush is an area with pretty homes and lots of businesses; **Bensonhurst** is a mostly Italian area. Currently the old harbour area, **Red Hook** in South Brooklyn, is changing. Young people and families particularly are converting the old warehouses into living and working space. Although lack of time makes visitors tend to leave it off the itinerary, Brooklyn is definitely worth a visit. Stars such as Mae West, Eddie Murphy, Barbra Streisand and Woody Allen come from Brooklyn, and Henry Miller, Arthur Miller, John Dos Passos, Truman Capote and Norman Mailer lived here. Its independence and its location opposite Manhattan increasingly attract artists, writers, painters, filmmakers and musicians. The two films *Smoke* and *Blue in the Face* by Wayne Wang (director) and Paul Auster (script), which take place exclusively in the borough at the corner of Third St. / Seventh Ave, are declarations of love for Brooklyn.

Brooklyn Heights and DUMBO

Those who enjoy a stroll should take the 45-minute walk from Manhattan across ▶Brooklyn Bridge. The walkway is one floor above the street busy with traffic. At the ramp of the bridge stands the headquarters of the Jehovah's Witnesses, founded in 1872, on whose façade giant letters proclaim »The Watchtower«, the name of their well-known periodical (Furman St.).

Walking across the Brooklyn Bridge

Brooklyn Heights (subway: High St.) stretches out at the mouth of the East River, between Brooklyn Bridge and Atlantic Avenue. This neighbourhood, which was placed under monument protection in 1965, has a charm all its own: narrow tree-lined streets, some still with cobblestones, and many pretty sandstone or brick houses, some of them from before 1860 with small front gardens. Number 24 Middagh St. is said to be the oldest house, built in 1824. Truman Capote wrote *Breakfast at Tiffany's* among other works in the basement of 70 Willow Street; Arthur Miller lived at number 155. Along the East River is the romantic Brooklyn Promenade, also called the **Esplanade**. The Brooklyn-Queens-Expressway runs under the small strip between Orange and Remsen Street. The view from here across the river to Manhattan is spectacular – particularly in the afternoon and early evening – and has been photographed and filmed thousands of times.

★ **Brooklyn Heights**

> ! **Baedeker TIP**
>
> ### By ferry into the sunset
> The most beautiful sunset over New York can be seen from Fulton Landing; the Fulton Ferry, which runs between Manhattan and Brooklyn, takes passengers there. It starts from Pier 11 (south of the South Street Seaport) and ends directly under the Brooklyn Bridge (Apr–Oct daily 10am–6pm, in the summer noon–8pm; www.nywatertaxi.com).

★ ★
◀ View

The southern end of the promenade leads to Montague Street, the neighbourhood's main street with numerous shops and restaurants. The **Brooklyn Historical Society** (128 Pierrepont St. / Clinton St.) explains the history of the area, including an account of the sale of the Dodgers, the legendary baseball team, to Los Angeles in 1957 (open:

Montague Street

☼

Borough Hall in Brooklyn

Wed–Fri noon–5pm, Sat 10am–5pm, Sun 12am–5pm). Built in 1848 by Gamaliel King in the Greek Revival Style, **Borough Hall** (209 Joralemon St., subway: Jay St., Borough Hall) was once the city hall. Every Tuesday and Saturday there is a farmers' market here. On **Atlantic Avenue**, the southern boundary of the Heights, there are numerous oriental bars, restaurants and deli shops; the area is also called Little Arabia. In the **New York Transit Museum** photos, tickets, old network maps and other exhibit items tell the changing story of the longest subway in the world (entrance: Boerum Place and Schermerhorn St.; open: Mon–Fri 10am until 4pm, Sat, Sun noon–5pm). Historical subway trains are parked in a disused subway yard.

On the East River Old Fulton, which runs almost parallel to Brooklyn Bridge and then Front St. lead to the former harbour known as **DUMBO**, standing for »down under the Manhattan Bridge overpass«. The »new village« is an up and coming area. Artists first moved into the huge warehouses; currently many are being converted to flats, studios and shops. The DUMBO Art Under the Bridge Festival in mid-October gives a good impression of the scene.

Other Sights in Brooklyn

Prospect Park, a national park with old trees, broad lawns, playgrounds and a small zoo lies in the heart of Brooklyn. Its main entrance is on Flatbush Ave. opposite the oval **Grand Army Plaza** with the 24m/78ft-high Soldiers' & Sailors' Arch (1870), modern sculptures and a John F. Kennedy monument (subway: Grand Army Plaza or Prospect Park). Immediately west of the Grand Army Plaza is the most beautiful building of the prettiest neighbourhood Park Slope: the **Montauk Club** was built in 1891 and modelled on the Ca' d'Oro in Venice. The frieze is decorated with scenes from the history of the Montauk people, who once lived in eastern Long Island. Prospect Park was donated in 1858 by the Litchfield family and designed by the landscape architects Olmsted and Vaux, who considered it to be their masterpiece (they also designed the more famous ► Central Park). There is rowing on Prospect Lake in the south of the park in the summer, and ice skating on Kate Wollman Rink. Other attractions are Litchfield Mansion, the former home of the donor, and Leffert's Homestead, a farmhouse from the year 1776, which was brought here in 1918 and is now a museum with furnishings of that time.

> ## ! Baedeker TIP
>
> ### Dining with a view and chamber music
> The skyline of south Manhattan and classical American cuisine can be enjoyed in the luxury restaurant River Café (1 Water St./Old Fulton St., tel. 718-522-5200; Mon–Sun noon–3pm, 5.30pm–11pm). Chamber music concerts take place regularly from Thursday to Sunday on a barge on the East River: Barge Music, Fulton Ferry Landing (information: tel. 718-624-2083; www.bargemusic.org).

Greenwood Cemetery

Greenwood Cemetery (25th St./Fifth Ave., subway: 25th St.) is a completely different world and is located about 1.5km/0.9mi southwest of Prospect Park. There are hundreds of Victorian style mausoleums, monuments and statues in this cemetery, which was opened in 1840 and designed in the style of a romantic park. Enter the cemetery through the Gothic Revival style brownstone gatehouse with a 30m/97.5ft gate tower, which is decorated with reliefs. Along with graves from earlier times, which were moved here from Manhattan, numerous prominent people from the 19th century found their final resting place here, among them Peter Cooper (1791–1883, railway magnate and inventor); Samuel Finley Breese Morse (1792–1872, inventor of the telegraph that was named after him; on his grave: »S. F. B. M.«); Elias P. Howe (1819–1867, inventor of the first functional sewing machine); and Lola Montez (1818–1861, dancer known for her influence on the Bavarian King Ludwig I; on her grave: »Mrs Eliza Gilbert«). Among the largest grave monuments is the »Niblo Tomb« (at Crescent Water) of the theatre and restaurant owner William Niblo as well as the »Whitney Tomb« (on Ocean Hill) of the

cotton magnate Stephen Whitney. A visit at the end of May/beginning of June, when the cherry trees and rhododendrons are blooming, is especially pleasant.

✳ Brooklyn Botanic Garden

The Botanic Garden borders on Prospect Park to the north-east. Designed by the Olmsted brothers in 1910, it has not lost any of its attraction in its 90 years of existence. More than 12,000 different kinds of plants grow on the 20ha/49.4ac of land. The main attractions include a garden of decorative herbs, the Cranford Rose Garden with a large collection of roses, a Japanese hill and pond garden with a teahouse and Shinto shrines as well as a new greenhouse with an impressive collection of Bonsais. A visit to the garden at the end of April/beginning of May, when the Japanese cherry trees are in blossom, is especially enjoyable. For visually impaired visitors there is a garden in which the plants are arranged according to their scent (1000 Washington Ave.; subway: Eastern Parkway, Lines 2, 3; Prospect Park, lines B, Q, S; open: Apr–Sept Tue–Fri 8am–6pm, Sat, Sun, holidays from 10am, Oct–Mar only until 4.30pm). A visit to the Botanic Garden can easily be combined with a visit to the ► Brooklyn Museum.

Willow Street

The three brownstone houses at 155 to 157 Willow Street are among the most beautiful and interesting buildings of the Federalist Period, which lasted from the War of Independence until the 1830s. At this time architects kept themselves to simple façades without elaborate decorations. A tunnel runs from the basement of one of the houses to a former stable that has been converted to a residential house.

Beach fun at Coney Island

Watching butterflies metamorphose, crawling into a model anthill or making your own video: all this and much more is offered in the Children's Museum. The Children's Museum was founded in 1899 in Bedford-Stuyvesant, and is one of the first children's museums ever – and one of the best in America today. Its mission is to give children a living impression of the various aspects of technology, ethnology and natural history. Anyone travelling to New York with children should not miss it. The museum also has an important collection of dolls, rocks, shells, fossils, costumes and African artefacts (www.brooklyn-kids.org; 145 Brooklyn Ave.; subway: Kingston Ave., continue with Bus 43 to St Marks Ave.; open: Tue, Wed, Thur 11am–5pm, Fri 11am–7.30pm, Sat, Sun 10am–5pm, closed Tue in winter).

★
Brooklyn Children's Museum

⊙

Coney Island and Brighton Beach

It takes one hour to get to **Coney Island** by subway (Subway: Coney Island/Stillwell Ave., Brighton Beach). It is located at the southern end of Brooklyn on the Atlantic and is the only seaside beach in New York City. Until the Second World War it was popular among the rich and the beautiful with casinos, elegant restaurants, chic hotels, luxuriously equipped bathing areas and all manner of attractions. Hardly anything is left of that one-time luxury; those who can afford it have settled in the remote villages of Long Island, the Hamptons or on the New Jersey coast. Today Coney Island is a place for rather less expensive entertainment and hundreds of thousands of New Yorkers populate the beach in the summer. In the last few years Oceana, a new neighbourhood, has been developing here.

In Brighton Beachon the east side of Coney Island lies Little Odessa, where about 60,000 Jews from Eastern Europe have settled around Brighton Beach Avenue since the 1970s. Here people speak – and cook – Russian. The restaurants Odessa (1113 Brighton Beach Ave., tel. 718-332-2323), Primoski and National (282 and 273 Brighton Beach Ave.) are popular; more inexpensive is the little Theater Café & Grill (1031 Brighton Beach Ave).

A stroll along the **Boardwalk**, a beach promenade several miles long, leads to Coney Island. The somewhat run-down **amusement park** (open: summer daily 6am–1am) is a collection of souvenir and snack booths, with a Ferris wheel (named after the inventor George Washington Ferris) and a rollercoaster (Cyclone).

New York Aquarium

The New York Aquarium, located in about the middle of the Boardwalk, is quite popular (Surf Ave., West Eighth St., tel. 718-265-4740, www.nyaquarium.com; subway: Stillwell Ave.; open: daily 10am to 5pm, May–Aug. until 6pm, Sun until 7pm). In the warmer months (June–Sept) the Aquatheater has shows with dolphins and sea lions, in the colder months with Beluga whales. Visitors can also watch the daily feeding of the sharks, penguins, seals, walruses, whales and electric eels.

★ ★ Brooklyn Bridge

C 19

Location: Between south Manhattan and Brooklyn across the East River

Subway: Manhattan: Brooklyn Bridge-City Hall; Brooklyn: High St.

Mighty construction of stone and steel

South-east of ► City Hall the lengthy ramp of the Brooklyn Bridge ascends, the oldest bridge over the East River. The plans for the first steel hanging bridge in the world, which rests on two mighty piers about 40m/130ft over the water, were drawn up by the engineer Johann August Röbling, originally from Mühlhausen in Thuringia. He died two years later from injuries incurred during a work accident. His son Washington Roebling continued the work. In 1872 he suffered from the bends after he left a caisson too soon, before the pressure had been equalized. His wife Emily took over the construction project; the partially lamed Roebling directed the work from home and watched through his telescope from the window of his house in Brooklyn. The bridge was inaugurated in May 1883 after 16 years of construction. It is 1,052m/1,150yd long without the ramps (the en-

9am – and ends with a small public celebration in the park around the church.

Peace Fountain, sculpted by Greg Wyatt, has stood south of the church since 1985. The grounds of Columbia University stretch out a little further north (►Harlem).

⋆ Central Park

E 10–6

Location: In the centre of Manhattan, between 59th and 110th St.

Subway: Visitor Center (The Dairy): 68th St.; Belvedere Castle: 81st St.; North Meadow: 96th St.

Central Park, the green oasis, lies in the middle of Manhattan and is an idyllic contrast to the sea of skyscrapers that reaches right up to the park.

Sun worshippers in Central Park

200 gardeners and 1,400 assistants take care of New York's green oasis

Its size is 340ha/840ac (= 5% of the entire surface area of Manhattan; Monaco: 195ha/481.9ac) and stretches from 59th to 110th St. (length 4km/2.5mi) and from Fifth Ave. to Central Park West, the extension of Eighth Avenue (500m/546.8yd wide). The park is bordered on the east and west by premium residential areas. Thus some of the richest people in New York live on the **Upper East Side**, on Fifth and Park Avenue; and the so-called Museum Mile, Fifth Avenue along Central Park, is the location of some of the most important museums of the city. The **Upper West Side** by contrast has a much broader appeal.

Getting around in Central Park   Romantic carriage rides start at Central Park South. On Central Park Drive, which runs around the park, a path is reserved for bikers, joggers and inliners. But disciples of other forms of physical exercise, like practicing yogis, rock climbers or anglers can also be found in the park. All together the park has over 90km/55.9mi of paths, 8,968 benches and reputedly 26,000 trees. Bird experts get their money's worth, too: 258 of the over 800 bird varieties of North America live in Central Park, at least when passing through. Information and programme: www.centralparknyc.org, tel. 212-794-6564

The idea of a park for the quickly expanding New York was born in the 1840s. It was laid out from 1859–1870 on what was then the northern periphery of the city according to plans by Frederick Law Olmsted and Calvert Vaux and modelled on the Bois de Boulogne in Paris. Ten million wagon-loads of earth had to be brought in and the ground cleared of rocks and boulders. The many bridges and the four somewhat lower east-west roads were present from the beginning. Central Park is closed to cars at weekends so that bikers, roller skaters, inliners and the still active horse drawn carriages can use the broad streets exclusively. Apart from that the park is populated by strollers, picnicking families and dog walkers, who expertly walk several dogs at a time. The much more frequented southern part of the park is gentler, while the northern part (above 86th St.) is left in its natural state, with a more fascinating landscape and less visitors. The park is in general very safe. But, as in any of the world's large cities, you should still stay on the well-lit main paths and avoid the dark corners after nightfall. | **History**

A Walk in the Park

It's best to enter the park from Grand Army Plaza. There is a pond directly at the south-east entrance (60th St.), **The Pond**, with a bird sanctuary on its west side, and to the north is the **Wollman Rink**, where visitors can roller-skate, inline skate and play hockey in the summer, and in the winter ice skate (it is possible to hire skates at the rink).

In the zoo large animals such as polar bears roam rather small living quarters. Take a look at the small monkeys and snakes in the so-called Tropic Zone and the penguins in the Polar Circle, an exemplary polar landscape (open: daily 10am–4.30pm, Sat, Sun until 5.30pm; subway: Lexington Ave. /63rd St.; www.centralpark zoo.com). | **Central Park Zoo**

The Dairy, a park building by Olmsted and Vaux west of the zoo, is the seat of the park administration (**Visitor Center**; open: Tue–Sun 11am–5pm; tel. 212-360-3444). Park maps and information on all park activities are available here. | **The Dairy**

The Mall, an avenue of elm trees with sculptures of poets and composers, begins at the **Sheep Meadow**, a huge lawn where, until 1934, | **The Mall** sheep still grazed. Self-promotion New York style can be witnessed here: amateur preachers, athletes and freaks, ball-playing youths, picnicking families and frustrated variety artists make this a colourful venue. Cross the Mall to get to **Bethesda Terrace** featuring a fountain decorated with figures by Emma Stebbin in the middle. Beyond it **The Lake** stretches out, a branching romantic expanse of water, on which Venetian gondolas even float. Boats, bikes or inline skates as well as food are available in **Loeb's Boathouse** (behind Bethesda Terrace).

On its north side, on the highest point, stands **Belvedere Castle** (weather station), which was modelled after a European castle; inside there is a small exhibition on the park's fauna. To the west is the **Delacorte Theater**, where in the summer free Shakespeare and other plays are performed (entrance: West 81st St.).

Strawberry Fields

Opposite West 72nd St., Strawberry Fields is a memorial to John Lennon, who was killed in front of the Dakota Building on Central Park West in 1980. Fans still lay flowers on the mosaic set in the pathway bearing the single word »imagine«, the title of Lennon's famous song.

East of the Lake

East of the Lake is the small **Conservatory Pond**; on the west side a statue commemorates the fairy tale writer Hans Christian Andersen (Georg Lober, 1956), and the bronze group to the north *Alice in Wonderland* (Jose de Creeft) is especially popular with children. On the adjoining **Great Lawn** ball games often take place; in the summer concerts are held by the New York Philharmonic Orchestra.

Behind the ► Metropolitan Museum of Art stands the Egyptian obelisk **Cleopatra's Needle**, which comes from Heliopolis where it was erected in around 1500 BC by Thutmose III. The obelisk once stood in Alexandria and was given to New York at the end of the 19th century by the Khedive Ismail Pasha. Today, however, Cleopatra's Needle is completely weathered. Its partner stands in London along the Thames. The final stop is the so-called **Reservoir**, a large fenced-in lake. The water reflects the bordering skyscrapers and the 2.5km/1.6mi-long path around the Reservoir is especially popular with runners. North of the Reservoir there are fewer facilities – one is the **Conservatory Gardens** in the French style – instead there is more untamed natural beauty (entrance 105th St. and Fifth Ave.).

! **Baedeker TIP**

Open air

In summer, the Summer Stage programme organizes free concerts in the open air. The annual theatre festival is called »Shakespeare in the Park«, though that doesn't mean it consists exclusively of Shakespeare plays. Tickets are available from 1pm daily at the Delacorte Theater (tel. 212-539-8750) – expect long queues! Infos: tel. 212-794-6564, www.centralpark.com. Live jazz, salsa and funk are the focus of the Harlem Meer Festival, every Sunday in summer outside the Charles A. Dana Discovery Center (tel. 212-860-1370, www.centralparknyc.org).

At the extreme north-east is the **Harlem Meer**, where rowing boats can also be hired; in the winter the western part is transformed into an ice skating track. Beyond 110th St. (now Central Park North) ►Harlem begins.

In Central Park there are several places to get refreshments: **Loeb's Boathouse**, a small restaurant on The Lake (open: 9am until sunset); and the **Tavern on the Green**, near the park entrance, Central Park West/67th St. (11.30am–3pm, 5pm–9pm, Sat, Sun from 10am until 10pm resp. 9.30pm; chamber music 11am–3pm; table reservations are advised especially at weekends, tel. 212-873-3200).

Refreshment stops

Chelsea

A–D 12–14

Location: West Manhattan   **Subway:** 14th St., 23rd St.

Chelsea is an area in south-west Manhattan, which extends roughly between 14th and 34th St. and between Fifth Ave. and the Hudson River. Historic Chelsea, known as the Historic District, between 9th and 10th Ave. and 19th and 23rd St. is a quiet residential area which still has many buildings from the 19th century. Oil-smeared streets with taxi traffic and garages mark the scenery in West Chelsea, the area west of 10th Ave. between 21st and 24th Street which has developed into a magnet for young art. The piers on the Hudson are a Mecca for sports fans and Eighth Ave. the centre of the gay scene.

Sightseeing in Chelsea

A good starting point is the **General Theological Seminary** (9th Ave./ 20th, 21st St.), the oldest seminary of the Episcopal Church in America. The inner courtyard is worth a look; the westernmost building was built in 1836 and is the oldest example of the Gothic Revival style in New York. The seminar owns the world's largest collection of Latin Bibles. Opposite is **Cushman Row** (406–418 W 20th St.), which has won several prizes as New York's most beautiful street block. The seven buildings in the Greek Revival style were built between 1839 and 1840. Following 22nd Street past St Paul's church leads on to the legendary **Chelsea Hotel**, which was originally built in 1884 as an apartment building (23rd St., between Seventh and Eighth Ave.; ►Baedeker Special p.66). Rock musicians and other colourful characters like Salvador Dali and Thomas Wolfe used to stop here. At the western end of 22nd St. is the Chelsea Art Museum. Here the New Museum of Contemporary Art has found a temporary home until its new building in the Bowery is opened in late 2007 (►p.116).

Historical Chelsea

◄ Chelsea Art Museum

Golf course on the Piers; practice in front of an impressive backdrop, and never lose a ball

FITNESS COUNTS

New York's concrete jungle has much to offer those addicted to fitness, and not only in Central Park, where athletes can be found at any time of the year and where ice skating is obligatory in the Christmas season, as it is in Rockefeller Center. Just think of the skyscrapers that invite sports fanatics to »take the stairs«: once a year in the Empire State Building a popular race to the 102nd floor is held – and at least the runners who reach the finish line at almost 400m / 1300ft high can breathe better than in the smog at ground level.

Of all the countless health clubs in New York the **Chelsea Piers** are the most popular among athletes. New York's largest fitness club was created on four former piers between 17th and 23rd Street, pointing like fingers into the Hudson River. Once, large transatlantic steam ships docked at the piers that were opened in 1910, and in 1912 the relatives waited for the survivors of the *Titanic* catastrophe here. The era of the large transatlantic steamers ended in the 1960s, and the quays declined until the police didn't even dare go there. At the beginning of the 1990s a New York businessman showed interest in the area. His daughter, a passionate ice skater, had not been able to find an ice rink in all of New York. He discovered a gap in the market: the city needed an ice rink and he wanted to build it on the only available free space in the Big Apple, the Chelsea Piers. But the city said that the investor could only have the pier he had chosen if he took them all – **rent: $200,000** per month. Thus the 120,000 sq m/143,500 sq yd complex, after an investment of more than **$100 million**, was a bit bigger than planned – »really only a hockey rink gone wild«, as he himself admitted.

Golfing on the piers

Apart from skiing, riding and playing tennis, almost every other imaginable type of sport can be done here. One whole quay is available to inliners, on one pier there are two ice rinks, a third pier has the fitness area, and a fourth is exclusively for golf. There is also a five-block long building, the Field House, with numerous fitness areas, wellness zones, restaurants and all sorts of shops. The inline tracks, the ice rinks and the golf course can be used by anyone for a few dollars.

Only the Sports Center and the Field House, the actual fitness area, are members only ($100 per month).

Ex-soldier as a trainer

Here an ex-trainer in the »leather-necks« (that's what the soldiers of the United States Marine Corps are called) can really get you to build up a sweat, and you can tone up your muscles on the newest fitness equipment, as well as ascend the 15 x 33m/ 16.4 x 36yd **artificial climbing wall**, the largest on the American east coast. Of course all sorts of sports disciplines such as football, basketball, swimming (indoor pool), Asian martial arts and even beach volleyball are available. In addition there is special training for business management and children's gymnastics. Since the ice rinks were built on Chelsea Piers, the city also has an ice theatre company, which trains here daily for the season's gala performance; and the golf course, with its artificial green, the 600,000 cubic metre/762,847 cu-

bic yard netted area and the split-second ball return, refutes the criticism that golf ruins the landscape. Anyone looking for real adventure can take a kayak course – with the goal of paddling around Manhattan and, as the trainer remarks with a grin, braving dangers like »shipping, city garbage and corpses«.

Open around the clock

The fitness area closes at midnight, the golfing range is open until 3am and the ice rink never closes. Chelsea Piers can only show profits if the facilities are used regularly. But New York won't close down the investors: the number of visitors has surpassed all estimates. So it is no wonder that next to the 28 available sports, 20 films have been made here and in the almost ten years of its existence over 230,000 birthday parties have been celebrated here. Detailed information: Chelsea Piers, 23rd St./Hudson River; tel. 212-336-6666, www.chelseapiers. com

✳
Chelsea Piers

The Recreation Area, where once ocean liners and freighters docked, seems like an oasis in the city of millions with its golf courses, skating rinks, swimming pools, promenades and jogging paths on the bank of the Hudson (▶ Baedeker Special p.208). In nearby West Street is Chelsea Studios, in which well-known TV series like *Law & Order* are filmed.

Meatpacking District

Even more than West Chelsea, the so-called Meatpacking District is on the way to replacing SoHo and TriBeCa as New York's trendy neighbourhood. The area in the vicinity of the meat market, around Gansevoort/14th St., attracts visitors with its giant warehouses, restaurants and trendy shops.

✳
High Line Park
Green oasis on stilts ▶

High Line Park starts here, too, New York's most recent attraction. The green oasis, which is being praised highly, but only partially complete, runs presently from Gansevoort to 20th St. for about 2.5km/1.5mi along the path of a railway that was built in the 1930s and closed down in 1980 (www.thehighline.org); entrances at Gansevoort St., 14th and 16th St. (lifts), 18th and 20th St.

West Chelsea

The area west of Ninth Avenue is especially trendy. Artists wanting to win a place in the progressive art scene have their galleries or studios between West 22nd and West 29th St., if possible on West 26th, the new **Gallery Row**. Numerous galleries have moved here because ▶SoHo has become too commercial for them or the rents near the

Chelsea Piers Recreation Area, once ocean liners and freighters docked here

►Museum of Modern Art have become too expensive. The Dia Center for the Art was the vanguard (which has since then opened a museum in Beacon on the Hudson River (►p.168), and a row of galleries have followed such as Matthew Marks, Metro Pictures, Paula Cooper, Barbara Gladstone and many more (►Practicalities, Museums and Galleries). Recently exclusive shops have been opening here too, like the Comme des Garçons shop which was built by Takao Kawasaki based on an idea by Rei Kawakubo (520 W 22nd St.). Modern dance is practiced in the Joyce Theater (175 Eighth Ave./19th St.; tel. 212-242-0800).

Madison Square Garden

Madison Square Garden, located between Seventh and Eighth Ave. and 31st and 33rd Street, is a concrete cylinder, a stadium with 20,000 seats. Alongside sporting events of the Knickerbockers basketball team and the Rangers hockey team, other major sporting and musical events take place here. Beyond that the complex includes a theatre with 5,600 seats, cinema, bowling alleys, exhibition areas, offices, shops and restaurants. Pennsylvania Station was originally located here. Today's **Penn Station** (1968) for Amtrak long-distance and commuter trains to Long Island and New Jersey is below ground.

General Post Office

The »Roman temple« with its Corinthian columns, a classic example of the Beaux Arts style, originally stood opposite the old Pennsylvania Station. The latter was built in 1910, the General Post Office in 1913 according to plans by the architects McKim, Mead & White. In 1963 the old Penn Station was torn down despite massive public protest and in its place an unimaginative new building was built; thus the General Post Office seems somewhat out of proportion without its counterpart. In the course of the expansion of Midtown westwards there are plans to replace the underground **Penn Station** with an entry building above ground. The General Post Office is seemingly ideal for this purpose. The plans of SOM architects provide for preserving the façade with the imposing outdoor steps, which is under

! **Baedeker** TIP

Big Cup

The Big Cup, a friendly (gay) café with a relatively young clientele, is a good starting point to investigate the scene (8th Ave./corner 22nd St., on the east side of 8th Ave.); here, the two free weeklies of the gay scene are available: *HX Magazine* and *Next Magazine*.

monument protection, and the old post office counter hall for use by US Mail, while converting most of the building behind it into the new Penn Station. The main element of the construction is a 40m/130ft-high fan-shaped glass hall, which will bisect the block north-south and through which daylight is to fall onto the underground train platforms. The opening of the new Penn station is planned for the year 2008.

Jacob K. Javits Convention Center Further west on Eleventh Ave. between 34th and 38th St. (subway: 34th or 42nd St.) stands the Jacob K. Javits Convention Center, a massive convention centre by the architects I. M. Pei and James Ingo Freed. In its giant glass walls the New York skyline is reflected by day.

Garment District The Garment District stretches between Eighth Ave. and Broadway to 40th Street. Here, countless fashion and textile producers have their offices. In the so-called Accessories District between 23rd St. and Herald Square there are numerous sewing and tailoring businesses. The backbone of the Garment District is Seventh Avenue, also known as »Fashion Avenue« in this section south of ► Times Square. **Macy's** is located here as well, the largest department store in the world (Seventh Ave. and 34th St.). Not far to the east the ►Empire State Building looms up.

★ ★ Chinatown

C 17/18

Location: South Manhattan   **Subway:** Canal St., Grand St.

Masses of people, exotic smells, vegetable and fish shops, rundown houses, colourful pagodas, countless small shops with cheap watches, scarves and other odds and ends, ubiquitous Chinese script – that's Chinatown, Asia in America.

www.explore chinatown.com Currently about 150,000 people live in the 120 year old area. That makes Chinatown the largest Chinese city outside China. With up to 400 restaurants, over 300 flourishing textile businesses (thanks to cheap labour) and seven (!) Chinese daily newspapers Chinatown is an independent metropolis in the middle of Manhattan. And it's growing: Little Italy was more or less bought up and large parts of the Lower East Side are already in Chinese hands. Other Chinese neighbourhoods are Sunset Park (Brooklyn; predominantly Hong Kong Chinese live here), Elmhurst (Queens; mostly Taiwanese) and Willowbrook (Staten Island).

The first Chinese settlers were sailors who came to New York in 1847 on board the junk *Kee Ying* and stayed; they were followed about 20 to 25 years later by Chinese who came to work as coulees on the building of the transcontinental railroad to California and who lived on the land that belonged to John Mott and Joshua Pell. The large inflow of up to 2,000 a month began in 1965 when immigration from the Far East was made easier. Even the immigration reform of 1986 could not stop it. »The snake« is what the journalist Gwen Kin-

China in New York: Pell St. →

kead calls the pipelines of human smuggling from China, Taiwan or Malaysia into the USA. The smugglers, the so-called snakeheads, demand up to $50,000 per person, which are either paid by relatives in the USA or by the immigrants in the form of years of labour. Chinatown has always been self-contained. About 40 family clans form the social network. They provide old age care, job referral, child care and unofficial legal judgments. Since the clans are quarrelling today they have lost influence. Police statistics state that the Chinese neighbourhoods are the safest in New York – because no one reports anything. But crime is a problem. The power is in the hands of organized gangs that make up a Chinese mafia.

In Chinatown

The core of the Chinese area stretches between Canal St., Broadway and the Bowery, the two main streets are Mott Street and Pell Street. One of the oldest houses in Manhattan stands on the corner of Pell St. and the Bowery: the **Edward Mooney House** of 1785. The plaza opposite was named after the monument to the Chinese philosopher Confucius (551–479 BC). The large arch on the east of the plaza is the entrance to Manhattan Bridge.

Kim Lau Memorial South-west on Chatham Square, the Kim Lau Memorial commemorates Chinese-American soldiers killed in action. In 1997, the year in which the British crown colony Hong Kong was given back to China, the statue of the anti-British »opium warrior« Lin Ze-xu was erected as a demonstration of Chinese self-confidence.

Eastern States Buddhist Temple In the **Eastern States Buddhist Temple**, between restaurants and souvenir shops, over 100 Buddha figures sit in the smoke of countless incense sticks (64 Mott St.).

Museum of Chinese in America ⏲ A small **Museum of Chinese in America** tells about the origins of the Chinese and their working conditions (70 Mulberry St./Bayard St.; open: Mon, Fri 11am–5pm, Thur until 9pm, Sat, Sun 10am–5pm).

Columbus Park The area Columbus Park, the only open land in Chinatown and a popular meeting place for New York Chinese, was part of the Five Points Slum in the 19th century. Martin Scorsese's film *Gangs of New York* (2002) tells the history of this notorious slum.

Municipal Building behind City Hall Park

Across from the U. S. Courthouse is the district court, built in 1912 by Guy Lowell in the shape of a hexagon with a Roman temple façade. Here Sidney Lumet made the famous film *Twelve Angry Men* in 1957 with Henry Fonda in the leading role.

New York County Courthouse

The U. S. Federal Building on the other side of the plaza was built in 1967 by Alfred Easton Poor, Kahn Eggers (26 Federal Plaza). The small windows make the façade look like a chessboard. Occupants include the New York branch of the U.S. Department of Immigration.

U. S. Federal Building

The Criminal Courts Building (100 Centre St.) was built in 1939 by Harley Whiley Corbett. The so-called Night Courts are held in this building on weekdays between 5pm and 1am, and are usually open to the public. A new prison was built to replace the notorious city prison »The Tombs«, which meanwhile has been demolished. The »Bridge of Sighs« connects the courthouse to the prison.

Criminal Courts Building and Prison

★ The Cloisters

Location: Fort Tryon Park at the northern tip of Manhattan

Subway: 190th St., continue with Bus 4

The Cloisters, the museum for medieval art, is located in Fort Tryon Park high above the Hudson River at the forested northern tip of Manhattan. Although it comes from the 1930s, the building seems astonishingly authentic.

⊙ Opening hours:
Mar–Oct
Tue–Sun
9.30am–5.15pm
Nov–Feb
until 16.45pm

The architect Charles Collens put parts of four cloisters from the Middle Ages together and added to them. The striking main tower is a replica of the tower of the French cloister St-Michel-de-Cuxa (12th century). The Romanesque cloister of The Cloisters comes from there as well. The basic stock of the collection goes back to the sculptor George Grey Barnard (1863–1938), who brought back many works of art from his trips to Europe. In the 1925 Metropolitan Museum of Art bought the collection. The money came from John D. Rockefeller Jr., who also donated the land (including the bank of the Hudson opposite) and the means to build the museum. In clear weather there is a unique view of the Hudson, the Washington Bridge and the (undeveloped) western river bank. The admission ticket is also valid for the ► Metropolitan Museum on the same day (**guided tours** Tue–Fri, Sun 3pm; tel. 212-923-3700,

? DID YOU KNOW ...?

■ The larger of the two cloisters in the lower floor comes from the Cistercian monastery Bonnefont-en-Comminges south-west of Toulouse (13th/14th century). The medicinal herbs and spices in the garden were also cultivated in the Middle Ages. The adjacent cloister is from the monastery Trie (from Tarbe, southern France); it was built in the 15th century and destroyed 100 years later by the Huguenots.

The exhibition of Romanesque and Gothic building parts, illustrated manuscripts, painted glass, artefacts of enamel, glass, ivory and silver as well as paintings and sculptures is chronologically organized. It begins with the Romanesque period (around AD 1000) and ends with the Gothic period (around 1550).

The core of the museum is the cloister on the main floor and entrance level, from the monastery Saint Michel de Cuxa in the northeastern Pyrenees (12th century), which was dissolved during the French Revolution but is inhabited by monks again today. The small cloister from the St Guilhem monastery founded in 806 by Montpellier is from the 13th century. Among the main attractions are the seven tapestries that depict a unicorn hunt (**Unicorn Tapestries** Room; made around 1500 near Brussels as replicas of Parisian designs). The tapestries show a hunt for the innocent unicorn, with its infamous murder and ensuing re-surrection; both the execution and

The Cloisters *Floor plan*

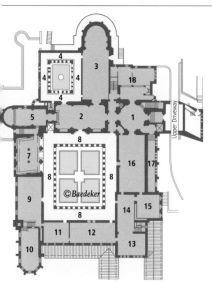

Museum for sacred medieval art and architecture

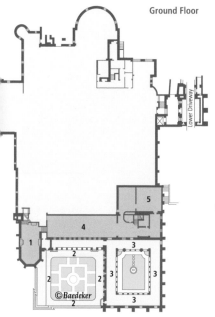

Main Floor

1 *Entrance Hall*
2 *Romanesque Hall*
(portals from France)
3 *Fuentidueña Chapel*
Apsis of the church San Martin de Fuentidueña at Segovia (central Spain)
4 *Saint Guilhem Cloister*
Cloister of the Benedictine abbey St-Guilhem-le-Désert (southern France)
5 *Langon Chapel*
Part of the church Notre-Dame du Bourg in Langon (southwest France)
6 *West Terrace*
7 *Pontaut Chapter House*
Chapter house of the monastery Notre-Dame de Pontaut (southwest France)
8 *Saint Michel de Cuxa Cloister*
Cloister (in part supplemented) of the monastery St-Michel-de-Cuxa (southern France)
9 *Early Gothic Hall*
(sacred statuary)

10 *Gothic Chapel*
(► Lower floor)
11 *Nine Heroes Tapestries Room*
Tapestries of the nine heroes of world history
12 *Unicorn Tapestries Hall*
Tapestries with scenes of a unicorn hunt
13 *Boppard Room*
Stained glass windows from the Carmelite monastery St. Severin in Boppard on the River Rhine
14 *Burgos Tapestry Room*
Flemish tapestry from the Cathedral of Burgur (northern Spain)
15 *Spanish Room*
(Campin Room)
Merodé wing altar from Flanders; Gothic painted ceiling from Castile
16 *Late Gothic Hall*
Hall in Late Gothic style of a medieval refectory
17 *Froville Arcade*
Gothic arcade from the monastery Froville (Lothringen)
18 *Books & Reproductions*

Ground Floor

1 *Gothic Chapel*
patterned after the church interior of the Gothic cathedral St-Nazaire in Carcassonne
2 *Bonnefont Cloister*
Monastery cloister

Bonnefont-en Comminges (southern France)
3 *Trie Cloister*
Cloister of the monastery Trie near Toulouse (southern France)
4 *Glass Gallery*
5 *Treasury*

the multi-levelled interpretation make the tapestries a high point of European textile art and courtly elegance of the late Middle Ages.

The six glass windows in the **Boppard Room** come from the Carmelite monastery St Severin in Boppard on the Rhine (1447) and came into the possession of the Cloisters by a circuitous route in 1937. Along with Gothic ceiling paintings from Castile and furniture from the 15th century in the **Campin Room**, the altar triptych, whose centrepiece shows the Annunciation (around 1425), by Robert Campin from Tournai is particularly worth taking a look at. The **Gothic chapel** on the ground floor, an imitation of the cathedral St Nazaire in Carcassonne, contains grave monuments from the 13th and 14th centuries. Along with sculptures and painted glass from the 15th century in the **Glass Gallery**, look out for the altar pictures *Birth of Christ* and *Dream of the Three Kings from the Orient* from the school of Rogier van der Weyden, and the courtyard of a house in Abbéville.

A special attraction of the **Treasury** is the book of hours of the Duc Jean de Berry (*Belles Heures*), a prayer book illustrated by the Limburg brothers before 1410.

Medieval art in north Manhattan: the Cloisters

Columbus Circle

D/E 10

Location: Central Park West, 59th St.   **Subway:** Columbus Circle

The busy Columbus Circle on the south-west corner of Central Park is one of the squares created by ► Broadway in its course through Manhattan. The outstanding feature is that the streets here form a circle, which happens nowhere else in New York. In the centre of the circle, on a pedestal, stands Columbus (Gaetano Russo, 1894).

The west side is occupied by the **Time Warner Center**, completed in 2004 (architect: David Childs, SOM). With its two 229m/750ft-high, diagonally cut glass towers, it takes up the course of Broadway and continues the tradition of double towers on the western edge of Central Park. On 55 floors, along with the media corporation of the building owner Time Warner, there are various exclusive shops, first class restaurants, the Mandarin Oriental luxury hotel, concert halls

Time Warner Center

(»**Jazz at Lincoln Center**«; information: www.jalc.org) and high-priced condominiums. On the northern edge of Columbus Circle stands the 207m/678ft-high, 44-floor former Gulf & Western Building, from the year 1969, today the Trump International Hotel Tower. Since its renovation by Philip Johnson and Costas Kondylis it has been covered by a skin of tinted glass.

East Village

C 15/16

Location: South of 14th St. and east of the Bowery   **Subway:** Astor Place

East Village, once the northern part of the Lower East Side, is the area east of Broadway between 14th and Houston Street. In the 19th century the wealthier New Yorkers lived here, and later immi-

grants from Germany, Poland, Russia and Puerto Rico displaced the rich, who moved northwards. In the 1950s, with ▶ Greenwich Village becoming increasingly favoured by the chic set, the artists, literary types, musicians and students who had been driven out of the Village discovered this neighbourhood.

St Mark's Place, actually the extension of Eighth St., developed into the centre of the **hippy scene** and along with the surrounding side streets was renamed the East Village. In the 1980s art galleries and trendy restaurants moved here and the area became the centre of the New York sub-culture. Within a short time the neighbourhood changed into a popular residential and entertainment area. Even though the East Village cannot be called middle class, the times when no one dared go out at night around Tompkins Square are over. Particularly at weekends, the countless hot spots and restaurants around St Mark's Place are teeming with life, and during the daytime numerous small antique shops and boutiques are waiting to be discovered.

! *Baedeker* TIP

A relic
The Yaffa Café (St Mark's Place/97th St.) is a relic of wild times past with its garish decorations and secluded garden.

Astor Place
The cast iron sculpture *Alamo* (Bernard Rosenthal, 1967) on Astor Place marks the entrance to the subway station (Lafayette St./Fourth Ave.). On the south side of Astor Place stands the **Cooper Union Building**, a massive brownstone house, which was founded in 1859 by the railway magnate, inventor and philanthropist Peter Cooper in order to help gifted children from poor families get a free education. In 1860, in the Great Hall, President Abraham Lincoln delivered an impassioned speech against slavery.

Colonnade Row
The so-called Colonnade Row, four of originally nine once magnificent villas (429–434 Lafayette St.), was built in 1836 in the Greek Revival style. The white marble, however, lies hidden under a dark patina. Opposite is the **Public Theater** (425 Lafayette St.), which was opened in 1854 as the Astor Library and now hosts the New York Shakespeare Festival and Joe's Pub.
Not far from here is another house in the Greek Revival style. The **Old Merchant's House** was built in 1831, and shortly afterwards it was bought by the wealthy businessman Seabury Tredwell. It contains the original furnishings (29 E Fourth St.; open: Sun–Thu 12pm–5pm).

St Mark's
Stuyvesant St. leads to the church St Mark's in-the-Bowery (Second Ave. /10th St.). The second oldest church in New York, from the year 1799, stands on ground rich in history: the estate of the Dutch gov-

ernor Peter Stuyvesant was situated here (1610–1672; he is buried in the neighbouring cemetery). The church, built in the colonial style with a classical tower and Roman columned hall with cast iron screens, played an important role in the main period of the hippie movement, whose centre was St Mark's Place only two blocks away. Today cultural events are still held here. **Grace Church**, a little way to the west, is a masterpiece of Gothic Revival by James Renwick (1846; Broadway / Tenth St.).

Since the 1970s about 30,000 Ukrainians have lived in the neighbourhood, as shown by shops and restaurants such as the Kiev (117 Second Ave.), a church and a small Ukrainian Museum (**Ukrainian Museum**; E Sixth St., between Second Ave. and Cooper Square; open: Wed–Sun 1pm–5pm). On display in the new building is Ukrainian folk art, including examples of the famous Pysanky (painted Easter eggs) as well as woven and needle-worked textiles, ceramics, wood and metal work.

Little Ukraine

Towards the end of the last century a large German community lived in the East Village. Several buildings still testify to this, including the house once used by the German-American shooting club at

German community

More than two million books: Strand Book Store, 828 Broadway/12th St.

St Mark's Place 12 (1885), the Ottendorfer branch of the Public Library (135 Second Ave.; 1884) and the Stuyvesant Polyclinic, until 1918 known as the Deutsche Poliklinik (German Polyclinic) (137 Second Ave.; 1884). The English poet W. H. Auden lived at number 60 St Mark's Place until his death.

The descendants of the immigrants from Poland and the Ukraine share the little Tompkins Square Park with busy office workers, chess players and a few homeless people. East of the East Village is **Alphabet City**, which gets its name from the Avenues A, B and C and which was once a notorious area. Where heroin was sold until the end of the 1990s, there are now chic restaurants.

✱ Ellis Island

Location: West of the southern tip of Manhattan	**Subway:** South Ferry; the ferry to the island runs from/to Battery Park

Ellis Island, located west of the southern point of Manhattan off the shore of Jersey City, is one of the 40 islands in New York's waters. Originally a fortified site and ammunition depot, the island achieved fame as the immigration station for new arrivals between 1892 and 1917, when the federal government took over control of the flood of immigrants into New York (►Baedeker Special p.313).

🕐
Opening hours:
daily 9.30am–5pm

People who wanted to emigrate had to endure physical checkups and questioning before getting permission to continue on to Manhattan or New Jersey. The sick, single women or the politically suspect (about 2%) were sent back or interred on the island until their appeal had been heard and decided upon. The largest number arrived in the period from the 1890s until the beginning of the First World War, when about 17 million people were shunted through.

The crowds were sometimes so huge that every official had to question 400 to 500 people a day, meaning that the fate of entire families were sometimes decided in a few minutes – which earned Ellis Island the name »Island of Tears«. After 1917 Ellis Island served primarily as a camp and clearance area for the deported and politically persecuted; during the Second World War it was an internment camp for

Great Registry: immigrants were processed here

foreigners. An impressive description comes from **Egon Erwin Kisch**, author and journalist from Prague: »Am again a prisoner on the ship. I see New York through the closed porthole, which I have been approaching for fourteen days, war days on the *Pennland* (Holland-America Line)... The Immigration Officer said that my passport was not in order, for a Chilean visa from Paris was not enough for a transit visa to America ... While he spoke with me another official showed him a piece of paper, doubtless about me. – »I know,« he said. So I have to go to the »island« – a euphemism for Ellis Island, the Island of Tears ... Off the *Pennland*, on which we were for more than fourteen days, down with the baggage (mine stayed in Belgium) onto the ice-cold docks, where customs inspection takes place, then on a tender to the prison island guarded by the Statue of Liberty...« (»Notes 23–28.12 1939«; Landing in New York).

Photos, artefacts and films document the circumstances under which immigrants came to the USA. A computer can tell you when your ancestors came to Ellis Island. In the **museum** visitors follow the route that the immigrants had to follow: from the baggage room, where possessions were inspected, to the Great Hall or Registry Room in the second floor where the immigrants first had to answer officials' questions and then pass a medical examination. If everything went well the procedure took three to five hours, after which the immigrants received their papers.

Museum

At the northern end of the island is the Wall of Honor, in which about 500,000 names of immigrants are engraved.

One of the most beautiful views of downtown Manhattan can be seen from the Staten Island Ferry – and it's free of charge

CONQUERING THE HEIGHTS

New York is a city of contrasts: rich and poor, loud and quiet, high and low. A few streets away from extremely expensive shops there are poor neighbourhoods, and in the middle of the loud, colourful bustle there are peaceful corners where almost none of the constant noise of the city can be heard.

One of the many contrasts of the city can be seen when approaching New York in an aeroplane: if you look down on Manhattan, the heart of the metropolis on the Hudson River, you notice that the skyline does not form a continuous line, but instead the skyscrapers congregate in Midtown and at the southern tip while in the middle are at most buildings of medium height. The reason is **geological**: Midtown and the south of Manhattan are on a bedrock of massive granite, which allows tall buildings to be built; this is not possible on the ground in between.

Manhattan's skyline is probably the most famous in the world. But the skyscraper era actually began in the mid-19th century in **Chicago**. At first conventional stone and brick buildings were built: the more storeys added, the thicker the the lower walls had to be. Then the cast iron

Woolworth Building, the »Mozart« of the skyscrapers

beam was invented, and shortly afterwards the steel skeleton. The electrical lift had already been developed. In 1884 the first building with a steel frame was built in the city on Lake Michigan, which brought the Second City the title of the »highest building in the world« – the word **skyscraper** was born.

Motivation for New York

Now the New Yorkers were spurred to act, since they already recognized the advantages of high rise buildings. The steel skeleton allowed not only thinner walls and larger windows, which were in great demand then – they theoretically allowed buildings to be of unlimited height (optimal above all when land is very rare). In 1902 Manhattan saw its first skyscraper: the 21-storey Flatiron Building on the corner of Fifth Ave./23rd St. The building attracted onlookers long after its completion, above all men, for the narrow edge of the building with the open plaza in front was so windy that women's skirts were blown about. The Flatiron is only one example for the first of four phases

of New York high rise history. »Utility« was in the foreground at that time: the new structural possibilities were used mainly to put one storey on top of another, without regard for the surrounding streets and the amount of sunlight they got. Some of the early high rises nevertheless display **aesthetic architecture**, such as the Woolworth Building, the so-called »Mozart of the skyscrapers«, with its neo-Gothic stone ornaments. In 1916, a year after the completion of the Equitable Building, which shamelessly took up one whole block in the vertical and caused a storm of protest, the city passed the Zoning Law, **building regulations** that were intended to prevent the streets from being turned into canyons without light. The building of high rises consequently changed. The wedding cake style was developed, the second phase: the higher a skyscraper was built, the narrower it became on top.

Chrysler and Empire State

The best known examples are the Chrysler Building of 1930, with its Art Deco point which glitters like a diamond at sunset: it consists of cobalt-wolfram steel developed by Krupp, which has **diamond splinters** mixed into the alloy. Another example of the second phase is the Empire State Building on Fifth Avenue, which at 381m/1250ft was the tallest building in the world for over four decades after its completion in 1931. With its point, which was originally supposed to be an **anchor for airships** and now has a television antenna attached, it even measures 443m/1454ft. An airship never anchored at the Empire State Building – the era of airships was almost over – but on 28 July 1945 a B - 25 US Air Force bomber did fly into the building at the level of the 79th floor at about 300m/975ft in dense fog. The observation deck of the Empire State is closed about 40 days every year – from fear that the occasionally strong winds might blow the visitors away. When filming *Sleepless in Seattle* the main actors Meg Ryan and Tom Hanks were tied to the railing as a precaution. The Empire State Building is not only the most impressive building in Midtown by day: at night the point is illuminated – red-green in the Christmas season, blue-white at the opening of the Yankee's baseball season and red, white and blue on the birthday of a US president.

Incidentally, it is constantly stated that mostly Native Americans work as **ironworkers** on the steel skeleton because they have such a good head for heights. In fact, most of the ironworkers in Manhattan were and are »Newfies«, people whose families originally came from Canadian Newfoundland.

Modern Phase

After the second phase, in which the architects increasingly let historical echoes of contemporary art, above all the Beaux Arts, influence the building of high rises and which created some of the most beautiful New York skyscrapers, the »modern« phase followed – but with hardly any noticeable and few style-making buildings, apart from the **Seagram Building**, a modern classic, built in 1958 by the German-born Mies van der Rohe, and the Lever House by his student Gordon Bunshaft. At any rate these

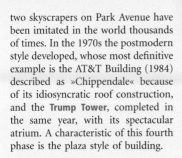

The steel skeleton grows: construction site of the World Trade Center, 1970

two skyscrapers on Park Avenue have been imitated in the world thousands of times. In the 1970s the postmodern style developed, whose most definitive example is the AT&T Building (1984) described as »Chippendale« because of its idiosyncratic roof construction, and the **Trump Tower**, completed in the same year, with its spectacular atrium. A characteristic of this fourth phase is the plaza style of building.

Stricter building regulations

In 1961 the Zoning Laws were revised; the building authorities had recognized that the regulations to date were not enough to allow space, air and light between the buildings. Now the builders had to make sure that part of the surface area was used for a public plaza; in exchange the houses could be built flat and did not have to recede as they got higher. But not everyone liked the box-shaped building style: Bunshaft built two office high rises for Manhattan in 1972 which remind critics of sailors' pants or knocked out teeth. The twin towers of the World Trade Center, opened in April 1973 and 417m/1,368ft and 415m/1,362ft high respectively, took the title of tallest building in the world away from the Empire State Building after 40 years. But the twin towers could only keep their first place for a short time: in 1973 Chicago beat the Big Apple with the 443m/1,454ft-high Sears Tower. In the meantime there are higher skyscrapers outside America. The 452m/1,484ft-high Petronas Towers stand in Kuala Lumpur (Malaysia) and the »king of skyscrapers« is the 509m/1,670ft Taipeh 101 in Taipeh, the capital city of **Taiwan**. But the Burj Dubai in the United Arab Emirates, which is planned to be 560m/1,838ft, is supposed to top them all in 2009. The Freedom Tower, the 541m/1,776ft-high new construction of the World Trade Center, will only be occupied up to 335m/1,100ft (70 storeys), above which will be a lattice skeleton and a point. But the skyline of Midtown and Downtown Manhattan remains the most famous in the world and the symbol for New York.

★ ★ **Empire State Building**

D 13

Location: 350 Fifth Ave./34th St.   **Subway:** 34th St.

After the collapse of the ▶ World Trade Center the Empire State Building is again the tallest building in New York and one of the most famous buildings in the world – 3.5 million people visit it every year. From the observatory on the 102nd floor there is an incomparable view of Manhattan; in clear weather the visibility is said to be 128km/80mi.

⏱ Opening hours: daily 8am–midnight

In 1929, construction began on the site where once the first Waldorf-Astoria Hotel stood. After only 19 months the 381m/1,250ft (with antenna 443m/1,454ft) colossus was complete; it was named after the nickname of the State of New York. The Art Deco building is a kind of city in itself – over 30,000 people live and work here. The building used 365,000 tons of steel, cement and granite; 100km/60mi of water pipes and 5,630km/3,498mi of telephone line were laid. 73 lifts travel through 11km/6.8mi of shafts, in only 45 seconds they transport people and freight up to the top. There are also stairs: runners at the peak of fitness require eleven minutes for the 1,860 steps in the annual Empire State Run up. The mast on the roof was originally intended to be an anchoring place for airships but is now used as an antenna for radio and television programmes.

In cinema, the building was the final place of refuge for the giant gorilla King Kong, before he plunged to his death – though the famous final scene of the film was made in a studio.

Thanks to the window frames made of stainless steel the Empire State Building radiates a special glow, both day and night. The top 30 floors are illuminated after dark until midnight by large searchlights, on special occasions even in

In the Empire State Building

colour: on Independence Day in red, white and blue, on Valentine's Day in red, and on St Patrick's Day in green (lighting schedule: www.esbnyc.com).

The building is worth a visit both in the daytime and the evening – there are two observatories, one on the 86th and the other on the 102nd floor – but the security checks for visitors are very strict since 9/11. A tip: in **hazy weather**, as is often the case in New York in the summer, enjoy the view during the **early morning hours**. Expect long queues. Tickets can be bought online: www.esbnyc.com.

★ ★ Fifth Avenue

C–J 15–4

Location: From Washington Square Park along Central Park northwards

Fifth Avenue has always been New York's most magnificent thoroughfare and, because there is no main square, it is also the centre of the city. The big parades start here (Steuben Parade, St Patrick's Day Parade), and it is also closed to traffic for other festivities.

Fifth Avenue starts downtown at Washington Square in ▶Greenwich Village, and runs straight to the Harlem River dividing Manhattan's streets into West (W) and East (E). At the end of the 19th century, the Rockefellers, Fricks, Forbes, Astors, Vanderbilts, Goulds and others who wanted to flee the congestion of southern Manhattan had townhouses built on its first mile or so, which earned it the nickname »**Millionaires' Row**«. Its new nickname, »Boulevard of Golden Credit Cards«, comes from luxury shops like Tiffany and Cartier between 49th and 59th St. The rich of the past century have settled further along, next to Central Park. Today the sights concentrated along Fifth Avenue (▶ Empire State Building, ▶ Rockefeller Center, ▶Museum of Modern Art, Trump Tower, ▶Central Park as well as the Museum Mile, to name but a few) exert an unparalleled attraction, not only on tourists but also on New Yorkers.

On Fifth Avenue

The **Flatiron Building** at the intersection Fifth Avenue, Broadway and 23rd Street made architectural history as the first skyscraper of Manhattan (▶Flatiron District). For those taking a stroll, the most interesting part of Fifth Ave. is between 34th and 59th Street. A special magnet for tourists is the ▶ Empire State Building (Fifth Ave./34th St.), whose observation platforms also give a good view of the course of the street. Art lovers should visit the nearby ▶Morgan Library and Museum (E 36th St.), and a very special pleasure is the little **Bryant**

WHERE NEW YORK'S MILLIONAIRES BLOW THEIR PROFITS

Great things are afoot in Manhattan: »triple profits«, »analysts' expectations surpassed«, is the positive news from everywhere on Wall Street. No question about it: many international, Dow-Jones indexed companies are again registering record profits.

This is also because of mass redundancies and the closure of inefficient companies. No wonder that there are meanwhile 13,000 millionaires in Manhattan – the rich could start their own town.

The big spenders

New York's rich are big spenders. Manhattan's real estate prices are at record levels, superstar restaurants are booming: a caviar omelette costs $1,000 at Le Parker Meridien, and the cheapest lunch at the Japanese Masa costs $300. The newest gag in the traditional restaurant »21«: a frequent-eater premium. Diners who spend more than $20,000 get a short trip on the Orient Express, since both have the same mother company. No wonder the presidential suite at the Mandarin Oriental Hotel in the Time Warner Tower didn't stay empty

long: it's a snip at $12,595. Or how about the costume ball of the Metropolitan Museum, tickets for about $3,500? A new haircut, perhaps, by Sally Hershberger, Hollywood's star hairdresser–starting at $600 for women. Or maybe you'd prefer earrings by Harry Winston for $185,000 plus the beach sandals by the jeweller H. Stern, which are set with gold feathers and diamonds and can be yours for a mere $17,000? Four-legged friends don't have to miss out on the fun either: a session in the Ritz Carlton's dog parlour costs $1,095 and includes a 22 carat gold dog tag. Evenings are spent at the Bubble Lounge where a bottle of champagne costs $1,900.

How about an island?

If those ideas aren't enough, the *Trader Monthly* gives more tips on how to dispose of your money.

Park behind the ►New York Public Library (476 Fifth Ave., between 40th and 42nd St.). Those interested in architecture should make a detour to E 42nd St., where there are several buildings worth seeing, including the ►Grand Central Terminal and the ►Chrysler Building.

Back on Fifth Avenue, the **Chase Manhattan Bank** (Fifth Ave./43rd St.) was built in 1954 to plans by Skidmore, Owings & Merrill and was one of the first glass buildings. In the block between Fifth and Sixth Ave., near 47th St., the diamond trade has established itself. For the most part it is in the hands of Chassidic Jews, who control 80% of American trade in the valuable gems. According to estimates the Diamond District employs 26,000 people. While the total sales turnover here is not known, the city collects almost $60 million in tax revenue from this area.

Continuing along, the 19 buildings of the ►Rockefeller Center are next and on the other side of the street

Not only for millionaires: the atrium in the Trump Tower

stands ► St Patrick's Cathedral with the Villard Houses behind it. The neighbouring 189m/621ft-high, 50-storey **Olympic Tower** (645 ◄ Olympic Tower Fifth Ave.) was built in 1976 according to plans by Skidmore, Owings & Merrill. The aluminium-covered building, once the New York headquarters of Aristotle Onassis's empire, unites shops, offices and condominiums under one roof for the first time. The public arcades inside, with palm trees and a waterfall, do not however create an atmosphere of real life.

In the **Tishman Building**, also called »666 Fifth Avenue«, a 39-storey, **Tishman Building** aluminium covered high rise from 1957, there is also a waterfall designed by the artist Isamu Noguchi.

11 E 52 St., between Madison and Fifth Ave., is the address of the **Austrian Cultural** Austrian Cultural Forum. Regular events take place in the narrow, **Forum** 24-storey, new glass and cement building by architect Raimund Abraham (information: tel. 212-319-5300, www.acfny.org).
On the corner of Fifth Ave./W 53rd St. stands St Thomas Church, built in 1913 by Cram, Goodhue and Ferguson in the neo-Gothic

style. In the side street there are three worthwhile museums, among them the ► Museum of Modern Art. A piece of information for architecture fans: the plans of the University Club, built in 1899 in Renaissance style (Fifth Ave./W 54th St.) were by McKim, Mead & White.

Carnegie Hall

A detour brings you to one of the most famous concert halls in the world, Carnegie Hall (154 West 57th St./Seventh Ave.). The steel magnate Andrew Carnegie donated the house with almost 2,800 seats; Tchaikovsky conducted the opening concert in 1891. Until the building of the ► Lincoln Center Carnegie Hall was the home of the New York Philharmonic orchestra. It was supposed to be demolished in the 1960s, but instead was placed under monument protection, the brick and glazed tile music temple built in Italian Renaissance style being carefully restored. Events still take place here (►Practicalities, Theater, Music and Ballet). The **Rose Museum** museum shows gifts from the artists who have performed here (open: daily 11am–4.30pm; guided tours during the season: Mon–Fri at 11.30am, 2pm and 3pm; information: tel. 212-903-9765, www.carnegiehall.org).

Cesar Pelli is the architect of the neighbouring **Carnegie Hall Tower**. The skyscraper with offices and extensions of Carnegie Hall was

FAO Schwarz, legendary toy shop on Fifth Ave.

erected over a concrete tube that was poured on site, and then covered with bricks and glazed tiles like the Hall itself. In its shadow just a few metres away is the 66-storey black **Metropolitan Tower** (Harry Macklowe, 1987). A block to the south is the third giant, Helmut Jahn's 70-storey **Cityspire** (1987) with its cupola reminiscent of the cathedral in Florence. Together, Carnegie Hall Tower, Metropolitan Tower and Cityspire make an impressive ensemble.

Moving towards Central Park, exquisite shops line up like pearls on a string. The department stores **Saks Fifth Avenue** (611 Fifth Ave., between 49th and 50th St.) and **Takashimaya** (693 Fifth Ave., between 54th and 55th. St.), are popular, as are »theme shops« such as the **Disney Store** (711 Fifth Ave./55th St.), **Niketown** – the multi-storied shop offers everything from the world of sports (6 E 57th St., between Fifth and Madison Ave.) – or **Tiffany**, the jewellery shop which opened in 1837 and was made famous by Truman Capote's tale and the film *Breakfast at Tiffany's* (727 Fifth Ave., www.tiffany.com).

Back on Fifth Avenue

The Corning Glass Building (717 Fifth Ave./56th St.) was built in 1959 to plans by Harrison & Abramowitz, the architects of the ► Rockefeller Center and the Metropolitan Opera in the ► Lincoln Center. The Steuben Shop in the ground floor offers a broad selection of glass, historical and modern.

Corning Glass Building

In 1984 the real estate magnate Donald Trump built a monument to himself on the corner of Fifth Ave./E 56th St. The 202m/663ft-high, 68-storey glass palace goes back to a design by Der Scutt. The six-storey-high atrium is certainly an eye-catcher (► picture p.235). Breccia marble from Italy was used for the walls and floors here, its colour mixture of pink, peach and orange makes everything appear gilded. A waterfall tumbles the 60m/198ft down to the ground. Restaurants, cafés and countless shops are housed here, above them are offices and condominiums, of which the largest on the top floor can be had for a mere $10 million. Trump Tower is connected with the also very attractive glass garden of the former IBM Building (590 Madison Ave., ►Sony Building).
Trump Tower would be only half as beautiful without the reflection of the **Crown Building** (730 Fifth Ave.) in its façade. The former Heckscher Building was built in 1921 (architects: Warren & Wetmore) in the French Renaissance style.

Trump Tower

Grand Army Plaza forms a dignified provisional finale to Fifth Avenue with the Pulitzer Fountain (1915) in its centre. Here are the former **Plaza Hotel** (59th St.), which was built in 1907 in the style of a French Château by Henry J. Hardenbergh, the south-east entrance to ► Central Park – the horse drawn carriages start their trips through the park here – and the giant toy shop **FAO Schwarz** (767

★
Grand Army Plaza

Fifth Ave./58th St.) in the **General Motors Building**, which was built in 1968 by Emery Roth & Sons with Edward Durell Stone. Unfortunately the 215m/705ft-high, 50-storey building has destroyed the much praised harmony of the Grand Army Plaza. Furthermore, take a look at the building of the **Metropolitan Club** (corner of 60th St.), from 1893 by Stanford White in the style of a Florentine palazzo.

Northwards, between the ►Frick Collection (70th St.) and the Museum of the City of New York (103rd St.), stretches the **Museum Mile** with the ► Whitney Museum, the ► Metropolitan Museum of Art, the ►Neue Galerie, the ►Guggenheim Museum and the Cooper Hewitt Museum.

✳ Financial District

A/B 19

Location: Lower Manhattan   **Subway:** Wall St., Rector St.

The financial district in southern Manhattan is so named for the New York stock exchange and the many banks and credit institutions in the area, primarily on Wall St., the city canyon which rarely sees sunshine.

Wall Street

Wall Street is named after a defensive wall that once ran along here (»The Wall«), which was supposed to protect the Dutch Nieuw Amsterdam from attacks by the Native Americans and the English. At noon Wall Street and its surroundings are so full of people that it is hard to move forwards; on holidays and on weekends the area is empty of people.

Trinity Church

For 300 years Trinity Church has stood at the start of Wall St., where it is now wedged between the high rises of the financial district (Trinity Place; www.trinitywallstreet.org). Today's building was erected in 1846 in the Gothic Revival style with brown sandstone (architect: Richard Upjohn). The 92m/300ft-high tower was the highest building in New York in the 19th century. There were two previous buildings of the same name: the first church, from the year 1698, was a simple building without a steeple, which burned down in 1776. The following building was dedicated in 1790 and torn down in 1839 because it was structurally unsound. The bronze doors by Richard Morris Hunt (1828–1895) on the three entrances from Broadway show Biblical scenes (main entrance and north portal) as well as events from the history of America and Trinity congregation (south portal). In the interior, the stained glass windows and the back wall of the altar with Christian scenes engraved in stone from Caen (France) are worth taking a look at (guided tours: daily 2pm).

In the **museum** the beginnings of New York and the church are explained, which in 1705 got most of its property from the English

Trinity Church between high rises

Queen Anne and is one of the richest Episcopalian congregations in the city (open: Mon–Fri 9am–5.30pm, Sat 9am–3.45pm, Sun from 1pm). In New York's oldest **cemetery** numerous historical personalities are buried, including Alexander Hamilton, buried in a pyramid-shaped tomb, the first US Secretary of the Treasury (1755–1804), who was shot in a duel by his opponent Aaron Burr (► Harlem, Morris-Jumel Mansion Museum), and Robert Fulton, who constructed the first functional steamship (1765–1815).

Opposite the church (Broadway/Wall St.) stands the high rise of the **Irving Trust Company**, a massive limestone block (1 Wall St.; architect: Ralph Walker, 1931). The exquisitely decorated Art Deco style lobby is worth a look.

From here it is only a few steps to Federal Hall. This building was completed after eight years in 1842 and inaugurated as the customs house on the intersection of Wall/Nassau St.; it represents the high point of neo-classical building in New York. Its Wall Street façade, which is in the shape of a Doric temple, is a simplified Parthenon without a frieze. The interior consists of a rotunda, which actually seems to be more Roman than Greek.

From 1862–1920 Federal Hall was a sub-section of the U. S. Treasury; it has been a museum since 1955. President George Washington, who took his oath of office in 1789 where his statue now stands, is remembered here in particular. At that time the old city hall (1701) stood here, which Pierre L'Enfant, famous as the urban planner of the nation's capital Washington, had modernized and which was the seat of the U.S. Congress in 1789/90 (open: Mon–Fri 9am–5pm).

**Federal Hall
National
Memorial**

Outside the New York stock exchange

The New York Stock Exchange (20 Broad St.), NYSE for short, is the largest stock exchange in the United States and, in spite of many crises, the most important in the world. On an average trading day about 1.5 billion stocks worth more than $46 billion change hands (record: Oct. 10, 2008 with 7.3 billion; in 2008 the total was 802,027 billion. In London the volume is about $30 billion). The value of all 3,507 companies listed on the NYSE in late 2008 sank more then 60% during the financial crisis as against mid-2007 to currently about $8.5 trillion. The New York stock exchange was founded in 1792: at that time a few stock dealers used to meet regularly under the sycamore trees along Wall Street in order to deal in government loans from the American Revolutionary War. The building with a façade in the style of a Roman temple, designed by George B. Post, was built in the year 1903. In the legendary trading room there is seemingly chaotic activity. Since 9/11, visitors are no longer permitted entry. Current information at: www.nyse.com, tel. 212-656-3000. Those interested in the history of Wall Street should instead go to the **Museum of American Finance** (48 Wall St.; subway: Wall St.; open: Tue–Sat 10am–4pm, www.moaf.org).

23 Wall St.   At 23 Wall St., corner of Broad Street, stands the fortress-like **Morgan Guaranty Trust Company** (architects: Trowbridge & Livingston). Close by is the Bank of Manhattan (40 Wall St.), now the **Trump Building** (H. Craig Severance, Yasuo Matsui, 1929). The tower, with its pyramid like crown, is 282.5m/927ft high. The banking house with two rows of giant Greek columns (55 Wall St.) was built in 1841 for the New York stock exchange and designed by Isaiah Rogers; in 1907 it was renovated and expanded by the architects McKim, Mead & White. Opposite is the 40-storey office high rise of the **Morgan Bank**, a tower of granite and reflecting glass built in 1988 to plans by Roche, Dinkeloo & Assocs. At a height of 289.6m/951ft it is the tallest building in the financial district. At this point, Wall St. meets Water Street. A short detour to the left leads to Wall Street Plaza (Water/Pine St.), built in 1973 to a design by the Chinese American I. M. Pei. There is a nice **view** across the East River from the somewhat higher plaza between the buildings at 55 Water St.

Fraunces' Tavern Museum   Follow Water St. south-west to reach a block with houses from the 18th century. Fraunces' Tavern was built in 1719 and taken over in 1763 by Samuel Fraunces, who opened an inn here; it is the oldest house in Manhattan (54 Pearl St./Water St.). George Washington spent his last days as general here in the winter of 1783: on 4 December he said farewell to his officers and withdrew to his estate in Mount Vernon near the city that would later become the capital named after him. In 1837 and 1852 the building burned down but it was rebuilt in 1907 in the late colonial style. Today's building is a new construction by William Mersereau from the year 1928 in 18th-century style. On the ground floor there is a restaurant (tel. 212-968-1776), and on the two upper floors a museum about the history of America (open: Tue–Sun noon–6pm).

Return along Pearl to Pine Street, where the beautiful Art Deco American International Building stands at 70 Pine St.; its lobby is worth taking a look at. A couple of steps north-east between Nassau and William, Pine and Liberty St. is the headquarters of the Chase Manhattan Bank with a huge plaza (1 Chase Manhattan Plaza). The design of the 248m/813ft-high, 60-storey high rise of steel and glass – an example of International Style – was by Gordon Bunshaft from the offices of Skidmore, Owings & Merrill. Its completion in 1960 marks the beginning of the modernization of the financial district. On the plaza stands the large sculpture *Four Trees* by **Jean Dubuffet** (1972). The 14m/46ft-high, 25-ton sculpture made of aluminium, steel and plastic was called »a monument of the spirit, a landscape of esprit« by the artist. The second large sculpture *Sunken Garden*, a lowered plaza with a fountain and seven basalt blocks, is at the same time the light source for the bank under the plaza. It is the work of the Japanese artist Isamu Noguchi (1961–1964).

American International Building

◄ Chase Manhattan Bank

The intersection of Liberty and William St. and Maiden Lane is named after the artist Louise Nevelson (1900–1988, ► Famous People). The sculpture *Shadows and Flags* (1977) in the middle of the street, which consists of seven iron figures of varying heights, is her work.

Louise Nevelson Plaza

The Federal Reserve Bank in William St. was built in 1924 in classical style and is known as the Fed (entrance is in Liberty St.). It is one of twelve Federal Reserve banks, which circulate US dollars. Here – and not in the US gold depot Fort Knox in Kentucky – about half of the world's gold is stored, amounting to 700,000 gold bars. Only about 2% belong to the United States, the rest to 60 other countries and organizations such as the International Monetary Fund. A giant security system guards them. The safe is about 30m/98ft underground, is half as big as a football field and has 122 numbered cells in which the bars are stacked like bricks. Each one is 99.5% pure and weighs 12.5kg/27.6lbs. Most of the gold came to the USA during the Second World War. If a national bank sells its gold today, it is simply carried from one cell to another. The bank refuses to divulge who has sold how much gold (tours by appointment: Mon–Fri 9.30am–3.30pm, tel. 212-720-6130; www.newyorkfed.org).

Federal Reserve Bank

Marine Midland Bank

The 223m/725ft dark glass tower of the Marine Midland Bank (Gordon Bunshaft from the offices of Skidmore, Owings & Merrill, 1967) stands at 140 Broadway on a receded base; the 7m/23ft-high *Red Cube* by Isamu Noguchi (1973) is a real eye-catcher.

Equitable Building

Opposite the Marine Midland Bank towers the Equitable Building, built in 1915, a giant 160m/525ft-high massive stone block (120 Broadway). It casts the whole area in shadow and protests about this caused the Zoning Law to be passed in the year 1916. This law stated that high rises had to be built terraced, so that they became narrower with increasing height.

33 Maiden Lane

The office high rise reminiscent of a knight's castle, 33 Maiden Lane, is the work of Philip Johnson, the old master of the International Style, who obviously helped himself here from the smorgasbord of architectural history.

Liberty Plaza

The small plaza on Liberty St. (between Broadway and Church St.) is a popular meeting place for the lunch crowd from the surrounding offices and banks especially at midday – the bronze sculpture depicting a financier searching through his briefcase by J. Seward Johnson Jr. hints at this. The east side of the plaza is occupied by the 245m/804ft-high former U. S. Steel Building, today **One Liberty Plaza** (Skidmore, Owings & Merrill, 1972).

Flatiron District & Union Square

D 14

Location: Between Fifth and Park Ave., and 14th and 29th St.

Subway: 23rd St., 14th St.

The Flatiron Building at the intersection of Fifth Ave. and 23rd St., one of the first and most unusual skyscrapers in New York, is the centre of the new trendy area with restaurants ranging from the cosy to the off-beat and select shops.

★
Flatiron Building

The striking triangular shape of the »Flatiron« gave the building its name. It is New York's first skyscraper in the – then new – steel skeleton construction. The architect D. H. Burnham could not build in any other way on the acutely angled land at the intersection of Fifth Ave. and Broadway. The building was erected in 1902, is 76m/250ft high and with its 20 floors looks more like an oversized apartment building.

The Flatiron Building heralded the skyscraper era →

Madison Square Park The small park between Fifth and Madison Ave., on 23rd and 26th Street, named after an American president James Madison (1751–1836) is not very significant. But its surroundings are interesting. To the south is the Flatiron Building, and to the east three buildings stand out:

The **Metropolitan Life Insurance Company Building**, the originally ten-storey main building (1 Madison Ave.) of the large insurance company, was built in 1893 by Napoleon LeBrun. 16 years later the tower, which was based on St Mark's Campanile in Venice, was added. For two years the now 213m/699ft-high, 50-storey building was the tallest in the world.

Also on Madison Square is the **Appellate Division Courthouse**, the tallest court building in New York state. It was built in 1900 in a historicizing tradition. The sculptures portray several great law-makers, among them the Chinese Confucius, the Persian Zarathustra, the Greek Solon and the Indian Manu.

! *Baedeker* TIP

Excellent lunch address

The organic supermarket chain »Whole Foods« (for instance at Union Square, www.wholefoodsmarket.com) have a varied selection of excellent dishes and salads, which can be eaten in the adjoining restaurant.

Cass Gilbert, who was also in charge of the design of the Woolworth Building (▶City Hall & Civic Center, p.215), designed the **New York Life Insurance Building**, constructed in 1926–1928. Until it was demolished in 1925 the famous Madison Square Garden stood in its place, the palace of entertainment designed in 1890 by Stanfort White.

Museum of Sex ⏱ A bit further north the Museum of Sex applies itself to the subject of New York and sexuality (233 Fifth Ave./27th St.; open: Sun–Fri 11am–18.30, Sat until 8pm; minimum age 18 years) ▶Practicalities, Museums and Galleries.

Theodore Roosevelt Birthplace ⏱ The house between Broadway and Park Ave., a bit further south, is an exact replica of the house where Theodore Roosevelt (1858–1919) was born. »Teddy«, the 26th president of the USA, lived here until he was 15. Almost half of the furniture is original (28 E 20th St.; subway: 23rd St.; open: Tue–Sat 9am until 5pm).

Gramercy Park Gramercy Park, between E 20th and 21st St. in the neighbourhood of the same name, was designed around 1830 by Samuel Ruggles, in order to attract buyers of real estate. It is the only private park in the city. Only locals and guests of the neighbouring Gramercy Park Hotel may use it.

Union Square At Union Square, where Broadway and the Bowery meet, New York justifies its reputation as the »Entertainment Capital of the World«. In the early 20th century the first film studios opened here; there were theatres, opera houses, concert halls and nickelodeons. On the »Ladies Mile« stood the original Macy's, Tiffany and other legendary shops. Here also is a lively area with numerous shops, cafés and bars. On Mondays, Wednesdays, Fridays and Saturdays there is a giant **farmer's market** here. The façade of the building south of the square is decorated with a striking triptych, *Metronome* (Kristin Jones, Andrew Ginzel). The six illuminated numbers on the left represent the time of day, the six on the right the time yet remaining in the day. From the centre of the artwork a spurt of steam is released at noon and midnight every day. On the right the current phase of the moon is shown.

✦ ✦ Frick Collection

F 10

Location: 1 E 70th St.   **Subway:** 68th St.

The private art collection of the steel producer Henry Clay Frick from Pittsburgh (1849–1919) is housed in his ostentatious former townhouse. It was built in 1913/1914 to plans of the architects Carrère and Hastings in the French neo-classical style and was intended to be superior to the house of Frick's former partner Andrew Carnegie (today the home of the Cooper Hewitt Museum).

In 1935, after the death of Adelaide Frick, widow of the collector, the house was opened as a museum. The private character has been preserved in the museum. The excellent collection comprises paintings

The city palace of the art collector Henry Clay Frick

Frick Collection Plan

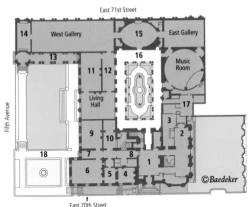

East 71st Street

14 | West Gallery | 15 | East Gallery
13 | | 16 | Music Room
11 12
Living Hall
17
3
9 | 10 | 2
18 | 7 | 8 | 1
6 | 5 | 4
©Baedeker

Fifth Avenue

East 70th Street

1	Entrance Hall	5	Ante Room	9	Fragonard Room	12	North Hall	15	Oval Room
2	Reception Hall	6	Dining Room	10	South Hall	13	Portico	16	Garden Court
3	Museum Shop	7	West Vestibule	11	Library	14	Enamel Room	17	Green Room
4	Boucher Room	8	East Vestibule					18	Terrace

🕐
Opening hours:
Tue–Sat 10am–6pm
Sun 11am–5pm
www.frick.org

of old masters, bronzes of the Italian Renaissance and enamels from Limoges, which are presented in the intimate surroundings of the rooms furnished in the Empire style.

The **Boucher Room** on the ground floor, styled like a French boudoir, shows eight allegorical portrayals, *The Arts and Sciences*, which François Boucher (1703–1770) painted for Madame de Pompadour's boudoir in Crécy Palace. The **Dining Room** is decorated with English paintings of the 18th century, among them Hogarth's *Miss Mary Edwards* (1724) and *Path in St James' Park* by Gainsborough (1783). The main attraction in the **Fragonard Room** is the painting cycle created for Madame du Barry and Louveciennes Palace *Les Progrès de l'Amour* by Jean-Honoré Fragonard (1732–1806).

In the richly furnished **Living Hall** (salon) paintings by Giovanni Bellini, *The Ecstasy of St Francis* (around 1480), Titian, *The Man with the Red Turban* and *Pietro Aretino*, El Greco, *St Jerome*, and Hans Holbein the Younger, *Sir Thomas More* and *Thomas Cromwell* are displayed.

Among the pictures in the corridors are Vermeer's *The Officer and the Laughing Girl* (around 1656) and *The Music Lesson* (1660) in the **South Hall**. Goya painted the picture *Don Pedro, Duke of Osuna* (around 1790), Renoir the *Mother and Two Children* (1870). The dresser and bureau were created by Jean-Henri Riesener around 1780 for Marie-Antoinette. The **Library** mainly displays portraits, including a portrait of the art collector Henry Clay Frick by Johansen (1943) and *George Washington* by Gilbert Stuart.

In the **North Hall** the portrait of Comtesse d'Haussonville by Ingres (1845), *Portal of Valenciennes* (1709/1710) by Watteau and Monet's *Winter in Vetheuil* are especially worth seeing. A glass roof lightens the **West Gallery**, which contains Rembrandt's self-portrait from the year 1654 and his *Polish Rider* (1658), Veronese's *Wisdom and Strength* and *The Choice of Hercules*, *The Smithy* by Goya (1818), portraits by El Greco, van Dyck, Hals, Bronzino and Velázquez's *Philipp IV of Spain* (1664). The adjoining **Enamel Room** contains, among others Jan van Eyck's *Virgin and Child, with Saints and Donor*, *St Simon* by Piero della Francesca and a four part altar by the same artist from the church S. Agostino in Borgo San Sepolcro (Italy). In the **Oval Room**, Frick's former study, there are two portraits by van Dyck and Gainsborough displayed facing each other. In the **East Gallery** are the *The Sermon on the Mount* by Claude Lorrain, portraits by Jacques Louis David, Goya and Whistler. This leads to the **Garden Court**, a glass-covered inner courtyard with a small table, benches and a bronze angel by Jean Barbet. In the **Lecture Hall**, lectures and introductions to the collection are occasionally held.

✶ Gracie Mansion

Location: East End Ave./E 88th St. (in Carl Schurz Park)   **Subway:** 86th St.

This house, which was built in 1799 by Ezra Weeks for the Scottish importer Archibald Gracie in the Federal Style, has been the residence of the mayor of New York since 1942.

It has been renovated and expanded several times. Since the current mayor Michael Bloomberg doesn't live here but in his own home, Gracie Mansion is currently open to the public (tours: Tue–Thur on appointment, tel. 212-570-4773, www.nyc.gov/gracie). It lies in the north of **Carl Schurz Park**, which is especially popular in the summer, and is located along the bank of the East River between 84th and 90th Street. It was named after the German-American journalist and politician Carl Schurz (1829–1906; ▶ Famous People). A pretty promenade runs along the bank of the East River. The first stretch is named after John Finlay, the publisher of the New York Times. From here there is a nice view of the Queensboro Bridge, Roosevelt and Ward's Island and Hell Gate, the connection between the East River and Long Island Sound.

Yorkville, the area between East 79th and 96th St. as well as East River and Lexington Ave., was once the **German quarter** of Manhattan, and 86th Street was known as the »German Broadway«. Today the names of a few cafés, restaurants and shops are a reminder of this.

> **!** **Baedeker TIP**
>
> **Excursion to Death**
> June 15, 1904 marked the end of Little Germany in New York. Edward T. O'Donnell, *Ship Ablaze* (Broadway), relates the background of how 2,000 residents of Little Germany died in a boating catastrophe.

The German population has shrunk to a small core since real estate speculation and the removal of older houses pushed the rents up. German settling in this area began at the end of the 19th century and reached its high point before the beginning of the Second World War. The rapid decline of Yorkville as German quarter began about 1960. The so-called **Henderson District** (on the East River) consists of 24 pretty terraced brick houses from the late 19th century and is a sought after address today.

★ ★ Grand Central Terminal

E 12

Location: E 42nd St./Park Ave.　　　**Subway:** Grand Central

In 1871 the railway magnate Cornelius Vanderbilt opened the first railway station here, from which the trains of the private railway line New York Central left for Chicago and Canada.

Today's building by the architects Reed & Stern, a masterpiece of Beaux Arts style, in which Baroque and Renaissance elements have been merged, was opened in 1913 and elaborately renovated a short time ago. Today commuter trains depart from here. At its heart is a giant station hall, and above the elaborate marble floor domes an artificial sky with over 2,500 stars (Paul Helleu). The double staircase is also impressive, based on the Paris opera house and reminiscent of the glory days of train travel. From above the information windows a giant brass clock shines, and the candelabra are plated with gold and nickel (information: www.grandcentralterminal.com; tours: Wed 12.30pm with the Municipal Arts Society, meeting point is the kiosk, tel. 212-935-3960). There are numerous restaurants and shops in the side corridors, among them the famous **Oyster Bar**, which has excellent seafood cuisine (tel. 212-490-6650); also Cypriani, Métrazur and Michael Jordan's Steakhouse. On the lower floor the Grand Central Market, a shopping level with a broad selection and fast-food for every taste, is an inviting place to have a look around.

MetLife Building

In 1963 the Pan Am Building (today MetLife Building) was built over the Central Terminal ▶ Park Avenue (the railway station has direct access to the lobby).

42nd Street
Philip Morris
Building

Back on 42nd Street, there are several interesting buildings: diagonally across from Central Station is the 26-storey Altria Building

Grand Central Terminal is a pivotal point for commuters

(former Philip Morris Building, 120 Park Ave.; Ulrich Franzen, 1983).

Other interesting buildings on 42nd St. are the Home Savings of America Building (former Bowery Savings Bank; 110 E 42nd St.), whose richly appointed teller hall is an absolute must (York and Sawyers, 1923). **Home Savings of America**

The neighbouring 56-storey Chanin Building (122 E 42nd St.) is a successful example of Art Deco style (Sloan & Robertson, 1929); here, take a look at the beautiful lobby. **Chanin Building**

The architectural high point of the street is indisputably the ►Chrysler Building, built in 1930. Opposite is the 45-storey Mobil Building (150 E 42nd St.). It was built in 1955 of stainless steel to plans by Harrison & Abramovitz and was supposed to prove that glass and aluminium are not the only building materials of the future. **Mobil Building**

Daily News Building The former Daily News Building (220 E 42nd St.) was built in 1930 in Art Deco style for the newspaper that had the largest circulation of the time – film buffs will recognize it as the building of the *Daily Planet*, which Clark Kent (alias Superman) entered and exited, either on foot or by air. The façade is impressive: the rising, prominent vertical bands of light brick make the 37-storey building seem taller than it really is. The flat roof designed by the architects Howells and Hood is also unusual. The extension along Third Ave. followed in 1958 to plans by Harrison & Abramovitz. Take a look at the Art Deco lobby with its large rotating globe.

Ford Foundation Building Architectural history was also made in 1967 by the Ford Foundation Building, which was designed by Kevin Roche and Dinkeloo, headquarters of the Ford Foundation (320 E 43rd St.; entrance on 42nd St.), founded in 1936. The L-shaped ground plan of the 12-sto-rey building includes an almost 1,400 sq m/1,674 sq yd winter garden. The intention of the builder and architects was to create an environmentally sound building.

Tudor City Opposite the Ford Foundation the so-called Tudor City, completed in 1928, stretches between E 40th and E 43rd Street. The complex, in the neo-Gothic Tudor style, consists of twelve buildings with about 3,000 apartments, a hotel and two parks, and is an oasis in the middle of Manhattan. When the colony was built, the UN headquarters (▶ United Nations Headquarters) did not yet exist, and there were industrial sites and slaughterhouses on the East River; for this reason there are hardly any windows facing the river.

✳ **Greenwich Village**

B/C 14–16

Location: Between 14th and Houston St. and west of Broadway

Subway: Fourth St./Washington Square, Sheridan Square, Eighth St.

New Yorkers just call it »The Village«. Greenwich Village stretches between 14th and Houston St. and between the Hudson River and ▶Broadway; the small part west of Sixth Ave. is also called West Village.

When the village of Greenwich was founded in 1696, it lay far outside the city. By 1811, when the chessboard-like street grid of Manhattan was adopted, Greenwich was already a small city, whose small, winding streets had names that remain to this day. In the course of the 18th and 19th centuries the area developed into a refined residential area, to which old brick buildings bear witness. It became important when from about 1900 for about 30 years it was the living and meeting area for New York's Bohemia, who patronized the small theatres and many bars. During prohibition, bars known as **speakeasies** met the demand for illegal alcohol. The number of poets, authors and painters who lived in the Village is legion, and included James Fenimore Cooper, Edgar Allan Poe, Richard Wright, Henry James, John Dos Passos, Marianne Moore, Mark Twain, Sinclair Lewis and Dorothy Thompson, Thomas Wolfe, Hart Crane, Mary McCarthy, E. E. Cummings, William Styron and Edward Albee as well as Edward Hopper, William Glackens and Rockwell Kent.

Today Greenwich Village is a respectable residential area; there are a few modern high rises, but the impression of a city with many homes with pretty inner courtyards and the winding narrow streets remains. The rents are among the highest in New York. A stroll through the historical area, whose centre lies immediately west of Washington Square, is most worthwhile. In the evening in particular it is a popular attraction with its overwhelming selection of legen-

The extravagant marble arch commemorates George Washington's inauguration

dary jazz clubs (among them the Blue Note and the Village Vanguard), theatres, cafés and restaurants.

✳ Washington Square

The main square of the area is Washington Square. Once execution grounds, paupers' graveyard and parade grounds, it is now a place where New York romps; at weekends a microcosm of the city with people of all races, nations and ages, who play, make music, roller skate or just enjoy the sun. The square is dominated by the mighty **Washington Centennial Memorial Arch**. The 26m/85ft-high triumphal arch (by Stanford White) was erected in 1892 to commemorate the inauguration of George Washington. In the north of the square stands a statue of the first president (Alexander Calder, 1918), and south of the arch is a monument to Garibaldi (Giovanni Turini; 1888). The Italian independence hero lived on Staten Island from 1848 until 1854.

The Grey Art Gallery

The square is bordered by the buildings of **New York University**, the largest private university in America, founded in 1831 by Albert Gallatin. In New York University's gallery predominantly American art from about 1940 until the present is on display (100 Washington Square East between Washington and Waverly Place; open: Tue, Thu, Fri 11am–6pm, Wed until 8pm, Sat until 5pm; www.nyu.edu/greyart).

Northwest of Washington Square lies **The Row**, a group of elegant townhouses in the classical Federal Style. They inspired Henry James to write the novel *Washington Square* (1881). From here it is not far to the **Washington Mews**, former stables on a pretty cobbled street which today belong to New York University.

The **Northern Dispensary** (165 Waverly Place), a three-sided building on the corner of Waverly Place, was built in 1831 during a cholera epidemic. In **McDougal Alley**, a small street north-west of Washington Square, Gertrude Vanderbilt Whitney (1875 until 1942) opened a gallery at the beginning of the 20th century that later developed into the ▶Whitney Museum of Art.

The brick built **Judson Memorial Church** south of Washington Square commemorates the Baptist Adoniram Judson, who went to Burma as a missionary in the early 19th century. The church has magnificent stained glass windows by the New York artist John La Farge.

Bleecker Street

Bleecker Street, of which Simon & Garfunkel sang on one of their first albums, is the commercial centre of the Village with its many theatres, restaurants, bars and antique shops. The **Bayard Building**

(65 Bleecker St.) is the only New York building by the Chicago architect Louis Sullivan (1898).

At 100 Bleecker St. stands the sculpture *Bust of Sylvette* by Pablo Picasso. The 11m/36ft, 60-ton concrete sculpture rises four storeys high in front of the three towers of the faculty residences of New York University (I. M. Pei, 1966). Despite its size, the sphinx-like figure radiates an unusual grace.

Until the 1960s the gay and lesbian scene in New York was considered to be immoral. A full-blown rebellion took place on 27 June 1969, after the police stormed Stone Wall Inn (51 Christopher St.) and arrested some of the homosexual clientele. Three nights of resistance followed. This and many other actions led to a change in the law, which gave gays and lesbians the same rights as the rest of the population. Today people in the Village don't hide their sexual inclination

Jefferson Market Library

anymore. »Christopher Street Day« is celebrated all over the world to commemorate the »Stonewall Rebellion«. **Sheridan Square**, where **Christopher St.** and Seventh Ave. intersect, is the second centre of the Village after Washington Square.

The Jefferson Market Courthouse Library (425 Sixth Ave./10th St.) is an especially interesting building. Built in 1876 in wonderfully overloaded Venetian Gothic, it was a courthouse until 1945 and reopened in 1967 as a branch of the ►New York Public Library.

Jefferson Market Library

Other streets worth checking out in the Village are Minetta Lane, Bedford Street – no. 75 is the oldest remaining Village house (1799), the winding Commerce Street, and Grove Street, as well as St Luke's Place (between Leroy and Hudson St.) with a group of completely preserved houses from the year 1855, and Hudson Street with the **St Luke-in-the-Fields** church (no. 485) from the year 1822 which was badly damaged by fire at the beginning of 1981. In spite of later changes to the building it still looks like a village church. In this part of Hudson St. there are countless antique shops. One of the newest trendy neighbourhoods is the so-called **Meatpacking District**, the area between the Village and ►Chelsea.

Other streets

✶✶ Guggenheim Museum

G 8

Location: 1071 Fifth Ave./88th St.   **Subway:** 86th St.

The Guggenheim has one of the world's best collections of modern art – from classical modern works to the most recent offerings. The museum is the creation of the Swiss mining industrialist Solomon R. Guggenheim (1861–1949).

🕐
Opening hours:
Sat–Wed
10am–5.45
Fri until 8pm
www.
guggenheim.org

Guggenheim originally collected old masters until the German artist and later museum director Baroness Hilla Rebay introduced him to non-objective art. In 1943 the Swiss collector commissioned the architect Frank Lloyd Wright (1869 until 1959) to plan a museum building to display the works of art in the »Solomon R. Guggenheim Collection of Non-Objective Paintings« which had been housed tem-

Idiosyncratic construction: Solomon R. Guggenheim Museum

porarily since 1939. Fourteen years passed until all of the city's requirements were met, and building finally began in 1957. Wright never saw the opening: he died six months before the museum was completed in 1959.

Wright's only museum and his only building in New York is a great work of architectural art, even though there are a number of critics who doubt its suitability as a museum. For Wright himself his aesthetic form meets the function halfway. »A museum,« so he postulated, »is an organic structure with one large room on one continuous storey.« He detached himself from the usual division of museums into halls and created one single cylindrical 28m/90ft interior in which the only light source is daylight through a glass dome. A conically widening, 432m/472.4yd-long spiralling ramp with a 3% incline winds around the room and exhibits the works of art in over 70 niches and small galleries. As already mentioned, lighting is from daylight – along with some indirect lighting along the ramp. This arrangement of space results in an easy to survey and systematic exhibition and leads the visitor clearly in the direction of the logical order of the exhibits, which, after taking a lift to the top, goes downwards.

Frank Lloyd Wright's museum building

The foundation had to fight more than 20 court cases until they were allowed to build a highly necessary extension – which Wright had already planned in 1951 (10m/33ft higher than the present extension) – next to the rotunda which is under a preservation order. In 1992 the 14-storey gallery house with several double stories was finished (architect: Charles Gwathmey). The spiral is now used only for temporary exhibitions; the main collection is in the extension. But even now there is still not enough room for the New York foundation – actually a »collection of collections« – since the Thannhauser, Niedendorf, Dreier, Peggy Guggenheim and Panza collections, among others, were added to the Guggenheim complex. Guggenheim had to expand: there are now branches in Venice, Bilbao, Berlin and Las Vegas.

The collection consists of more than 8,000 paintings and sculptures – from the famous pictures of the Thannhauser collection including those by Camille Pissarro, the oldest Guggenheim artist, all the way to Pop Art. This excellent overview of classical to contemporary modern is displayed in a rotating selection of about 350 masterpieces. The Munich art dealer Justin K. Thannhauser, who died in 1976, willed the museum his collection of 75 impressionist and post-impressionist masterpieces. In another gallery art from the time between the World Wars is exhibited, chronologically a continuation of the Thannhauser Collection with works by Kandinsky, Mondrian, Mirò, Chagall and Léger. The collection donated by the Italian Count Panza consists of 200 works of Minimal and Concept Art, monochrome painting and environments.

Collection

★ Harlem

F–K 1–6

Location: North of Central Park   **Subway:** 125th St.

Express subway trains, as once immortalized by Duke Ellington in *Take the A-Train*, take less than ten minutes to go from Times Square to 125th St., Harlem's shopping street. Since the turn of the millennium Harlem, the predominantly African American neighbourhood in north Manhattan between 110th and 162nd Street, has been experiencing its second Renaissance.

Peter Stuyvesant founded the settlement Nieuw Haarlem (named after the Dutch city) in a hilly area in 1658, and it kept its rural character for a long time. In 1832 the first train connection to the urban south of Manhattan was built, and Harlem developed into a refined summer resort. One by one, settlements of solid brownstone houses like Morningside, Hamilton or Washington Heights (named after the later president, who had his troops camped here in the War of Independence against the English) were built. After the turn of the 20th century the subway connection from Harlem to south Manhattan started a building boom, but the apartments turned out to be unrentable. So Philip A. Payton Jr., an African American real estate agent, persuaded the owners who were concerned about their income to rent the empty apartments to the steadily growing African American population. Thus the »Black capital of America« was founded. As early as 1910 almost all of Harlem's residents were African American. With them came writers, painters and musicians. In the 1920s the neighbourhood flourished in the first **Harlem Renaissance**.

The renaissance of African American self-confidence was promoted by African American writers, painters and musicians and celebrated in legendary clubs like the Cotton Club or the Apollo Theater – though in times of segregation only in front of a white audience. The collapse began after the stock market crash in 1929, when the area sank into the bitterest poverty and misery. In the 1970s and 1980s Harlem was a synonym for decline, oppression, drugs and violence. The demography shifted as well. Today **125th Street, also known as Martin Luther King Jr. Boulevard**, is the centre of African American Harlem; in East Harlem, east of Fifth Ave., the immigrants from Puerto Rico (El Barrio) are

Maxine Brown, Beverly Crosby and Ella Peaches Garrett in the Lenox Lounge

concentrated; in the far north those from the Dominican Republic and Honduras. The signs that Harlem – apart from a few skyscrapers – was built around the turn of the century as a residential area for the upper middle class are still visible. The buildings are of a better quality than in other Manhattan neighbourhoods and the streets are broader than any others in New York (like Lenox Ave., next to 125th St. the real centre of Harlem). Although very little is left of the middle class polish of that time, the signs of recovery cannot be missed. The population is growing, and the crime rate has dropped here even more than in the rest of New York. A new business opens almost every day. Tourism has discovered the reawakened cultural life of the city and the tourist attractions. About 40,000 tourists visit this neighbourhood every year, and the number is growing.

Is it dangerous to walk around in Harlem? It would be negligent to deny that there are dangers. But anyone who follows the usual rules that apply in any large city will be as safe here as Downtown. In the evenings it would be better to go directly to a certain destination in Harlem, like a jazz or dance club or a theatre. In the meantime Harlem Heritage Tours or Harlem Spirituals, among others, offer guided bus and walking tours through Harlem (information: tel. 212-391-0900, www.harlemspirituals.com and ► Practicalities, Tours and Guides).

Guided tours

Sightseeing in Harlem

Columbia University

✳ Columbia University, located between 114th and 120th St. and Amsterdam and West End Ave. (subway: 116th St./Columbia University), was founded in 1754 as King's College and as such is the oldest university in New York. Alongside Harvard, Yale and Princeton it is one of the most respected universities in the country. With about 19,000 students Columbia is not the largest university in New York (New York University on Washington Square has 40,000 students). Among its graduates are more than 50 Nobel Prize winners as well as Isaac Asimov, J. D. Salinger, James Cagney and Joan Rivers. In 1897 building was begun on today's campus, with architect Charles McKim, who also designed the **Low Library**, in charge. The classical columned building with its impressive outdoor stairway today houses the university administration. The statue of the alma mater is by Daniel Chester French (1903). The university library is the Butler Library at the southern end of the campus. Immediately east of the Low Library is **St Paul's Chapel**, which was built in 1904 to plans by John Howell. Its style is a mixture of Italian Renaissance, Gothic and Byzantine architecture; occasionally free concerts are held here. There are various sculptures on the campus including ones by Rodin, George Grey Barnard, Jacques Lipchitz, Kees Verkade and Henry Moore. On the other side of Broadway is Barnard College for women, which was opened in 1889.

! **Baedeker TIP**

Hearty southern cooking
Probably the best soul food in Harlem, in any case better than Sylvia's Kitchen: the fried or BBQ chicken at amy Ruth's is served with mashed potatos and baked beans or buttered corn. The baked macaroni and cheese is also very popular, but unfortunately none of it is lowfat. If anyone wants to try the generous desserts, it's better to skip the main course! Harlem folk art decorates the walls. (113 West 116th St., tel. 212-280-8779, www.amyruthsharlem.com).

St John the Divine

▶Cathedral of St John the Divine

Riverside Church

It is worth visiting Riverside Church to see its 120m/394ft-high tower (first a lift, then about 150 steps), from which there is a great view. The church was inspired by the cathedral in Chartres and was built in 1930. It has a glockenspiel with 74 bells (Sun noon and 3pm) as well as an organ with 22,000 pipes; in the interior take a look at the 16th century stained glass windows from Brugge and a Madonna by J. Epstein (Tours Mon–Fri 9am–4pm, 490 Riverside Drive/122nd St.; subway: 116th St./Columbia University).

Riverside Park

Grant's Tomb, the imposing grave in honour of Ulysses S. Grant diagonally opposite, commemorates the 18th president of America and commander in chief of the Union troops in the American Civil War (1822–1885; John H. Duncan, 1890). It is in the northern part of

Riverside Park, which is on the eastern bank of the Hudson River between 72nd and 155th Street and divided by Henry Hudson Parkway. The park was designed in 1875 by Frederick Law Olmsted, who also designed ►Central Park. Numerous monuments stand here: the Jewish Martyrs Memorial (near 83rd Street) commemorates the Holocaust, the Soldiers' & Sailors' Monument (89th St.) those who fell in the Civil War, the Fireman's Memorial (100th St.) the New York firemen, and a statue of a figure on horseback the Civil War general Franz Sigel (1824 until 1902; 106th Street).

The legendary **Apollo Theater** (253 W 125th St.; subway: Lenox Ave./125th St.; tel. 212-531-5300, www. apollotheater.com) was opened in 1913, but until 1934 its doors were closed to African Americans. In the next 40 years Bessie Smith, Billie Holliday, Huddie Ledbetter, Duke Ellington, Count Basie, Dizzie Gillespie, Thelonius Monk, Ella Fitzgerald and Aretha Franklin were among its stars. At the beginning of the 1970s it was converted to a cinema and finally closed in 1976. Since its renovation in the 1980s amateur and comedy shows have taken place here.

Apollo Theater

Brownstones in 120th Street

Studio Museum

The Studio Museum, just a few blocks away, is the only official institution in the USA for African American art. In rotating exhibits art from the 20th and 21st centuries is shown (144 W 125th St.; subway: 125th St.; open: Sun, Mon–Fri noon–6pm, Satn 10am–6pm; www.studiomuseuminharlem.org, tel. 212-864-4500).

Schomburg Center

Those interested in African American culture should visit the Schomburg Center for Research in Black Culture (515 Lenox Ave., between 135th and 136th St.; subway: 135th St.; open: Mon–Wed noon–8pm, Thu, Fri 11am–6pm). The basis of the collection is the private collection of Arthur Schomburg (1874–1938). This bank employee, who was originally from Puerto Rico, protesting against the dominant opinion of his time that African Americans had no history, collected 5,000 books, 300 manuscripts, 2,000 prints and portraits as well as other material. The building was designed by Bond Ryder Associates, and has an octagon on one end and a tower at the corner of 135th St.

Of the older buildings in the area the many churches and religious establishments are especially interesting. The most famous of the approximately 400 churches in Harlem is the Abyssinian Baptist Church (132 W 138th St.; subway: Lenox Ave./135th St.), built in 1924 in the neo-Gothic style, where the father and son both named Adam Clayton Powell – the son was in Congress in 1944 – preached their fiery sermons. On Sundays there is a gospel worship service here at 11am.

The roomy brownstone houses in Strivers' Row (138th and 139th St. between Adam C. Powell Blvd. and Seventh Ave.) are among the most beautiful in all of New York. They were built in 1891 by architects in order to prove that affordable apartments could also be tasteful and spacious. Nowadays the pretty houses are traded by white speculators for high prices.

125th Street, Harlem's main thoroughfare

! *Baedeker* TIP

Gospel in the churches

The lively style of worship and the infectious music of the gospel choirs are the biggest attraction in Harlem. There are bus tours (for example Harlem Spirituals Gospel Jazz Tours, tel. 212-391-0900), but you can go to Harlem under your own steam, too. The most famous choirs are at the Abyssinian Baptist Church (see below), Metropolitan Baptist Church (151 West 128th St./Powell Boulevard) and Mount Moriah Church (2050 Fifth Ave.). Tickets are available at tourist information.

Donated by Archer M. Huntington (►Famous People), the complex built in 1908 in the neo-classical style is named after the scientist John James Audubon(Broadway, between 155th and 156th St.; subway: 157th St.). The sculptures on the main square were created by the sculptress and wife of the donor, Anna Hyatt Huntington. Several special institutes are housed in the building: the **American Numismatic Society** with an important coin collection, the **American Academy of Arts and Letters**, a group of respected American poets, painters, architects and composers, and the Hispanic Society of America, founded in 1904 by Huntington, a museum with exhibitions on the culture of Spanish-speaking ethnic groups from prehistoric times until the present. The collection of paintings includes works by Joaquín Sorolla y Bastida, El Greco, Velázquez and Goya, and the museum also displays archaeological finds, goldsmith work, Islamic art from the Middle Ages, carpets and porcelain from the times of the dispersion of the Moors, as well as craft items (open: Tue–Sat 10am–4.30pm, Sun 1pm–4pm).

★
◄ Hispanic Society of America

⊙

The well-restored country estate a little to the north is one of the oldest buildings in Manhattan. It was built in 1765 in the Georgian style by Roger Morris and served in 1776 as George Washington's headquarters, when American troops fighting the English had withdrawn to New York. In 1810 the trader Stephen Jumel bought it as his country estate. He and his wife Eliza furnished it in the French Empire style. In the museum many pieces of original furniture from the 18th and 19th century as well as paintings, drawings, silver, porcelain and crystal from the early USA are on display (65 Jumel Terrace, between 160th and 162nd St.; subway: 163rd St.; open: Wed–Sun 10am–4pm).

★
Morris-Jumel Mansion Museum

⊙

►The Cloisters

The Cloisters

Jewish Museum

G 8

Location: 1109 Fifth Ave./92nd St.   **Subway:** 86th St.

🕐
Opening hours:
Sat–Tue, Thu
11am–5.45pm
Fri until 4pm

Founded in 1904 by the Jewish Theological Seminary of America, the Jewish Museum is located on the so-called Museum Mile, a little north of the ►Guggenheim Museum. After the ►Museum of Jewish Heritage it is the second largest Jewish museum in New York. Since the 1940s it has resided in the former town home of the banker Felix M. Warburg, which was built in 1908 in the neo-Gothic style to plans by C. P. H. Gilbert (expanded in 1993 by Kevin Roche). The museum owns a large collection of Jewish art as well as historic Judaica. 4,000 years of Jewish history are on display in numerous galleries. Cult objects from synagogues and private households of many countries, including Torah scrolls with their gold and silver work, Shabbat lamps, Kiddush goblets, jewellery and implements from the extensive Harry G. Friedman collection are on display. The main collection also contains the Benguiat Collection, which in turn contains objects dating from the Middle Ages to modern times. Café Weissman serves kosher food.

Sculpture by Louise Nevelson

At Park Ave./92nd St., near the Jewish Museum, stands *Night Presence IV*, an almost 7m/23ft sculpture by Louise Nevelson (1972); nickel and copper have been added to the steel, which accounts for the black-brown colour.

✳ Lincoln Center for the Performing Arts

D 9/10

Location: 65th St./Columbus Ave..   **Subway:** 66th St.

New York's large centre for the performing arts was built under the directorship of W. K. Harrison, mainly in the 1960s. Events include theatre, opera, ballet and concerts. The building not only gave a neglected area of New York a new face, it also pointed the way for many other cities in the USA, in which similar cultural centres have been built since then.

The building costs of $165 million were raised privately; public funds were used only to buy the land. Different architects designed the individual buildings which still appear unified by their stark classical appearance. Italian travertine was used for all of the buildings. The artistic arrangement of the cultural centre was important to the builders and architects, so that a visitor would not only be attracted by the culture on offer and the architecture but also because of the works of art by famous artists. Information on the activities in the Lincoln Center: www.lincolncenter.org. Info and registering for guided tours in the »Atrium at Lincoln Center«, tel. 212-875-5350.

Lincoln Center Plaza

The site is centred on the plaza open to Columbus Ave., around which the three main buildings and side buildings are grouped. The fountain in the middle by Philip Johnson is made of dark marble. In August street theatre and other performances are held here, mostly free of charge.

Avery Fisher Hall

The first building to be erected was the one on the north side of the plaza, designed by M. Abramovitz in the form of an ancient Greek temple, and opened in 1962 as the Philharmonic Hall; it was later re-named Avery Fisher Hall and is the home of the New York Philharmonic Orchestra. The concert hall with 2,800 seats and an organ

Metropolitan Opera House in the Lincoln Center

New York City Ballet

with 5,500 pipes has been renovated several times in order to improve the acoustics. In the foyer, the 5-ton metal sculpture *Orpheus and Apollo* by Richard Lippold is worth seeing. Along with the New York Philharmonic, which gives four concerts a week from mid-September to mid-May, famous US and foreign orchestras and soloists are guests in the concert hall. The Philharmonic also gives concerts in the parks in the summer (▶Practicalities, Theatre, Music and Ballet).

Opposite Avery Fisher Hall is the **New York State Theater** (Philip Johnson, Richard Foster, 1964), home of the New York City Opera Company and the New York City Ballet. The three-storey foyer of the theatre with 2,700 seats is decorated with a bust of Mahler by Rodin, a mask of Beethoven by Bourdelle and two large statues of women by Elie Nadelmann.

Metropolitan Opera House (Met)

The main building of the Lincoln Center is on the west side of the plaza: the Met, one of the leading opera houses in the world and home of the Metropolitan Opera Company and the American Ballet Theater. Designed by W. K. Harrison and opened in 1966, the building impresses with its five tall, arched windows, which give a clear view of the richly furnished foyer. The two large murals in the foyer by Marc Chagall, *Les Sources de la Musique* and *Le Triomphe de la Musique*, are protected from the sun in the mornings and unfortunately cannot be seen then. The auditorium has room for 3,800 guests; the stage technology is from Germany and the large crystal chandeliers come from Austria. There are portraits of famous singers in the corridors, who have performed in the Met, (tours: Oct–June Mon–Fri 15.30, Sun 10.30; reservations recommended: tel. 212-769-7020, fax 212-769-8519; information: www.metopera.org).

Behind the Met, in Damrosch Park, there are outdoor concerts in the summer in the Guggenheim Bandshell.

Vivian Beaumont Theater

West of Avery Fisher Hall there is another courtyard with a large, square decorative basin in the middle of which stands **Henry Moore's** 6-ton bronze group *Reclining Figure* (1968). The Vivian Beaumont Theater, designed by Eero Saarinen (1965), houses the Lincoln Center Theater (1,140 seats). The little Mitzi E. Newhouse Theater nearby (300 seats), a kind of workshop theatre, is also very successful.

The narrow building by Skidmore, Owings & Merrill from 1965 stands between the Metropolitan Opera House and the Vivian Beaumont Theater. The museum archives materials on the history of theatre, film, dance and music, including a collection of sound carriers. The Bruno Walter Auditorium, named after the German conductor, is part of the library and media centre, a branch of the ►New York Public Library in which free concerts, exhibitions, lectures, poetry readings and film showings take place (open: Mon, Thu noon–8pm, Tue, Wed, Fri, Sat noon–6pm,Thu until 8pm; tel. 212-870-1630). Outside the museum stands **Alexander Calder's** black steel sculpture *Le Guichet* (1972).

Library & Museum of the Performing Arts ⊙

Across West 65th St. to the north New York's most important conservatory is housed in a building conceived by Pietro Belluschi in 1968, which along with a modern stage for opera, lecture halls and practicing rooms also includes **Alice Tully Hall** for chamber music and solo concerts. The Walter Reade Filmtheater is also here; it is here that the **New York Film Festival** takes place every year in the early autumn.

Juilliard School of Music

In the American Folk Art Museum (2 Lincoln Square/Columbus Ave., between 65th and 66th St.) rotating exhibits show folk art and applied art from America as well as from other countries, including textiles, quilts and also paintings and sculptures from the colonial period until the present day (open: Tue–Thu, Sat 11.30–7.30pm, fri until 7.30pm, www.folkartmuseum.org). Visit the main building of the museum on 53rd St., next to the MoMA (►Practicalities, Museums and Galleries).

American Folk Art Museum ⊙

Little Italy

C 16/17

Location: North-west of Chinatown   **Subway:** Spring St., Prince St.

North-west of ►Chinatown lies Little Italy, one of the smallest ethnic neighbourhoods in Manhattan. Because of the expanding Chinese community the area has almost lost its identity.

Once more than 40,000 people lived in the area between Canal, Houston, Elizabeth and Lafayette St., but today there are only about 5,000, mostly older Italian Americans, the younger generation having long since moved northwards to Nolita (= North of Little Italy). The most important north-south streets are Mulberry and Mott St.; east-west are Grand and Broome Street. There are countless Italian restaurants and cafés on Mulberry St., and Italian shops and men's clubs complete the picture. The centre of the neighbourhood is the **former police station** (240 Center St.), which takes up the whole block between Grand, Center and Broome St. The building was completed in 1909 in the style of a French hôtel de ville and was later converted into a multi-storey luxury apartment building. Little Italy is most worth a visit during the second week in September, during the Festa di San Gennaro (▶p.92); St Januarius is the patron saint of the neighbourhood. At that time there are sales and food stalls along Mulberry St. and other streets in Little Italy.

Lower East Side

C/D 17/18

Location: Between First Ave. and East River (downtown)

Subway: Delancey St.

None of the ethnic neighbourhoods in Manhattan is as difficult to pin down as the Lower East Side, where even today there are still some tenements, giant housing blocks where the immigrant families were housed from 1880 until 1914. Unlike ▶Harlem, which was originally a residential area for the upper middle class, the Lower East Side was built for the poor and until 1900 it was one of the most densely populated areas in New York.

At the beginning of the 20th century the Lower East Side was a purely Jewish area, to which about 500 synagogues and school buildings testify. But only a few still serve their original purpose, among them thee laborately restored **Eldrige Street Synagogue**, built in 1887 by orthodox Ashkenazi Jews from Eastern Europe (12–14 Eldridge St., between Division and Canal St.; tours Sun–Thu 10am until 5pm). The Chinese entered the area from Chatham Square across East Broadway (just as in ▶ Little Italy), and after the Second World War a new wave of Spanish-speaking immigrants from Puerto Rico, Central and South America washed across the Lower East Side. Since the 1980s young artists and musicians have moved here, so that the neighbourhood today has a very mixed population and a lively infrastructure. In particular, the area around Orchard St. with its many fashion, shoe, fur and other

Lower East Side Tenement Museum

shops has a special attraction. This area is very busy on Sundays (the Jewish shops are closed on Saturdays) with a bazaar-like atmosphere, reminiscent of North Africa or the Near East. Since the prices are low and the quality often unusually high many people from Uptown make major purchases here.

The Lower East Side Tenement Museum, at Orchard St. 90 in an apartment building from the turn of the century, is definitely worth a visit. It shows the life of the immigrants, full of deprivation in the late 19th century (guided tours are available upon request: Tue–Fri 13.20–4pm, Sat, Sun 11.15–16.45, in July and Aug. also Mon; tel. 212-431-0233, www.tenement.org).

★
Lower East Side Tenement Museum
🕐

★ **Manhattan**

A–J 1–19

The 58 sq km/22.4 sq mi borough Manhattan might be New York's smallest borough, but it is the best known and the centre of the city. Along with a few smaller islands, it consists of the 21km/13mi-long and only 3km/1.9mi-wide island of the same name between the Hudson River, East River and Harlem River, and is home to about 1.5 million people. On this, the most famous island in the world, the most important attractions, and most hotels, restaurants, musical theatres and jazz clubs are found – this is the reason that, for most visitors, Manhattan is New York.

Native Americans still lived on Manhattan Island at the beginning of the 16th century. But then the explosive development which would create a world metropolis began. Nowhere are the results of such development so clearly seen as here. The city's character is defined by its residents, immigrants or their descendants, who in part still live in certain neighbourhoods like Chinatown or Little Italy; but it is also defined by the stunning skyline of Manhattan, the most beautiful conglomeration of skyscrapers on the smallest area, a unique collection of historicizing building styles – classical, Gothic, Art Deco and modern.

★ ★
◄ Skyline

Manhattan is arranged like a chessboard; twelve consecutively numbered avenues run north to south, the altogether more than 200 streets from east to west.

The term **downtown** has become a worldwide synonym for »city centre«. Here it refers to the settlement area south of 14th Street where the streets mostly have names and not numbers. Many of the oldest, as well as the most modern and tallest buildings, are at the southern tip. In the ► Financial District beats the business heart of the city, immediately next to it along the Hudson is one of the city's

Design of the city

BENEATH MANHATTAN

The greatest number of high rises is amassed on the southern edge of Central Park (Midtown) and at the southern tip of Manhattan (Downtown). The main reason for this is the character of the ground.

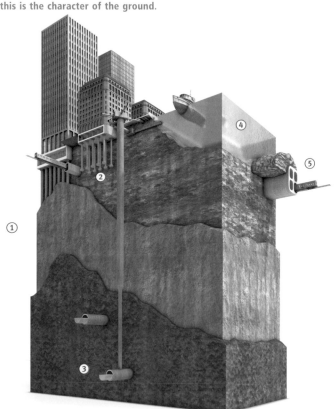

① Below the surface
In Midtown and Downtown bedrock lies just below the surface and provides a secure foundation, allowing the construction of very tall buildings.

② Levels 1 and 2
The shafts for electrical and telephone cables, water and steam as well as gas lie up to 9m/29ft deep (since the blizzard of 1888, 51 million kilometres/31.7 million miles of telephone cable have been buried underground). The subway tunnels run between 9m/29ft and 60m/197ft below ground; the subway station at 63rd St., for example, lies 60m/197ft underground.

③ Level 3
New York needs 5.3 trillion litres/1.4 trillion gallons of water daily. As of the 1970s a new water tunnel is being blasted through the bedrock about 240m/786ft below ground to supplement the current water pipes.

④ East River
The river is about 25m/82ft deep.

⑤ Road and train tunnels
The road and train tunnels run 50m/164ft below ground, for example the Queens Midtown Tunnel.

most beautiful green oases. In addition, some neighbourhoods bear witness to the fact that immigrants used to settle in their own ethnic groups.

Midtown, the busy centre of Manhattan and the heart of New York, stretches between 14th Street and ►Central Park. The most imposing skyscrapers stand here, which have shaped the city's features since the 1920s, among them the ►Empire State Building, the ►Chrysler Building, the MetLife Building and the ►Rockefeller Center. Midtown is also the Mecca of entertainment with the Theater District on Broadway and ►Times Square, Carnegie Hall, Radio City Music Hall and Madison Square Garden. **Uptown** is the area east and west of Central Park (► below). North of Central Park lies Upper Manhattan, ►Harlem where mainly African Americans and Hispanics live and where Columbia University is located.

Uptown: Upper West and Upper East Side

The Upper West Side stretches between Columbus Circle (near 59th Street; ►Lincoln Center) and 110th St. as well as between the Hudson River and Central Park West (subway: 86th St.). Unlike the Upper East Side (►below) this area is more down-to-earth, and the streets have names. Thus Eighth Ave. becomes Central Park West, Ninth becomes Columbus Ave. and Tenth becomes Amsterdam Avenue. The first building on the Upper West Side was the ►American Museum of Natural History. From 1880 the building of numerous luxury apartment buildings followed (►below). Today writers, actors and other artists as well as young families with children live here. In the last years a lively **restaurant scene** has developed here, which is easy to explore on foot. Along Amsterdam and Columbus Ave. between 66th and 86th Street there are countless restaurants and cafés, in which almost every cuisine in the world is represented. At the weekends New Yorkers meet here for their favourite pastime: brunch. Unfortunately there is often a wait for a table. But people don't mind, because they know the rule: where there's a queue, the food is good!

Upper West Side

Here is a list of some striking apartment buildings: **San Remo**, the double towered apartment building on Central Park West (no. 145 and 146/62nd St.), was built in 1929–1931 to plans by Emery Roth. Dustin Hoffman, Paul Simon and Diane Keaton are among its famous residents. The plans of the Art Deco **Century Apartments** (25 Central Park West) were by Irwin Chanin, 1931. The two-storied apartments of the **Hotel des Artistes** (1 West at 67th St.; George Mort Pollard, 1907) have been home to Isadora Duncan, Rudolph Valentino and Noël Coward. On the ground floor is the equally famous Café des Artistes.

The monumental Palazzo at 211 Central Park West (north of ►American Museum of Natural History) is one of the most posh ad-

Striking apartment buildings

◄ The Beresford Building

The most famous skyline in the world: south Manhattan

dresses in Manhattan. The former tennis star John McEnroe and the actor Rock Hudosn are among the celebrities who used to live here. The trademakr of the building, which was designed by Emery Roth, are the three towers on the roof. V arying façades and numerous decorative elements take away some of the building's weightiness.

The castle-like **Dakota** was built in 1880–1884 as the first private building on the Upper West Side (1 W 72nd St.). The contractor of this luxurious building was Edward S. Clark, Singer sewing machine heir. He commissioned Henry J. Hardenberg to produce the plans, who later also planned the Plaza Hotel. The luxury suites have been a roof over such heads as Judy Garland, Lauren Bacall, Leonard Bernstein and John Lennon, who in 1980 was shot outside the house by a mentally disturbed fan. The house has also been immortalized in film: in 1968 Roman Polanski filmed *Rosemary's Baby* here. A detour towards the Hudson River leads to more houses from the late 19th century. The ornate Beaux Arts building the **Ansonia Hotel** was built in 1899 to plans by Paul E. M. Duboy (2101–2119 Broadway, near 73rd St.). Its two swimming pools, a fountain in which seals played, as well as an internal mail chute system were legendary. Since the rooms in the hotel were especially sound-proof, it was popular among musicians. Among its guests were Arturo Toscanini, Enrico Caruso, Igor Strawinsky and the baseball legend Babe Ruth.

A little way north stand the **Apthorp Apartments**, another impressive apartment complex, which were built in 1906–1908 for William Waldorf Astor (2207 Broadway, between 78th and 79th Street).

Nearby is **Zabar's**, the famous New York delicatessen and household goods shop (2245 Broadway).

The Upper East Side, between Grand Army Plaza (near 59th Street) and 96th St., between Fifth Ave. and East River, is one of the most exclusive neighbourhoods in Manhattan. Here some of the richest residents live in ornate villas, the »Gold Coast Properties« on Fifth and Park Ave.; east of Lexington Ave. the middle classes are also represented. The Upper East Side is known for its exclusive shops and restaurants, and for some of the most important museums on the **Museum Mile**, on Fifth Ave. at Central Park.

Upper East Side

✶ Metropolitan Museum of Art · Met

F/G 8/9

Location: 1000 Fifth Ave./82nd St.   **Subway:** 86th St.

The museum known as the Met for short is among the most important art museums in the world, on a par with the British Museum in London, the Louvre (Paris) and the Eremitage (St Petersburg). Its opening exhibition in 1872 with Cypriot antiquities and a small art gallery was quite modest, but today the museum owns around 3.5 million works of art representing almost all epochs of art history.

The geographically and chronologically arranged exhibits range from the Egyptian Temple of Dendur to the façade of a Wall Street bank. Experts value the collections of Egyptian and Medieval art. The European Paintings department shows all famous painters, while the American Wing exhibits the most important American artists as well as authentic period rooms. The sheer quantity of art works is overwhelming: it is best to get to know the organization of the museum and then to concentrate on what you want to see.

www.met
museum.org
🕐
Opening hours:
Sun, Tue–Thu
9.30–5.15pm
Fri, Sat
9.30–8.45pm

The museum was opened in 1870 on the initiative of a few private citizens who thought that the time had come for the residents of New York (then almost one million) to have an art museum. The Metropolitan Museum of Art, called the Met for short, was first located on West 14th St., at that time the city centre. A short time later the city gave the museum a piece of land on the eastern edge of the newly created ▶ Central Park, on which Calvert Vaux, who

 DON'T MISS

- Temple of Dendur
- Frank Lloyd Wright's study
- Astor Court
- Rembrandt's self-portrait in the European painting collection
- Sculpture garden on the roof of the Met

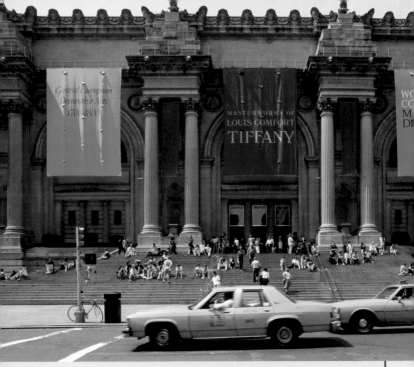

A museum of superlatives: the Metropolitan Museum of Art

was also in charge of the design of the park, built a red brick building in 1880 – which today can only be seen from Central Park itself. The current main building on Fifth Ave. followed in 1879–1898. The middle tract is by the architects Richard Morris Hunt and Richard Howland Hunt (father and son), while the two side tracts are by McKim, Mead & White. The newer additions were built under the guidance of architects Roche, Dinkeloo and partners: the Robert Lehman Wing (1975), the house of the Temple of Dendur in the Sackler Wing (1978), the American Wing for the American collection (1980), the Michael C. Rockefeller Wing for the ethnological department (1982), the Lila Acheson Wallace Wing for 20th century art (1987), the Henry R. Kravis Wing (1991) and the Milton Petrie European Sculpture Court, the garden courtyard for European sculpture. Even though the museum has over 300 exhibition rooms it can only display about one quarter of its collection, which grows faster (mainly through gifts) than the space can be expanded. In addition there are regular special exhibitions which are worth seeing.

Museum service Enter the museum at Fifth Ave. via the outdoor stairs, which is a popular place to sit when it is warm. In the so-called Great Hall, the

Metropolitan Museum of Art *Floor plan*

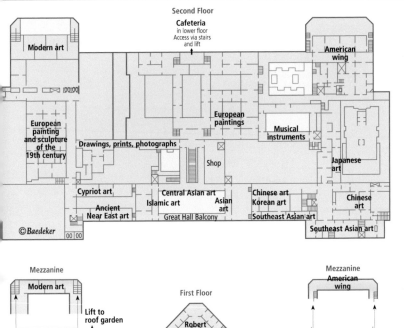

Second Floor

Cafeteria
in lower floor
Access via stairs
and lift

Modern art

American
wing

European
painting
and sculpture
of the
19th century

European
paintings

Musical
instruments

Drawings, prints, photographs

Japanese
art

Shop

Cypriot art

Central Asian art

Islamic art

Asian
art

Chinese art
Korean art

Chinese
art

Ancient
Near East art

Great Hall Balcony

Southeast Asian art

Southeast Asian art

©Baedeker

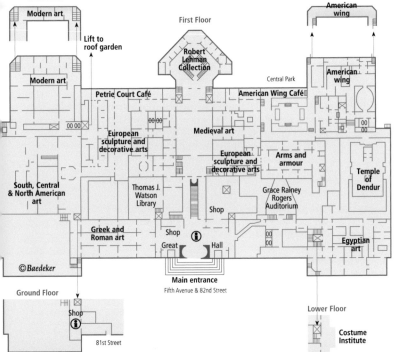

Mezzanine

Modern art

First Floor

Mezzanine

American
wing

Lift to
roof garden

Robert
Lehman
Collection

Central Park

American
wing

Modern art

Petrie Court Café

American Wing Café

European
sculpture and
decorative arts

Medieval art

European
sculpture and
decorative arts

Arms and
armour

Temple
of
Dendur

South, Central
& North American
art

Thomas J.
Watson
Library

Grace Rainey
Rogers
Auditorium

Greek and
Roman art

Shop

Shop

Great

Hall

Egyptian
art

©Baedeker

Main entrance
Fifth Avenue & 82nd Street

Ground Floor

Shop

81st Street

Lower Floor

Costume
Institute

The Temple of Dendur, a gift from Egypt

foyer, is the **information rondell**, where museum maps and brochures are available. On this floor there are also **museum shops** and two cafés (on the lower level a cafeteria and on the upper level a restaurant for museum members only). It is also possible to rent **audio guides** on the highlights of the museums here. To the right of the Great Hall lies the Grace Rainey Rogers Auditorium, where concerts and lectures take place regularly.

Daily at 10.15am and 3.15pm there is a **Museum Highlight Tour** around the best known works of art; guided tours in foreign languages can also be arranged by telephone (tel. 212-570-3711). ►The Cloisters, which is dedicated to the art of the Middle Ages, is also part of the Met.

First Floor

Egyptian art

The Egyptian collection on the first floor is among the most important in the world and spans more than three and a half millennia. The **Temple of Dendur** (1st century BC), which the Roman Caesar Augustus had built, had to be removed when the Aswan Dam was built so that it would not be submerged. It came to America as a present from Egypt and was rebuilt true to the original in an extension built especially for the temple. From the time of the Old Kingdom (3rd–6th dynasty, 2600 until 2160 BC) the **mastaba of the palace administrator Perneb** and the tomb chapel of Prince Raemkai (5th dynasty) are on display.

The Middle Kingdom (11th and 12th dynasty, 2040–1785 BC) is represented by grave offerings and painted stele from excavations in Thebes. Showpieces from the New Kingdom (18th–20th dynasty, 1552–1070 BC) are the helmeted head of Ramses II. and 14 statues of **Queen Hatshepsut** from the temple Deir el-Bahri near Thebes.

The Met owns the largest collection of **arms and armour** of the 14th until the 18th centuries from all over the world. The focal point is the Equestrian Court with armed knights mounted on horses. Among the main attractions are a Frankish strap helmet (6th century), a Viking sword (10th century), Japanese battle masks and revolvers from Samuel Colt's collection.

Arms and armour

The collection of Greek and Roman art goes back to the 3rd century BC with a series of idols from the Cyclades islands. The oldest part of the museum's collection are Cypriot vases, reliefs and jewellery, which the first museum director, Count Luigi Palma de Cesnola, brought over from Cyprus. Of particular importance are murals from a villa in Boscoreale, which was buried when the volcano Vesuvius erupted in AD 79, including the complete decoration of a bedroom.

Greek and Roman art

The medieval collection comprises items from the 4th to the 16th century, including Cypriot silver plates (6th century), cast iron choir screens from the cathedral of Valladolid (Spain), a Romanesque marble portal from the abbey church of Sangemini (Umbria), and Gothic church windows from the Parisian abbey St-Germain-des-Prés. In the Tapestry Room there are valuable pieces from Germany, France and Flanders. A part of the collection can be seen in the ▶The Cloisters.

Medieval art

The department for art and decorative art from Europe displays works from the Renaissance to the 20th century, including authentically furnished reconstructions of rooms from European palaces and private homes.

European sculpture and decorative arts

In order to receive the private collection of the banker Robert Lehman (1892–1969), whose value at the time of the donation was already estimated at $100 million, the Metropolitan Museum had to erect a new building. Here there are about 300 paintings and more than 1,000 drawings to be seen, including works by the Old Masters as well as artists of the 19th and 20th centuries, but also bronzes, majolica, glass, furniture and enamel in seven rooms in the two-storey Lehman Pavilion in the rear part of the first floor.

Robert Lehman Collection

The **American Wing**, more than 60 exhibition rooms (in the first and second floor), covers all aspects of American art and applied arts. The centre of the wing is the glazed Engelhardt Court with the

American Wing

façade of the United States Bank (from Wall Street) built in 1822–1824, the loggia of the villa of Louis Comfort Tiffany, known for his artistically coloured Art Nouveau glass, and the stairs of the architect Louis Sullivan from the demolished stock exchange in Chicago. In addition, the living room of the architect Frank Lloyd Wright and more than 1,000 paintings and sculptures can be seen.

Arts of Africa, Oceania and the Americas

Nelson Rockefeller had this wing built in memory of his son Michael, who died while on an expedition in the South Seas. The **ethnological collection** with several thousand objects shows African, Pacific and American art.

Modern art

The museum annex named after Lila Acheson Wallace, who died in 1984 and was co-founder of *Reader's Digest*, is dedicated to 20th-century art. Alfred Stieglitz's collection is the basis, which his widow Georgia O'Keeffe gave to the museum. The work of European and American artists are represented on three floors, including Henri Matisse, Wassily Kandinsky and Picasso; also Weber, Stella, Georgia O'Keeffe, Gorky, Hopper, De Kooning and Rothko, Eric Fischl or Matta. For a special experience, take a look at the **Cantor Roof Sculpture Garden** on the roof which includes works by Louise Bourgeois, Reuben Nakian and Louise Nevelson. From here there is a unique view of the Manhattan skyline. In the mezzanine there are photographs and the Paul Klee collection, which was left to the museum in 1984 by the Paris art dealer Heinz Berggruen. Beyond that, applied art is also shown: vases, glasses, jewellery, lamps and furniture.

Second Floor

European painting

The collection **European painting and sculpture** with around 3,000 works from the 13th to the 18th century takes up most of the room on the second floor. Among the attractions are works by Raphael, Titian, Tintoretto, Veronese, Giotto and Tiepolo, the Dutch masters Hals, Rembrandt, Vermeer and Ruysdael. French painting is represented by Poussin, de La Tour, Watteau and Jacques-Louis David, Flemish and German painting by Jan van Eyck, van der Weyden, Hans Memling, Rubens, Lucas Cranach, Dürer and Holbein the Younger, among others. A large proportion of the Spanish painting comes from the private collection of the New York department store owner Benjamin Altman: El Greco, Zurbarán, Velázquez, Murillo and Goya are especially noteworthy. Hogarth, Reynolds, Gainsborough, Constable and Turner represent English painting.

19th-century European paintings and sculpture

The French art of the 19th century is spread out over 21 exhibition rooms: Classicism, Romanticism and Realism are represented by J. A. D. Ingres, Turner and Delacroix. The focus of the collection is on the Impressionists and post-Impressionists with works by Edouard Manet and Claude Monet. The Met owns around 100 pictures by Edgar

In the sculpture department of the Met

Degas, one of the most comprehensive collections of this master in any museum. In addition Henri Fantin-Latour, van Gogh and Paul Cézanne, as well as Renoir, Seurat, Toulouse-Lautrec, Signac, Bonnard and Gauguin are displayed. In a long sculpture gallery stand sculptures by Auguste Rodin, Bourdelle, Maillol and Jules Dalou.

In ten galleries **Islamic art** from the 8th to the 19th century is documented. The objects come from Iran, Iraq, Egypt, Turkey, Spain and India. A set of doors from Samarra (8th/9th century) document early Islam, as well as a bowl with ornamental Kufic writing from the 10th century and Fatimid carving from the 10th and 11th centuries. From Persia there is a tiled prayer niche from Isfahan (1354) and a richly illuminated manuscript of the Persian national epic *Shah-Nameh* (14th century).

Islamic Art

The museum's collection of **Near Eastern** art spans a period from the 6th millennium BC to the 7th century AD. Among the most interesting objects are the statuette from Tell Asmar (3rd millennium BC), Sumerian rolling seals from the 3rd to the 1st millennium BC, a stone seated figure of Gudea from Ur (2100–2000 BC), ivory carvings from Anatolia (1900–1800 BC), a bronze helmet and gold container from northern Persia (around 1000 BC), ivory figures and tablets (9th–7th century BC) and relief pieces (9th century BC) from the palace of Assurbanipal II in Nimrud as well as fragments of the procession wall in Babylon (6th century BC).

Ancient Near Eastern Art

Among the objects from China, Japan, Korea, India and other countries across South and Southeast Asia there are art objects dating from the 2nd millennium BC to the 20th century, including paintings, sculptures, ceramics, bronzes, textiles and applied art. Of particular note are Astor Court, the reconstruction of a Chinese garden from the city of Suzhou, Chinese furniture from the Ming dynasty, a collection of monumental Buddhist sculptures and an important collection of Chinese painting from the Sung (960–1279) to the Ch'ing dynasty (1644–1911). In other rooms there are about 800 objects from India, Afghanistan, Pakistan, Thailand, Vietnam, Cambodia, Nepal, Tibet and Korea.

> **! Baedeker TIP**
>
> **View**
>
> A visit to the Roof Garden of the museum is a must. It is open from spring to autumn and holds a small selection of contemporary sculptures, supplies refreshments and, above all, has grandiose views of Central Park and the Manhattan skyline.

Drawings, Prints and Photographs

The collection of drawings, prints and photographs features some unusual works, including drawings by Carpaccio, Leonardo da Vinci, Michelangelo, Rembrandt and Matisse as well as photographs by Alfred Stieglitz, Edward Steichen, Margaret Cameron, Adolphe Braun and Thomas Eakins.

Musical instruments

This collection contains instruments from all parts of the world, and recordings convey their sound, including a French hunting horn made of ivory (around 1700), a southern German porcelain flute (around 1760), the first pianoforte (by B. Cristofori, Florence 1720) and three Stradivarius violins, including *Francesca* (1694) and *Antonio* (1721).

Ground Floor

Costume Institute

The **clothing museum** with its over 60,000 objects is one of the largest of its kind. Temporary exhibitions show men's and women's clothing as well as accessories from the 15th to the 20th century, theatre and film costumes (Hollywood) and folk costumes from all over the world.

The **Uris Center** has its own library and seminar rooms. Special programmes for children and young people are offered here (information at the information desk in the Great Hall).

★
Goethe House New York

The German Cultural Center, a branch of the Munich-based Goethe Institute opposite the Met (1014 Fifth Ave./83rd St.) offers a large number of events on German culture and a library as well as several German daily newspapers and periodicals (open: Mon, Wed, Fri 10am–5pm, Tue, Thu until 7pm, tel. 212-439-8700).

Next to the Goethe House is the apartment building 1001 Fifth Avenue, built in 1978 to plans by Philip Johnson. The architect related the façade to the house on the right, which was designed by McKim, Mead & White.

1001 Fifth Avenue

✳ Morgan Library and Museum

D/E 13

Location: 29 East 36th St.   **Subway:** 33rd St.

Once known as the Pierpont Morgan Library, the new name reflects the fact that this is both a library and an excellent art museum and unites bibliophile treasures with paintings and sculptures, which the banker John Pierpont Morgan (1837–1913) and his son collected from about 1890 onward.

John Pierpont Morgan came to New York from Göttingen in Germany when he was 20 years old. In 1860 he founded J.P. Morgan & Co. and in 1901 he and others started what was to become America's largest steel producer, U.S. Steel Corp. Moreover he was probably the most important private art, manuscript and book collector of his time. He originally commissioned the Renaissance-style palatial building in the years 1903–1906 to house his collection. It was designed by the architects McKim, Mead & White. It was expanded with an annex after the collection was opened to the public in 1924. Today the museum also serves as a philological research library. It was expanded between 2000 and 2006 on plans by **Renzo Piano**. The Morgan now occupies a new, enlarged campus that integrates the three historical buildings with three new steel-and-glass pavilions. There is a new entrance on Madison Avenue, and the interior now features a lecture hall on the lower level, a new restaurant and shop, and a fully equipped Reading Room, as well as 50% more exhibition space.

🕐
Opening hours:
Tue–Thu
10.30am–5pm
Fri 10.30am–9pm
Sat 10am–6pm
Sun 11am–6pm
Tel. 212-685-008
www.morgan
library.org

Morgan Sr. collected immense treasures. Of particular note are a Gutenberg Bible, a Psalter from Mainz from 1495, a sacramentary from the monastery in Weingarten, a missal from Constance, Catherine of Cleve's book of hours, a Venetian pictorial bible from 1471, a bull by Pope Hadrian IV from the year 1155 and books by the first English printer William Caxton. Among the many manuscripts and autographs are pieces by Machiavelli, Byron, Keats, Dickens and Heine as well as music manuscripts by Mozart, Bach, Beethoven, Schubert, Brahms, Chopin and Berlioz. The collection also contains books and illustrations (by Dürer among others), etchings and drawings (more than 250 by Rembrandt), Assyrian-Babylonian cuneiform tablets, rolling seals and papyri.

Collection

Floor 1   Entering through the new and striking entrance on Madison Avenue, visitors find a variety of rooms and exhibition spaces on Floor 1. The Morgan Stanley Galleries show loan exhibitions of original manuscripts, drawings and rare books, while Medieval and Renaissance treasures are found in the Clare Eddy Thaw Gallery. Mr Morgan's Study, where Pierpont Morgan once held meetings – also known as the West Room – contains paintings and sculpture from his original collection of which the most outstanding objects are the famous wedding portraits of Martin Luther and Katharina von Bora by Lucas Cranach the elder. A Tintoretto (*Portrait of a Moor*), a painting by Hans Memling (*Man with a Carnation*), two Bohemian board figures from the 15th century and Italian small statuary from the Donatello school are also on display. Another treasure is a Stablo triptych, a fine gold and enamel object by Godefroi de Claire (around 1150). The heart of the campus is Gilbert Court, suffused with natural light; adjacent to this the impressive Rotunda leads on to Mr Morgan's Library, packed floor to ceiling with European literature from the 16th through to the 20th century. The Morgan Shop near the entrance is well-stocked with books, cards and reproductions of exhibits. In the Morgan Dining Room, the menu is inspired by New York's cuisine of the early 20th century.

Floor 2   Since its re-opening, the Morgan has double its previous exhibition space, much of which is on Floor 2, devoted to exhibiting the various collections.

Reading Room   The museum also serves as a research library for the humanities; naturally lit, the Reading Room at the top of the building provides a working environment for scientists and researchers.

Lower Level   In the Gilder Lehrman Hall on the lower level, lectures and readings take place.

✶✶ Museum of Modern Art · MoMA

E 11

Location: 11 W 53rd St. and W 54th St.

Subway: Fifth Ave.-53rd St., Rockefeller Center

The Museum of Modern Art, also called the MoMA or Modern, was founded in 1929 by the three friends Abby Aldrich Rockefeller, Lillie P. Bliss and Mary Quinn Sullivan, wives and daughters of rich industrial barons, and today it has the largest and most important collection of modern art in the world.

In the evenings at the MoMA, crowd control does not present a problem.

The first exhibition in November 1929 was in the Rockefellers' town house at today's location, and was opened with 100 French Impressionist paintings (all loaned). The collection grew through generous donations and soon needed its own museum. The building was dedicated in May 1939 in a modern style considered controversial at the time (English International Style) by the architects Philip Goodwin and Edward Durell Stone and has since then been expanded on numerous occasions. In 1964 the east wing and the sculpture garden were added according to plans by Philip Johnson, in 1984 the Argentine architect Cesar Pelli doubled the exhibition area with an annex. Under his guidance the 44-storey apartment tower was built over the main house (the sale of the luxury apartments financed the continuation of the collection). At the end of 2004 the MoMA was reopened after the conversion and expansion by the Japanese architect Yoshio Taniguchi, the façade of black granite, glass and aluminium continuing seamlessly on from the old building.

Opening hours:
Wed–Mon
10.30–5.30pm
Fri until 8pm
www.moma.org

? DID YOU KNOW ...?

■ The »museum of museums« is one of the most expensive in America, with an admission price of $20. There is no admission charge on Fridays after 4pm. Avoid the long queues by reserving tickets in advance: tel. 212-220-0505 and at www.moma.org.

Museum services Guided tours are only given for groups by prior arrangement (tel. 212-708-9685). Audio tours explain the museum highlights. Information on film showings, special exhibits and other events is available on tel. 212-708-9480. There are two cafés in the museum (on the first and fourth floors), a restaurant, »The Modern«, in the lobby on the first floor (tel. 212-333-1220) and a well-stocked bookshop. The **museum shops** of the MoMA are almost an attraction in themselves (two other MoMA Design Stores can be found opposite the museum, 44 W 53 St., and in SoHo, 81 Spring St.: open: Sat–Thu 10am–6.30pm, Fri 9.30am–9pm, www.momastore.org).

DON'T MISS

- Van Gogh's *Starry Night* (1889)
- Monet's *Water Lilies* (around 1920)
- Picasso's *Demoiselles d'Avignon* (1907)
- *La Danse* by Matisse (1909)
- Brancusi's *Bird in Space* (1928)
- Gerhard Richter's *October 18, 1977*
- Sculpture Garden

This »canon of art history« includes over 100,000 works of art. The works are exhibited on four floors (the fifth and sixth floors have temporary exhibits) chronologically from top to bottom: paintings and sculptures from classics of post-Impressionism (on the top floor) to contemporary star artists (second floor), prints and book illustrations (second floor), drawings, an architecture and design collection, a photographic collection from the invention of photography in the early 19th century up to the present (third floor), as well as the largest film collection in the USA.

In the Museum

Foyer The heart of the new building is the 33m/108ft-high foyer (also called ground or first floor), with its two entrances (from 53rd and 54th Street). On the east side a giant window gives a view of the famous **sculpture garden**, which has also been expanded, where Rodin's bronze *Balzac* stands guard separated from the street by a high aluminium wall. From here, an escalator goes up to the **main gallery** in the second floor. In the middle stands **Barnet Newman's** *Broken Obelisk*, on the wall Claude Monet's triptych **Water Lilies** (around 1920). From here a connecting passage with pictures by Willem de Kooning, Jasper Johns and Brice Marden leads to the **contemporary gallery**, which is reserved for contemporary art from 1970 onwards.

Fifth floor The following short description of the museum begins on the fifth floor, where European art from 1880 until 1940 is shown. Paul Signac's portrait of the art dealer and collector Félix Fénéon (1890) starts the exhibition off, followed by works by Cézanne (*Bathers*, around 1885), Van Gogh (*Starry Night*, 1889; his only oil painting in the museum), Gauguin, Seurat, Rousseau, Matisse (the MoMA has

Museum of Modern Art *Floor plan*

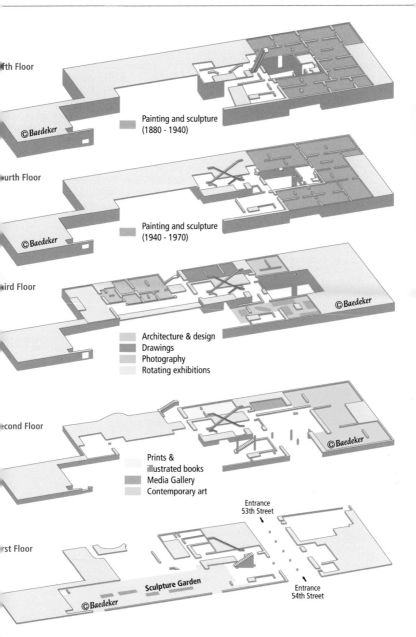

Fifth Floor

Painting and sculpture
(1880 - 1940)

©Baedeker

Fourth Floor

Painting and sculpture
(1940 - 1970)

©Baedeker

Third Floor

Architecture & design
Drawings
Photography
Rotating exhibitions

©Baedeker

Second Floor

Prints &
illustrated books
Media Gallery
Contemporary art

©Baedeker

First Floor

Entrance
53th Street

Sculpture Garden

©Baedeker

Entrance
54th Street

the largest collections of his works, including *La Danse*, 1909, and *Swimming Pool*, 1932), and Picasso, whose **Les Demoiselles d'Avignon** (1907) is considered to be the first cubist painting ever, as well as Dubuffet, Giacometti and Bacon.

Fourth floor The continuation of the history of art, its development in the second half of the 20th century including American art follows on the floor below, beginning with Pollock's *She-Wolf* (1943), on with Giacometti's *The Palace at 4 a.m.*, Jasper John's *Targets*, Warhol, Bruce Nauman, Eva Hesse and Joseph Beuys.

Second floor Contemporary art or the art scene since 1970 is the theme on the second floor, in the **Contemporary Galleries**, with works by Sigmar Polke, On Kawara, Blinky Palermo, Georg Baselitz, Gordon Matta-Clark, Kippenberger, Jeff Koons, Mathew Barney, Tuymans, Andreas Gursky, Kentridge, Jeff Wall, Rachel Whiteread and Gerhard Richter among others.

Third floor The third floor is dedicated to architecture and design since the late 19th century. Furniture by Gerrit Rietveld, *Red and Blue Chair* (1918), and many excellent objects as well as architecture in models and drawings (Mies van der Rohe, Le Corbusier, Frank Lloyd Wright) are displayed. Those interested in videos are bound to find something they like in the Film & Media Gallery. The excellent **photography collection** spans the beginnings of the form in 1839, through the classical and on to contemporary photography.

Sculpture Garden Among trees, flowers and benches stand numerous works in the Sculpture Garden, including those by Max Ernst, Alexander Calder, Henry Moore, Maillol, Matisse, Nadelman, Nevelson, Picasso's *She-Goat* and one of Auguste Rodin's *The Citizens of Calais*.

Nearby museums Near the MoMA are two other interesting museums, the **American Folk Art Museum** and the **Museum of Arts & Design** (▶Practicalities, Museums and Galleries).

National Museum of the American Indian

A 19

Location: 1 Bowling Green   **Subway:** Whitehall St., Bowling Green

At the southern tip of Manhattan, on the little square called Bowling Green, stands the US Custom House. It holds the Museum of the American Indian.

The US Custom House was built in 1907 in the classical style, a beautiful granite palace by the architect Cass Gilbert, the builder of the Woolworth Building. Chester French created the sculpture group at the portal whose figures represent America, Asia, Africa and Europe. The Museum's collection goes back to the legacy of the banker **George G. Heye** and belongs to the Smithsonian Institution today. At the end of 2004 it opened a large museum on the Native American cultures in Washington DC. In the former US Custom House rotating exhibitions of the Smithsonian Institution are to take place in the future including story tellers and dance groups (open: daily 10am–5pm, Thu until 8pm; Info: www.americanindian.si.edu).

Cunard Building

North of the museum is the Cunard Building, one of the most beautiful city post offices. It is housed in a neo-Renaissance building built in 1921 by Benjamin W. Morris for the passenger shipping line Cunard (25 Broadway). The large teller hall decorated with mosaics is especially impressive.

Once the extravagant seat of the US Customs Department, today the Museum of the American Indian

Shrine of Saint Elizabeth Ann Seton

South of the museum stands the former James Watson House, built in 1793 by John McComb in the Federal Style. The columned veranda followed in 1806. Elizabeth Ann Seton lived here (1774–1821) from 1801 until 1803. In 1975 she became the first woman born in America to be raised to sainthood by the Roman Catholic church (7 State St., between Pearl and Whitehall St.; open: Mon–Fri 8am–5pm, Sat before and after Mass at 12.15pm, Sun before and after Mass at 9am and noon).

★ Neue Galerie

G 8

Location: 1048 Fifth Ave./86th St.   **Subway:** 86th St.-Central Park West

The gallery is located in a a stylish city palace, which was built in 1914 by the architects of the New York Public Library Carrère & Hasting in the best part of New York, and lovingly restored.

Opening hours:
Thu–Mon
11am–6pm
www.neuegalerie.-
org

The Neue Galerie, whose name is based on the name of a famous Viennese gallery, displays Austrian and German art of the first half of the 20th century.

Among the works collected by Roland Lauder, the heir to the famous cosmetic company, and his Austrian friend, the art dealer Serge Sabarsky, are some by Gustav Klimt, Max Beckmann, Oskar Kokoschka, Paul Klee, Wassily Kandinsky or Egon Schiele. In addition there are also very beautiful furnishings and clocks from the Wiener Werkstätten as well as some sculptures (www.neuegalerie.org).

Viennese coffee-house charm

Apart from art there is Viennese coffeehouse charm on offer in the Café Sabarsky (open: Mon, Wed 9am–6pm, Thu–Sun until 9pm tel. 212-288-0665). The museum shop sells replicas of applied art objects as well as select books on art and literature.

★ New York Botanical Garden

Location: Bronx River Parkway/Fordham Road, Bronx   **Subway:** Bedford Park Blvd., continue with Bus 26; Metro-North from Grand Central

New York Botanical Garden, one of the oldest and largest botanical gardens in America, borders on the ▶Bronx Zoo to the north.

It was founded in 1891 and modelled on the Royal Botanical Gardens in Kew Gardens in London. A large part of the 1 sq km/0.4 sq mi park on both sides of the Bronx River is taken up by the Hemlock

Forest, which once covered the entire Manhattan Peninsula. Look out for the Enid A. Haupt Conservatory, built in 1901, a greenhouse styled after Crystal Palace in Kew Gardens. In eleven galleries plants from three climate zones grow, including orchids, ferns, cacti and tropical plants. In the Lorillard Snuff Mill of 1840, where tobacco leaves were once ground up for snuff, there is today a café, whose terrace on the Bronx River is an inviting place to take a rest. The main attractions of the Botanical Garden are the Rose Garden with countless varieties of roses, the Rock Garden (in a natural ravine of the Bronx River plants from all of the rocky and mountainous regions of the world flourish) and the Everett Children's Adventure Garden, where you can experience the growth of plants close up.

Opening hours:
Apr–Oct
Tue–Sun
10am–6pm
Nov–Mar
only until 5pm

www.nybg.org

✳ New York Public Library

D 12

Location: 76 Fifth Ave./42nd St.   **Subway:** Grand Central, 42nd St.

The New York Public Library, second in the United States only to the Library of Congress in Washington, is despite its name a private institution and was created from the union of three private libraries.

The impressive building in Beaux Arts style was designed by the New York architects Carrère & Hastings, who are also responsible for the home of the ►Frick Collection, among other buildings.

The steps in front of the New York Public Library

Opening hours:
Tue, Wed
11am–7.30pm
Mon, Thu–Sat
11am–6pm

Tours:
Tue–Sat
11am and 2pm

Main hall

Today's building was built between 1897 and 1911, on a site where there was once a pauper's cemetery and then the Croton Reservoir which provided the city's drinking water. Half of the cost of $9 million was carried by the steel industrialist Andrew Carnegie. The exterior staircase, which is flanked by two stone lions (Edward Clark Potter) is a popular lunch spot in the summer for people who work in the surrounding offices.

The giant main hall in the third floor has room for 550 people. Within a few minutes any book listed in the catalogue is made available by an ingenious computer system (total stock of the library: more than eleven million books, including copies of all of the telephone books in the United States, 14 million manuscripts and 10,000 periodicals from 128 countries). The library's special treasures include a Gutenberg Bible, a letter from Christopher Columbus, a copy of Galileo's publications and a handwritten draft of the Declaration of Independence by Thomas Jefferson. The Public Library has 85 branches, including the Library for the Performing Arts in the ►Lincoln Center, a reference and lending library for the subjects theatre, film, music and dance, as well as the ► Schomburg Center for the Research in Black Culture.

Bryant Park

Behind the library is Bryant Park, named after a publisher of the *New York Evening Post*. In 1854 the first New York World's Fair was held here, and today it is one of the prettiest places in the middle of Manhattan. Along with a café and a restaurant (both immediately behind the library) there is a box office here for all musical and dance events. Statues in the park are dedicated to the journalist and politician William Cullen Bryant (1794–1878, sculptor: Herbert Adams, architect of the pavilion: Thomas Hastings in 1911), Gertrude Stein (1874–1946; Jo Davidson, 1923) and Johann Wolfgang Goethe (1749–1832; Karl Fischer, 1832).

In the spring and autumn fashion shows are held here, and in the summer the **Bryant Park Film Festival** (information: www.bryantpark.org; tel. 212-768-4242).

American Standard Building

On the south side of Bryant Park is the American Standard Building (40 West 40th St.), which was built in 1924 by Raymond Hood, the architect of the ► Rockefeller Center. On the north side towers the 192m/630ft-high, 50-storey **Grace Building** (1114 Ave. of the Americas). It was built in 1974 by Skidmore, Owings & Merrill, who tried here – as they did with a second building at 9 West 57th St. – to retract the upper floors by means of a curved form and thus to achieve a slender silhouette.

Chase Manhattan Bank

At the corner of West 43rd St. and ►Fifth Ave. there is a branch of the Chase Manhattan Bank (1954 by Skidmore, Owings & Merrill), one of the first glass buildings in New York.

✴ Park Avenue

LocationFrom Union Square northwards

Park Avenue, together with ► Fifth Ave., is one of Manhattan's most expensive streets. It starts at Union Square and runs in a straight line northwards. In the 19th century the railway tracks of the private New York Central ran along here. From 1903 these were placed underground and a broad boulevard was constructed, which was built upon bit by bit. Some of the skyscrapers have made architectural history.

The following descriptions refer to the part of the avenue between 42nd St. and 59th Street. The **starting point** is ► Grand Central Terminal (42nd St. / Park Ave.).

The 59-storey former Pan Am Building was built in 1963 above the Grand Central Terminal (200 Park Ave.). Many architecture critics are of the opinion that the collaboration between Emery Roth, Pietro Belluschi and Walter Gropius produced the ugliest skyscraper in Manhattan.

MetLife Building

The building was already suffering criticism while it was being built because it blocked the view of Park Ave., which until then had been unobstructed. The building was sold in 1980 by Pan Am to the insurance company Metropolitan Life. The large foyer has works of art by Josef Albers, György Kepes and Richard Lippold.

Beyond 45th Street and in the shadow of the MetLife Building stands the Helmsley Building, built in 1929 by Warren & Whetmore (230 Park Ave.); it was originally the seat of the New York Central Railroad Company, whose main railway station was the adjacent Central Terminal.

Continuing along Park Ave. towards Central Park, on the left is (no. 270, between E 47th and 48th

Park Avenue, MetLife Building

St.) the 53-storey building which was built in 1960 for the Union Carbide Company by Skidmore, Owings & Merrill. Today it houses the headquarters of the Chase Manhattan Corporation. The silver-grey 50-storey tower opposite (no. 277) was built in 1962 and designed by Emery Roth & Sons.

Waldorf Astoria

The world famous hotel stands on the block between 49th and 50th Street. It was built in 1931 according to plans by Schultze and Weaver and replaced the original Waldorf Astoria Hotel, which stood on the grounds of the Empire State Building until it was demolished (▶Baedeker Special p.66).

St Bartholo-mew's Church

A block further on is St Bartholomew's Church (109 East 50th St.), designed in 1919 by the architect Bertram Goodhue in the Byzantine style. Its Romanesque entrance hall goes back to the church built in 1903 by the architects McKim, Mead & White (Madison Ave./44. St.). The bronze reliefs on the portal are by A. O'Connor. The altar inside the church is by Lee Larrie, who became famous primarily for the sculptures in the ▶ Rockefeller Center (open: daily until dark; subway: 51st St., Lexington Ave.).

General Electric Building

Immediately adjacent is the General Electric Building (570 Lexington Ave.), whose peaked point is a high point of Art Deco style. The 51-storey building was built in 1931 and designed by Cross & Cross for the Radio Corporation of America (RCA Victor), which moved into the ▶Rockefeller Center in 1931. The lobby is also worth seeing.

Seagram Building

The black metal, 160m/525ft-high, 38-storey building with bronze coloured windows, the headquarters of the whisky company, was built in 1958 and planned by Ludwig Mies van der Rohe and Philip Johnson (375 Park Ave./53rd St.). It is the only Mies van der Rohe building in New York and documents the International Style, which was developed in the USA. At least the architect was able to build here what he had proposed in 1920 in his famous design for Friedrichstrasse in Berlin. The interior was designed by Philip Johnson, among others, with works by Picasso, Rodin and Chagall. In the Four Seasons, the Seagram has one of the best restaurants of the city (▶Practicalities, Food and Drink).

Racquet and Tennis Club

Opposite the Seagram Building is the Racquet and Tennis Club, built in 1918 in the neo-Renaissance style (McKim, Mead & White; 370 Park Ave., between E 52nd and E 53rd Street).
Immediately behind the old tennis club is the **Park Avenue Plaza** (Skidmore, Owings & Merrill, 1981). Its 44 stories rise up over a glazed plaza with various shops.

Lever House

Architectural history was made by the Lever House (390 Park Ave., between E 53rd and E 54th St.), though it appears insignificant today sandwiched between giant sky-scrapers. It was built in 1952 as the administrative headquarters of the food company Lever Brothers and designed by Skidmore, Owings & Merrill. The 21-storey tower above a two-storey horizontal block was New York's first glass and steel high rise. Temporary exhibits are held in the lobby.

A detour leads to the **Citicorp Center** (153 East 53rd St., corner of Lexington Ave.), the white high-rise giant (279m/915ft, 46 stories) with the angled roof. The original plan was for solar panels to supply the building with heat from here, but the construction proved to be insufficient for this purpose. The

Citicorp Center, a giant high rise with an angled roof

aluminium tower rests on four 38m/125ft pillars, which stand in the middle of each of the four sides. The skyscraper was completed in 1978, designed by Hugh Stubbins and is considered to be a symbol of the reinvigoration of the city after the economic crisis. In order to gain permission to build that high, a public plaza had to be built in the interior of the site with connections to public transport; there are many shops and cafés here.

St Peter's had sold the land to the Citicorp Bank on the condition that they build a new church. Today the church built on the north-west corner is practically crushed by the high rise. The artist Louise Nevelson designed the interior; the Erol Beker Chapel is especially worth a visit.

St Peter's Church

In the shadows of the Citicorp Center, on the corner of Third Ave. and 53rd St., stands an office building built in 1986 by Philip Johnson and John Burgee. Because of its oval floor plan it is called »the lipstick«, and its critics also call it »the disposable lighter«. In comparison to other high-rise giants it seems insignificant, but it compensates for any lack of height through its striking shape and the high quality materials used.

✶
885th Third Lipstick

Cross 55th Street to get back to Park Avenue and pass the Central Synagogue (architect: Henry Fernbach), which was built in 1870 and is the oldest synagogue in New York with uninterrupted use.

Central Synagogue

The Mercedes Benz Showroom (430 Park Ave./57th. St.) was designed by Frank Lloyd Wright in 1953.

Mercedes Benz showroom

Queens

Location: East part of Manhattan,
north-east of Brooklyn

**With 313 sq km/121 sq mi Queens is the largest New York borough
and lies on Long Island north-east of Brooklyn. Every visitor has at
least seen it in passing, on the bus or taxi ride to Manhattan, since
two of the three large New York airports are here, John F. Kennedy
International and LaGuardia Airport.**

Queens was rather insignificant until the middle of the 19th century.
That changed when it was incorporated into New York in 1898 and
after the building of the Queensboro Bridge in 1909. Today, 2 million
people live here, and they are said to speak 120 different languages
and dialects. Astoria or »Little Athens« is the largest Greek community outside of Greece, Flushing proudly calls itself »Little Seoul«,
and there is also a Hindu temple here, as well as a large Puerto Rican quarter and a significant Dom-
inican community. In the 1920s
and 1930s Queens was an important film metropolis, to which the
American Museum of the Moving
Image bears witness. Beyond that
there is little worth seeing, unless you are interested in modern art,
the location of the 1864 World's Fair or the tennis stadium in Flushing Meadows.

? DID YOU KNOW ...?

■ Here is the key to the often 2 or 3-number
addresses in Queens: 36-01 43rd Ave. means:
the Museum for African Art is on 43rd
Avenue, near the intersection with 36th
Street.

Sightseeing in Queens

✱
**Isamu Noguchi
Garden Museum**

The building is as unusual as the work of the artist Isamu Noguchi
(1904–1988), who is rooted in American and Japanese culture. In a
former studio of the artist are sculptures, stage decorations (for Martha Graham and George Balanchine among others), furniture and
other designs; adjoining are a museum shop and a cafeteria (9-01
33rd Road, between Vernon Blvd. and 10th St.; tel. 718-204-7088,
www. noguchi.org;open: Wed–Fri 10am–5pm, Sat, Sun 11am–6pm).
A shuttle bus runs from Manhattan (from the Asia Society, Park Ave.
and 70th St.) to the museum at weekends.

**Socrates
Sculpture Park**

One block north is the Socrates Sculpture Park. The former industrial area along the East River, where works by freelance artists can be
seen, offers a very nice view of Roosevelt Island and the Manhattan
skyline (Broadway/near Vernon Blvd.; www.socratessculpturepark
.org).

Queens Plan

NASSAU

Rikers
Island

East River

Little
Neck
Bay

MANHATTAN

East River Drive

Triborough Bridge

Steinway
Piano Factory

LaGuardia
Airport

Throgs Necks Bridge

Bronx Whitestone Bridge

Cross Island Parkway

Clearview Expressway

Socrates
Sculpture Park

★ Isamu Noguchi
Garden Museum

Queensboro
Bridge

Queens–
Midtown
Tunnel

Museum of
the Moving Image

Museum of
African Art

★ P.S.1
Contemporary
Art Center

Ditmars Blvd.

Grand Central Parkway

Northern Blvd.

Astoria Blvd.

Broadway

31st Street

Roosevelt Ave.

Northern

Avenue

Greenpoint

Brooklyn Queens Expwy

Queens Boulevard

Long Island Expressway

Flushing
Town Hall
Shea
Stadium
Flushing Meadows
Corona Park
Hall of
Science

Louis
Armstrong
House

Bowne House
Queens
Historical Society

Queens
Botanical
Garden

Queens
Museum

Colden Center

Whitestone Expwy

Northern Boulevard

Willets Pt. Blvd.

Bayside Ave.

Francis Lewis Blvd.

Bell Blvd.

Kissena
Park

Van Wyck Expressway

Jewel Ave.

Main St.

Utopia Parkway

Kissena Blvd.

Northern Boulevard

Cunningham
Park

73rd Ave.

Union Tnpk.

Alley
Park

Queens County
Farm Museum

Grand Central Parkway

Westside
Tennis Club

Elliott Avenue

Metropolitan Avenue

Grand Avenue

Central Avenue

Myrtle Avenue

Grand Central Expressway

Hillside Ave.

Jamaica Avenue

Jamaica Center
for Arts & Learning

Hillside Avenue

Francis Lewis Boulevard

Belmont Park
Race Track

Montefiore
Cemetery

BROOKLYN

Williamsburg
Bridge

Bedford Avenue

Lafayette
Avenue

Flushing
Myrtle
Avenue

Bushwick Avenue
Broadway

Cooper Street

Forest
Park

Jackie Robinson Parkway

Fulton Street

Jamaica Avenue

Atlantic Avenue

Liberty

Van Wyck Expwy.

Jefferson Ave.

Guy Brewer Boulevard

Sutphin Blvd.

Linden Boulevard

Merrick Boulevard

Farmers Blvd.

Springfield Boulevard

Laurelton Parkway

Brookville
Park

Eastern
Parkway

Empire Blvd.

Atlantic Avenue

Liberty Avenue

Conduit Boulevard

Rockaway Boulevard

Aqueduct
Race Track

Nassau Expressway

Shore Parkway (Belt Parkway)

Rockaway Boulevard

Linden Blvd.

Utica Avenue

Ocean Avenue

Flatbush Avenue

Nostrand Avenue Highway

Ralph Avenue

Rockaway Parkway

Remsen Avenue

Flatlands

Linden Boulevard

Avenue

Shore Parkway (Belt Parkway)

Cross Bay Boulevard

✈
John F. Kennedy
International Airport

I-678

Avenue P

Avenue U

Marine
Park

Floyd
Bennett Field

Flatbush Avenue

Shore Parkway (Belt Parkway)

Marine Parkway Bridge

Channel Drive

★ Jamaica Bay
Wildlife Refuge Center

Beach Channel Drive
Rockaway Fwy.

Rockaway Beach Boulevard

Rockaway
Beach

Rockaway
Point Blvd.

Beach

Rockaway Inlet

Atlantic Ocean

1 mi
2 km

©Baedeker

The P.S.1 keeps art lovers up to date on the latest developments.

P. S. 1

★ After renovation and expansion (the plans were by Frederic Fisher, a student of Frank O. Gehry) the very young art scene is now given an introduction at the P. S. 1 Contemporary Art Center. The former elementary school (P. S. 1 is short for Public School 1) from 1890, together with the New Museum of Contemporary Art, fill a gap in the city (22-25 Jackson Ave./46th Ave.; subway: 23rd St.-Ely Ave., Long Island City-Court House Square, 45th Rd.-Court House Square; open: Thu–Mon noon–6pm, information: www.ps1.org, tel. 718-784-2084).

American Museum of the Moving Image

In the year 1920 Paramount Pictures opened in Queens what was then the biggest film studio in the city, Astoria Studios, where famous actors like the Marx Brothers, W. C. Fields, Gary Cooper and Gloria Swanson worked. The depression of the 1930s led to the film industry's move to Hollywood. Astoria Studios then filmed newsreels and training films for the army, eventually standing empty. In the 1980s Astoria Motion Picture and Television Foundation took over the complex. Since then it is used by some independent producers, and among other films Francis Ford Coppola's *Cotton Club* and Woody Allen's *Radio Days* were produced here. In 1988 the film museum was opened in one of the studio buildings (architects: Gwathmey & Siegel). Among the film properties there are also the chariot that Charlton Heston rode in *Ben Hur* and costumes from *Star Wars*. In addition, films are shown regularly (35th Ave. / 36th St., subway: Steinway St.; open: Wed, Thu noon–5pm, Fri until 8pm, Sat, Sun 11am–6pm).

After a visit to the film museum it is pleasant to stroll through **Astoria** or »Little Athens«, as the former Greek neighbourhood is called. Though today the area is more multi-cultural, Greek restaurants, shops and cafés can still be found on Steinway Street and 30th Avenue.

! *Baedeker* TIP

Summer parties at the P. S. 1

In the summer, young architects and designers transform the forecourt of the P. S. 1 into an abstract playground – an ideal atmosphere for weekend dance parties. In the past years the young public has been attracted by a grove of hammocks, water sprayers and a huge sandpit which served as a dance floor.

Steinway pianos

The subway station Steinway St. is named after Henry Steinweg, who originally came from Seesen in the Harz Mountains in Germany and who opened his first piano factory in 1870 in Long Island City. The famous Steinway pianos are still produced here today (1 Steinway Place, between 38th St. and 19th Ave., tours by appointment only, tel. 718-721-2600).

Flushing Meadows Corona Park

Two World's Fairs were held on the grounds of Flushing Meadows Park in 1939/40 and 1964. The »Unisphere«, a 42m/138ft-high massive steel globe, originates from this time. This is home to various institutions, including the National Tennis Center, where the famous U.S. Open is held every year, the 55,000 seat Citi Stadium, home of the famous baseball team the **New York Mets**, the Louis Armstrong Stadium (18,000 seats), golf courses, an ice skating rink and much more (location: in the north of Queens, between Roosevelt Ave., Long Island Expressway, Grand Central Parkway and Van Eyck Expressway; subway: Mets Willets Point).

Queens Museum of Art

The Queens Museum of Art gives an overview of the famous New York skyline with its model of all five boroughs at a scale of 1:1200. The model was made for the last World's Fair. The museum is in the New York City Building (in Flushing Meadows Corona Park, 49th Ave., near 111th St.; subway: 111th St.; open: Wed–Fri 10am–5pm, Sat, Sun noon–5pm).

New York Hall of Science

The New York Hall of Science, a hands-on museum of science and technology is also in the park (open: Sept–March Tue–Thu 9.30am–2pm, Fri until 5pm, Sat, Sun 10am–6pm; April–June Mon–Thu 9.30am–2pm, Fri until 5pm, Sat, Sun 10am–6pm; July, Aug. Mon–Fri 9.30am–5pm, Sat, Sun 10am–6pm; www.nyhallsci.org).

Unisphere in Flushing Meadows

Louis Armstrong House

The jazz legend Louis Armstrong (1901–1971) lived in Corona with his wife Lucille from 1943 until his death. The house is furnished with original furniture and many souvenirs and it is open to the public (34-56 107 St., between 34th and 37th Ave., tel. 718-478-8274, www.satchmo.net; subway: 103rd St.-Corona Plaza; open: Tue–Fri 10am–5pm, Sat, Sun noon–5pm).

Bowne House

The Quaker John Bowne's house from the year 1661 is one of the oldest buildings in the city and today is a museum. The furnishings (both furniture and utensils) for the most part go back to the 17th and 18th centuries (37-01 Bowne St., Flushing; subway: Main St., currently closed for renovations).

✱ Jamaica Bay Wildlife Refuge Center

The nature reserve Jamaica Bay Wildlife Refuge lies south of John F. Kennedy Airport and can be reached by subway directly from Manhattan. It is also known as Birdland, a place for bird-lovers all year round. More than 300 varieties of birds live in the bay which is protected from the Atlantic by the Rockaway Beach peninsula. The almost 3km/1.8mi-long nature trail winds through marshes and high ground. There are beautiful views from here, including views of

Manhattan. The only village, Broad Channel, lies along Cross Bay Blvd. (subway: Broad Channel, from here about a 20min walk to the visitor centre; open: daily 8.30am–5pm; guided drives and hikes are also offered, tel. 718-318-4340).

★ ★ Rockefeller Center

E 11

Location: Fifth Ave., between 47th and 52nd St.   **Subway:** Rockefeller Center

The Rockefeller Center is a complex of 19 skyscrapers between Fifth Ave. and the Avenue of the Americas. It was built by the richest citizen of America, John D. Rockefeller Jr., whom New York also has to thank for Rockefeller University, Fort Tryon Park with ▶The Cloisters, and the UN headquarters (▶United Nations), for which he donated the land.

The 4ha/9.8ac plot originally belonged to Columbia University, from whom John D. Rockefeller bought it in 1928. Between 1931 and 1940, during the worst depression, 228 houses had to be torn down first so that, with its 12 buildings, the largest private business and entertainment complex in the world could be built. In 1932 the RCA Building (today GE Building) was opened. A team of seven architects was responsible for the plans, including Wallace K. Harrison, who created the United Nations Headquarters and the Lincoln Center. From 1957 a second building phase and a further five buildings followed. Alongside countless offices, which see 250,000 people enter and leave daily, the Rockefeller Center has 30 restaurants, dozens of shops on ground level and, in the underground passages, television studios, exhibition rooms and in the winter an **ice rink**. The generous plazas are virtually a museum featuring frescos, sculptures and reliefs. More than two dozen artists are represented with over 100 works. At the end of 1989 the Japanese Mitsubishi Estate Company bought 51% of the Rockefeller Center from the – at that time – 88 Rockefeller heirs. Since 2001 the entire complex has belonged to the real estate company Tishman Speyer, which had to raise $1.85 billion to pay for it. In the meantime the value has probably risen in the face of the increasing real estate prices in Manhattan.

City in the city

> **? DID YOU KNOW …?**
>
> ■ Construction workers set up the giant Christmas tree at the Rockefeller Center for the first time in 1931. They wanted to make a positive statement in economically difficult times – a tradition that continues to this day.

The following description of the Rockefeller Center begins at the entrance to the pedestrian walkway **Channel Gardens** (Fifth Ave.,

Tours
Tel. 212-698-2000
www.rockefeller-center.com

opposite ▸ St Patrick's Cathedral). To the right and left are two 7-storey buildings, on the right the British Empire Building (1932), on the left the Maison Française (1933). Between these the 70m/76yd-long promenade **Channel Gardens** (named after the English Channel) leads to the Lower Plaza, which is used as a skating rink in the winter and as a terrace for cafés and restaurants in the summer. During the Christmas season the most impressive Christmas tree in the USA stands here. A marble tablet quotes John D. Rockefeller's credo. The gilded statue of **Prometheus** (1934, Paul Maship), who according to legend brought fire to humankind, stands in front of the west wall of the sunken garden. The flags of the countries accredited by the UN wave around the plaza.

GE Building   Immediately behind the sunken garden is the main building of the Rockefeller Center, the 250m/820ft-high GE Building (General Electric Building; until 1990 the RCA Building standing for Radio Corporation of America) with the studios of the radio and television company NBC, which are open to the public (tel. 212-664-3700). Above the main entrance (30 Rockefeller Plaza) is the relief *Allegory*

City in the city: Rockefeller Center

of Wisdom and Knowledge by the American sculptor Lee Lawrie. The main hall is decorated with murals by José M. Sert. Originally a fresco by the Mexican Diego Rivera was here, which Rockefeller however found to be too political. On the 65th floor the restaurant **Rainbow Grill** is currently closed. On the 70th floor, 260m/852ft high, the **visitor's platform** known as Top of the Rock re-opened at the end of 2005 after being closed for more than 19 years. The view of the city's skyline is breathtaking. Above all, it is impressive to see the Empire State Building amongst the skyscrapers (entrance 50th St., between Fifth and Sixth Ave.; daily 8.30am–midnight; avoid waiting by making a reservation for a viewing time: www.topoftherocknyc.com, tel. 212-698-2020; guided tours through the building daily from 10am).

★ ★
◄ Top of the Rock

⏱

⏱

To the north-west, behind the GE Building, is Radio City Music Hall. It was built in 1930 by Edward Durrell Stone in Art Deco style and houses a theatre auditorium with 6,200 seats in which, since film showings ceased, sporadic shows and appearances by popular stars and rock groups take place. The elaborately furnished music hall can be viewed outside of show times (1260 Ave. of the Americas; tours: daily 11am–3pm, tel. 212-247-4777).

★
Radio City Music Hall

⏱

For those interested in architecture, a short detour from Radio City Music Hall to Sixth Ave., also called Ave. of the Americas, is worthwhile. At the corner of 47th Street stands the **Celanese Building**, which was built in 1973 by Harrison, Abramovitz & Harris. This office also designed the next two skyscrapers, the **McGraw Hill Building** and the **1251 Avenue of the Americas Building**, which is named after its address today (originally Exxon Building).
In front of the McGraw Hill Building (no. 1221) is a sundial, *Sun Triangle* (Athelstan Spilhaus, 1973). The point of the steel triangle shows the sun'ss position at the solstices and the equinoxes. The curves of the blue-painted steel *Cubed Curve* (William Crovello, 1971) provide an effective counterpoint to the straight lines of the Time & Life Building behind it, built in 1959 (1271 Sixth Ave.).

Detour to Sixth Avenue

Between 51st and 52nd St. stretches the Equitable Center (1285 Sixth Ave. to 787 Seventh Ave.). The focus is the 54-storey Equitable Tower (Edward Larrabee Barnes, 1985). In its lobby (entrance from Seventh Ave.) Thomas Hart Benton's fresco cycle *America Today* (1930) can be seen, depicting everyday life in America during the boom of the 1920s. The atrium is dominated by Roy Lichtenstein's *Mural with Blue Brushstroke* (1984/85). The Equitable Gallery is also in the atrium, in which there are temporary exhibitions of modern art.

Equitable Center

The CBS Building, built in 1965, is home to one of America's three media giants (Columbia Broadcasting System). The architect was the Finnish Eero Saarinen (1910–1961), whose only high rise is also called »Black Rock«.

CBS Building

The E. F. Hutton Building rises up behind the CBS Building (31 W 52nd St.; Roche, Dinkeloo and Assocs., 1987). The small plaza between the two buildings is dominated by the sculpture *Lapstrake* by Jesús Bautista Moroles (1987).

At the end of 1989 on Sixth Ave., between 52nd and 53rd Street, a work by the pop artist Jim Dine, *Looking on the Avenue* has been erected – three bronze sculptures, about 4, 6 and 7.5m high (13, 19 and 25ft), who portray variations on the famous *Venus de Milo*, not only without an arm, but also without a head.

✱ St Patrick's Cathedral

E 11/12

Location: Fifth Ave., between 50th and 51st St.

Subway: 47–50th St.-Rockefeller Center, Fifth Ave.-53rd St.

The Roman Catholic cathedral, seat of the archbishop, was built of light-coloured marble between 1858 and 1888 according to plans by James Rentwick in High Gothic style, and in 1910 dedicated to the Irish patron saint.

🕑
Opening hours:
daily
6.30am–8.45pm

The Lady Chapel on the east side was added in 1905. The cathedral, with its two slender towers each 101m/331ft high and a rose above the main portal which has a diameter of 8m/26ft, is an especially beautiful sight in the evening when illuminated. The dignified interior is 93m/101.7yd long and 38m/41.5yd at its widest and has around 2,500 seats. Massive marble columns support the dome. Among the rich furnishings, the stained glass windows, the main altar crowned with a canopy (dedicated in 1942) and the numerous side altars are especially striking; also look out for the figure of Elizabeth Ann Seton (1774–1821), who in 1975 became the first woman from the USA raised to sainthood, and is the founder of the order of the Sisters of Charity. The main organ has over 9,000 pipes.

Olympic Tower

The Olympic Tower (▶Fifth Avenue) built in 1976 stands next to the cathedral. East of the cathedral on both sides of the choir are the neo-Gothic rectory and the residence of the archbishop of New York (both also built by J. Rentwick in 1880).

✱
Villard Houses

Immediately opposite the rectory are the three-storied Villard Houses (457 Madison Ave.), which were built in 1884 according to plans by McKim, Mead & White for Henry Villard. The native Bavarian emigrated to the USA in 1860 under the name of Heinrich Hilgard and quickly attained wealth and respect as the publisher of the *New York Post* newspaper. The houses imitate the Palazzo della Cancelleria in Rome and are among the most effective neo-Renaissance buildings in New York. In the 1970s they were supposed to be de-

St. Patrick's Cathedral

molished because the value of the land had grown enormously. The solution was selling the air rights to the Helmsley Group, which built the 50-storey Palace Hotel instead. Today the south wing of the Villard Houses is the elegant hotel entrance.

★ St Paul's Chapel

B 18

Location: 209 Broadway, between Fulton and Vesey St.

Subway: Fulton St. and Broadway-Nassau St.

The church built in 1764–1766 is not the oldest building in New York, but of those that have survived from the 17th and 18th century it is the only public building that has not been changed substantially.

The architectural model was probably St Martin-in-the-Fields in London, whose architect James Gibb was also the teacher of Thomas McBean who built the New York church. The tower and veranda

Opening hours:
Mon–Sat
10am–6pm
Sun 9am–4pm

were built in 1796. The chair marked with a »G« on the left of the elaborate interior was used by George Washington (www.saintpaul-schapel.org, tel. 212-602-0974).

The small cemetery is an oasis of quiet especially in the spring and autumn; a monument is dedicated to the actor George F. Cooke. ►City Hall and the Woolworth Building (►City Hall & Civic Center) are nearby.

✳ SoHo

B/C 16/17

Location: Between Ave. of the Americas, Broadway, Houston and Canal St.
Subway: Spring St., Bleecker St.

SoHo, an acronym for South of Houston, has of course nothing to do with the neighbourhood in London. Bordered by Houston St. in the north, West Broadway (SoHo's main street) in the west, Canal St. in the south and Broadway in the east, the area of about one square mile was still a sleepy collection of warehouses and small factories 40 years ago.

Then artists discovered the area and moved their flats and studios into the lofts. In the course of time galleries, out-of-the-ordinary shops, restaurants, jazz and rock clubs joined them. SoHo became a trendy neighbourhood and the rents exploded. Meanwhile, most of the artists have »emigrated« to West Chelsea, but the 21st century tourist is still attracted by SoHo's cobblestone streets. On Saturday afternoons in particular (except for the summer months) the area is as busy as a beehive.

»Cast Iron« Nowhere else in America is there such a continuous ensemble of so-called cast iron houses as in SoHo (next to West Broadway particularly in Greene St., and also in Broome St.). These buildings, made of cast iron, are more than 100 years old. The use of cast iron made it possible to reproduce columns, arches, gates and other building parts, even whole façades, very cheaply: for the first time in the history of building, pre-fabricated, standardized building parts could be used. This led to an unforeseen variety of details which can still be admired today, including bizarre fire escape ladders. The elaborate decorations on the buildings belie the fact that SoHo was an area given over mainly to industrial production. The façades have unusually large windows for the time, through which light can reach the workplaces deep inside the building, and the elevated ramps on the streets make deliveries easier. A unique feature of these buildings are the cast iron floor plates with hundreds of glass lenses through which daylight could reach the lower floors as well. These can still be seen in many places in SoHo. In the 1960s the houses were almost demolished to make way for a street. The plan was stopped literally at the last moment. Today all of SoHo is under monument protection.

A stroll through SoHo, which neighbours ►Greenwich Village to the south, is highly recommended. Visitors to the area find galleries, boutiques and other interesting or way-out shops, as well as restaurants and bars. The most striking buildings include the **Singer Building** (561–563 Broadway), built in 1904 by Ernest Flagg as the offices and warehouse of the sewing machine company of the same name, the neighbouring house with its Italian Renaissance style (**565 Broadway**) and the **Haughwout Building** (488 Broadway), built in 1857. At the corner of Prince and Greene St. a mural by Richard Haas in trompe l'oeil technique from 1970 imitates the cast iron façade. Those interested in the history of fire fighting will enjoy dropping in at the **NYC Fire Museum**, a fire station built in 1904 in the Beaux Arts style (►Practicalities, Museums and Galleries, p.119).

Cast Iron: Little Singer Building

✴ Sony Building

E 11

Location: 550 Madison Ave./56th St.   **Subway:** 53rd St.

Built in 1984 as the headquarters of the telephone company A T & T, what is now the Sony Building attracted attention like no other in the post-war era.

It was constructed at a time when dollars were short, when the old rule that the higher the building the more important was the owner was no longer completely true. Instead originality was called for, and the postmodern era dawned. But it was the cause of some amazement that Philip Johnson, the grand master of New York architects who had studied under Walter Gropius and Marcel Breuer, who had brought Mies van der Rohe and Le Corbusier to the USA and who had propagated the International Style in the 1930s based on the German Bauhaus, was the one to introduce a new era of architectural history in the 1980s. His A T & T Building, which he designed with his partner John Burgee, is considered to be the first postmodern skyscraper in the world.

In the Bamboo Garden of »590 Madison«

From 1984 to 1991 the 38-storey building of pink and grey granite, which was »only« 195m/639ft high, served as the headquarters for the telephone company A T & T, after which the Japanese concern Sony took it over. Its trademark is the individually styled broken gable – critics say that it looks like a Chippendale dresser – and the massive, six-storey-high arched portal. Since the change in ownership the atrium, which once left a rather cool impression, has been transformed into a friendly public plaza. In the **Wonder Technology Lab** Sony exhibits its most modern communications technology (open: Tue–Sat 10am–5pm, Sun noon–5pm).

A little north of here is the former IBM Building which since the change in ownership has been named after its address, 590 Madison 590 Madison. The 183m/600ft-high, 43-storey skyscraper made of dark green granite and green toned glass represents an important enrichment of the New York skyscraper scene. It was built in 1984 to plans by Edward Larrabee Barnes. An especially popular meeting place is the four-storey-high, glazed bamboo garden at the foot of the building, a good place to flee the noise of the city. Outside the entrance stands a sculpture by Alexander Calder and in the glass house there is a sculpture by J. Chamberlain. Through the lobby of the 590 Madison Building, visitors can enter the **Trump Tower**, which stands in the same block facing ►Fifth Avenue.

590 Madison

✶ South Street Seaport

Location: On the East River

Subway: Broadway-Nassau St., Fulton St.

The South Street Seaport, once the core of New York Harbor and the gateway to the city, lies south of today's ►Brooklyn Bridge.

The goods for overseas trade that made New York so large and important were sent on their way from harbour buildings and piers which are still standing today or have been restored. In the 1860s, when shipping changed from sail to steam, the harbour moved from the eastern shore to the western shore of Manhattan on the Hudson River, where ships with greater draught could anchor and where there was more room to expand the pier. The area on the East Side declined and only the fish market remained. In 1967 the neighbourhood was carefully restored and transformed into a Living History Museum, with historic houses and cobbled streets from the 19th century. Today the South Street Seaport is one of the most popular sites within the city, attracting more than 13 million visitors annually. And it is not only tourists, but also New Yorkers who visit the outdoor museum with its old ships, numerous smart shops, galleries,

Ⓞ
Opening hours:
Mon–Sat
10am–9pm
Sun 10am–7pm

www.southstreet
seaport.org

souvenir shops, restaurants and cafés. The museum buildings, galleries and the historical ships charge admission; ask at the ticket booth about guided tours.

Historic ships   Between Pier 15 and 17 several historic ships are anchored. The showpiece is the four-mast bark *Peking*, built in 1911 by Blohm & Voss, with Hamburg as home port. It belonged, like its sister ships the *Passat* and the *Pamir*, which sank in 1957, to the legendary Flying P Liners, a total of 17 large sailing ships owned by the Hamburg shipping company Laeisz, which trafficked between Europe and South America. The *Peking*, which could load 4,700 tons, was sold to England in 1932 and served under the name of *Arethusa* as a stationary school ship. In 1975 she found her final mooring here in New York. The light ship *Ambrose*, built in 1908, is also moored at this pier. From May to September the schooner *Pioneer*, built in 1885, casts off for two to three-hour **harbour tours** (reservations: tel. 212-748-8786).

In the so-called **Museum Block**, between Fulton, Water, Beekman and Front St., there are 14 renovated buildings from the 18th and 19th centuries, which today primarily house museums.

The **visitor centre** and the museum shop are in the house at 12 Fulton Street. An exhibition here shows the history of the harbour; there is also information here on current events (open: daily, May–Sept. 10am–6pm, Oct–May only until 5pm; tel. 212-748-8600).

In the Cannon's Walk block, Water St. no. 207, 211 and 215, is the printing house **Bowne & Co.** from the 19th century.

The series of buildings constructed in 1811 and commissioned by the ship owner Peter Schermerhorn, the so-called **Schermerhorn Row**, is the showpiece of the South Street Seaport. Once they were warehouses, later in great demand as real estate. The Fulton Market Building (Benjamin Thompson &

South Street Seaport Museum

Pearl Street · Titanic Memorial · Street · Peck Slip

Water Street · Cannon's Walk Block · Beekman Street · Peck Slip Trompe l'œil Jasper Ward House

Water Street · Fulton Street · John Street · One Seaport Plaza · (i) · Front Street

Front · Burling Slip · Schermerhorn Row · Fulton Market

South Street

Franklin D. Roosevelt Drive · Fulton Fish Market

box office

South · Maritime Crafts Center · Pier 17 Pavilion · Pier 18 · Pier 17

F · D · A · Pier 16 · B

E · C

Pier 15 · East River

Pier 14

100 m
300 ft
©Baedeker

Historic vessels

A   Ambrose (light ship; 1908)
B   Lettie G. Howard (schooner; 1893)
C   Pioneer (schooner; 1885)
D   Peking (four-mast bark; 1911)
E   Wavertree (three-mast sailing vessel; 1885)
F   W.O. Decker (tug; 1930)

South Street Seaport, the entertainment pier on the East River

Assocs., 1983) is already the fourth market house on its location. Opposite was once the Fulton Fish Market. From about 1821 until the end of 2005 fish was sold here. Now the fish market is in the Bronx, in the north of the city.

In 1985 the old Pier 17 was roofed over; the new **Pier Pavilion 17** (Benjamin Thompson & Assocs.) with many shops and restaurants enjoys great popularity. The view from the terrace is beautiful. At no. 41 **Peck Slip** Richard Haas has painted a trompe l'oeil mural on the house, which shows a row of houses with shops as well as the Brooklyn Bridge.

Staten Island

Location: In the south of Manhattan

With just about 400,000 residents, the 22km/13.6mi-long and 12km/7.4mi-wide Staten Island is the smallest and also least important part of New York. For this reason it is also referred to jokingly as »the forgotten borough«.

The first settlers came in 1661, and for more than two centuries the island was mainly agricultural. It was incorporated into New York in 1898. Since 1964 the 1,298m/1,420yd-long Verrazano Narrows Bridge has connected Staten Island with Brooklyn.

Staten Island Ferry

The 20-minute ride on the Staten Island Ferry is a special experience which has the added bonus of being free of charge. The ferries run all year and around the clock between the southern point of Manhattan (Battery) and the northern point of Staten Island (St George Station). En route, enjoy the views of Manhattan's skyscrapers, the Statue of Liberty and Ellis Island, Governor's Island opposite, the quarters of the Coast Guard with a red brick fort and the elegant Verrazano Narrows Bridge.

Among the famous visitors to Staten Island are Giuseppe Garibaldi (1807–1882), who lived here in exile before returning to Italy, and Francis Ford Coppola, who filmed *The Godfather* here in 1971. The inglorious superlative characters include »Big« Paul Castellano, head of the Gambino gang and the most powerful mafia boss in New

Travelling by Staten Island Ferry

York, who had his headquarters here until he was shot in 1985; the island also boasts the world's largest rubbish dump.

Sightseeing on Staten Island

In addition to a large number of well-kept homes from New York's period of expansion, Staten Island offers several tourist sights scattered some distance apart. Most can be reached by bus from the ferry landing St George Station, and the bus ride is also very interesting since it offers a view of this rural area.

The largest private collection of Tibetan art in the Western world can be found on a hill on Staten Island. The building's architecture imitates a Tibetan monastery with a terraced garden; the museum's

✳
Jacques Marchais Center

Staten Island *Plan*

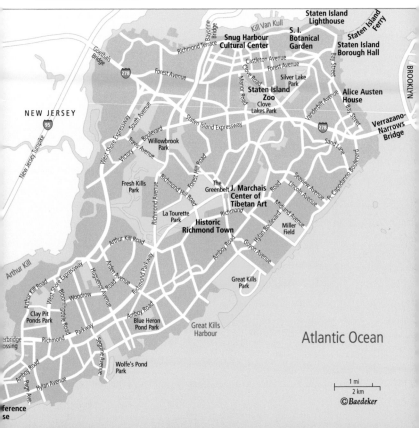

treasures were collected and donated by the New York art dealer Mrs Harry Klauber, who also sold Asian art under the name of Jacques Marchais. Next to Tibetan art, which constitutes the main part of the collection, there are also examples of art from China, Korea, Japan, Southeast Asia, India and Persia (338 Lighthouse Ave.; from the ferry landing on bus 74; open: Wed–Sun 1pm–5pm; tel. 718-987-3500, www.tibetanmuseum.com).

Historic Richmond Town

In Richmond, almost the centre of Staten Island, are 27 former seafarers' homes which give an excellent impression of life in colonial times. The oldest of the buildings, Voorlezer House, dates from the year 1696 and is the oldest schoolhouse in America. In the Moravian Cemetery is the mausoleum of the Vanderbilt family (▸ Famous People). Demonstrations of old crafts are given regularly, and information and a schedule is available here which also identifies which houses are open to the public (441 Clarke Ave.; after arriving with the Staten Island Ferry continue on bus 74; open: June–Aug Wed–Fri 10am–5pm, Sat, Sun 1pm–5pm, otherwise Wed–Sun 1pm–5pm; information on events: tel. 718-351-1611).

Alice Austen House

The American photographer Alice Austen, born in 1866, lived in this small cottage until her death in 1952. Today a selection of her pictures can be seen, which give an impression of what life was like on

Queen Mary 2, the world's largest passenger ship, passing the Verrazano Narrows Bridge

the island (2 Hylan Boulevard; from the ferry landing continue on bus 51; open: Thu–Sun noon–5pm; tel. 718-816-4506).

Snug Harbor was founded in 1831 in a park above a waterway into Upper New York Bay. Once a hospital with several residences for former seamen, today it is a cultural and event centre. The complex also includes the Newhouse Center for Contemporary Art, the Staten Island Children's Museum and a botanical garden (1000 Richmond Terrace, Building C; continue from the ferry landing on bus 40; open: daily from sunrise to sunset).

Snug Harbor Cultural Center

★ ★ Statue of Liberty

Location: Liberty Island

Subway: South Ferry; ferry from/to Battery Park, daily 9.30am–5pm

In the Upper Bay, about 4km/2.5mi south-west of the Battery, on the approx. 5ha/12.3ac Liberty Island (Native American Minissais, later Bedloe's Island, since 1956 Liberty Island), the »Statue of Liberty Enlightening the World« stands on the foundations of a fort built in 1811. The statue, 93m/305ft-high including the foundation and base, is a world-famous symbol for the USA.

The monumental statue, presented to the USA on its 100th anniversary by France, was designed by Frédéric Auguste Bartholdi (1834–1904, from Colmar) and was originally intended for the northern entrance to the Suez Canal. It was inaugurated on 28 October 1886 in the presence of US president Grover Cleveland, F. A. Bartholdi and F. de Lesseps, the builder of the Suez Canal. The statue consists of steel scaffolding covered with 300 copper plates (Gustave Eiffel), is 46m/50.3yd high to the point of the torch in the raised right arm, which is illuminated after dark, and weighs 225 tons. The goddess of liberty, crowned with a radiant diadem, stands on the broken chains of slavery and holds the Declaration of Independence in her left hand with the historic date »July 4, 1776« inscribed upon it. The massive star-shaped base was built according to plans by Richard M. Hunt. The construction materials could only be financed after a private fund drive. From the planning of the statue to its unveiling in New York, 20 years passed. Carved into the base is an excerpt

> **! Baedeker TIP**
>
> **A dubious pleasure**
>
> 354 steps up a narrow stairwell lead into the crown of the iron lady! A dubious pleasure when you consider the fact that the view from the base (a lift goes this far) or from the Staten Island Ferry is actually much better. These are the only possibilities anyway since 9/11, as the statue itself has been closed until further notice as a precaution against terrorist attacks.

One of the most famous symbols of the USA: the Statue of Liberty

from a poem composed by **Emma Lazarus** from the New World to the Old World:

»Give me your tired, your poor,
Your huddled masses yearning to breathe free,
The wretched refuse of your teeming shore.
Send these, the homeless, tempest-tost to me,
I lift my lamp beside the golden door!«

Tours

For millions of immigrants who came to the United States by ship, the Statue of Liberty was the first thing they saw of the New World and the manifestation of their hopes. But before they could disembark they had to endure the procedures on ►Ellis Island. The **Statue of Liberty Museum** in the base of the statue as well as the **observation deck** are open to the public. There is an extraordinarily beautiful view of New York from the observation deck, at a height of 50m/ 164ft (lift). Until 1916 it was possible to climb into the torch of the Statue of Liberty; since 2009 there is again free access to the **crown**, which had been closed after 9/11. The view of New York is extraordinarily beautiful. A glass ceiling in the base gives a view of the breathtaking interior design of the iron lady. **Tickets** must be reserved in advance (tel. 1-877-LADY-TIX or www.statecruises.com; info: www.nps.gov/stli).

Ticket orders ►

IMMIGRATION – A GROWING TREND

»Give me your tired, your poor, your huddled masses yearning to breathe free,« is the inscription on the base of the Statue of Liberty, which France gave to the USA in 1886 as a 100th anniversary gift. And between 1892 and 1954 more than 15 million people did emigrate to the land of opportunity.

No other US city saw as many immigrants pass through its gates as New York. Indeed, the expression used for the United States, the **melting pot**, originally referred to New York. The history of the city is the history of this melting pot, which has not been without its conflicts. In part, as Anthony Burgess once said, it is »the story of immigrants fighting against immigrants«.

From every corner of the world

The first European settlers in Manhattan were Walloons, who founded the settlement **Nieuw Amsterdam** in 1624 on the orders of the Dutch West Indies Company. In the following years Huguenots, Dutch, English and Germans joined them. Soon New Amsterdam developed into the North American colony with the most European cultures represented: in 1643 the roughly 500 residents spoke 18 different languages. They were not spared ethnic animosities and class conflicts, such as the Leisler Rebellion (1689 until 1691), in which Dutch artisans and small shop owners clashed with English and Dutch traders. In the 18th century, when New York became the leading port city of the New World, the flow of immigrants continued to grow and the population became more and more **ethnically and culturally diverse**. The number of Black Africans grew as well; in 1712 and 1741 there were even slave rebellions. In 1790 New York was the second largest city in the new nation after Philadelphia. Among the 33,000 residents most were of English or Dutch descent. Between 1815 and 1915 more than about 33 million people from all over

the world emigrated into the United States, three quarters of them through New York. They fled hunger, epidemics, political and religious persecution. A large number of **Irish and German Roman Catholics** also appeared in the city on the Hudson River, which disturbed the predominantly Protestant and Anglo-Saxon population. Street fights between native gangs and Irish immigrants were part of everyday life in the middle of the 19th century.

Second wave of immigration

In the middle of the 19th century New York was **the largest city in the western hemisphere**, with over 600,000 residents. The approximately 175,000 Irish were the largest ethnic group, followed by about 96,000 Germans, who settled on the Lower East Side in »Little Germany«. In the late 1880s a second immigration phase began when Russian and Polish Jews, Southern Italians, Greeks, Poles, Hungarians, Romanians as well as other southern and eastern Europeans fled changes similar to the ones that northern and western Europeans had

fled in the first half of the century. In 1907 twice as many people came into the country as in 1882, but the share of immigrants from northern and Western Europe sank from 87% to 19% at that time.

The immigrants around the middle of the century usually settled in ethnic neighbourhoods – the founding of **Little Italy** and **Chinatown** in southern Manhattan goes back to this time. The First World War had serious consequences for people of German descent. German language instruction was prohibited, the German theatre had to close, hamburgers were renamed »Salisbury steaks« and sauerkraut was called »liberty cabbage«. While Germans were still proud of their heritage before the war, afterwards they tried to hide it.

Fear of alienation

In 1920 about 20% of the residents of New York had been born abroad. The largest percentage consisted of Jews and Italians. Out of a fear of alienation a **quota** was introduced in 1924; every nation was permitted a certain annual quota of immigrants. This law

*Immigrants learning English
around 1919*

was aimed above all at Jews, Italians and southern and eastern European immigrants; Asians were not allowed to enter at all anymore. The law was not even repealed during the reign of **National Socialism in Germany**, when the persecuted tried to find refuge in the USA.

After the Second World War the flow of Spanish-speaking immigrants began which has continued to this day, initially predominantly from the American territory Puerto Rico, then also from the Caribbean and Central and South America. In 1965 the quota system was repealed, Congress instead fixing maximum numbers. Currently 675,000 immigrants are allowed to enter every year (excluding family members and political refugees).

Immigration continues

Currently more than 100 nationalities live in New York City, and speak about 120 different languages. About 90,000 immigrants settle here every year. Those who cannot make it legally try to enter illegally. The »tired, poor and huddled« still see a Mecca of freedom in New York – this is an unbroken trend. The terrorist attacks of 11 September 2001 on the Twin Towers of the World Trade Center have done nothing to alter this image. Immigration has not decreased since then, though the process has slowed down, primarily because the immigration regulations have been made stricter.

✶✶ Times Square

D 12

Location: Intersection of Broadway and Seventh Ave. between W 42nd St. and W 47th St.

Subway: Times Square

Times Square is the long intersection of Broadway and Seventh Avenue, between West 42nd and 47th St. A symbol of the Big Apple, the approximately 40 playhouses in its side streets make it the centre of the theatre world. Here, where city regulations require that all advertising be illuminated, the neon heart of the metropolis beats. An estimated one and a half million pedestrians cross the »world's intersection« daily, and more than 20 million tourists come here every year. Every New Year's Eve hundreds of thousands of revellers stand here and take part in the traditional countdown to the new year.

History

In the 19th century it was called »Longacre Square« and was the site of coachmen, saddleries and horse stables. The area was rather notorious, and the intersection of Broadway and Seventh Ave. was nicknamed »Thieves' Lair«. In 1904 the **New York Times** moved into its new publishing house »Times Tower« at the southern end of the square, which from then on carried its name (the editorial offices have since then moved their offices into a new building by Renzo Piano on Eighth Ave., between 40th and 41st St.). The narrow high rise with the address »1 Times Square« has since then changed owners several times.

Rise and decline

The square's rise to become the centre of New York's entertainment district began with the opening of the first house of the Metropolitan Opera in the year 1883 and with the opening of the Olympia Theater two years later by Oscar Hammerstein. In 1903 the Lyceum Theater (149 W 45th St.) followed, the oldest of the conserved houses, as did others. In the 1920s there were 80 houses in the Theater District, in which Charlie Chaplin, the Marx Brothers, Sarah Bernhardt, Houdini and others performed. The stars stayed in elegant hotels like the Astor. The illuminated advertisements were an attraction in themselves. For a few years Broadway was Times Square, and Times Square was New York – the »apotheosis of electricity«, as the French Odette Keun wrote in 1930.

The slow **decline** began with prohibition in the 1920s. The change became dramatic with the stock market crash in 1929, whose consequences restricted life in the theatres, varieties, restaurants and hotels. Striptease clubs opened in 42nd St., between Seventh and

Times Square today →

Eighth Ave. Dealing in sex, prostitution, drugs and violence became a symbol of urban decline, which had to be seen but which invited no one to stay.

At the beginning of the 1990s the situation turned around when businesspeople united with the authorities in a »clean-up« campaign. Then Disney invested, and many others followed. The first sign of success was the opening of the Marriott Marquis Hotel (1985). The opening of a branch of the exclusive Gap department store in 1992 at Broadway and Seventh Ave. served as a signal. In 1993 Bertelsmann moved to Times Square. In 1996 Disney opened a giant store on 42nd Street and Seventh Ave., in December 1996 the curtain rose again in the Victory Theater, the oldest theatre on Broadway which first opened in 1900, and in May 1997 in the New Amsterdam Theater opened. Where once the *Ziegfeld Follies* appeared, Disney shows are now performed. Along with cinemas and stylish restaurants, more and more tourist attractions are being opened, including **Madame Tussaud's wax museum** (▶ Practical Information, Museums and Galleries) and the **NASDAQ Market Site**, the visitor centre of the technology stock exchange for those interested in stocks – the wall familiar from television with the current prices is part of the centre (4 Times Square; open daily).

> ## ! *Baedeker* TIP
>
> ### New Year's Eve at Times Square
>
> Times Square turns into a fairground on New Year's Eve: at 6pm the illuminated New Year's Eve Ball is pulled up on a flag pole and the festivities begin with much music and spectacular sound effects. At 11.59pm the New Year's Ball starts moving so that it reaches the bottom of the flag pole at exactly midnight. The colourful fireworks start the new year with a bang and confetti pours out of the windows of the skyscrapers.

TriBeCa

A/B 17

Location: South of SoHo (Downtown)   **Subway:** Canal S.

TriBeCa, an acronym for Triangle Below Canal, is the neighbourhood between West Broadway, Canal, West and Chambers Street. The area was actually called Lower West Side until a clever real estate agent invented the acronym, which has meanwhile been generally accepted. Old warehouses and former factory buildings dominate, many of them brick built. The atmosphere is rather dry: people say that life takes place backstage here. In the 1980s many artists moved here who could no longer afford the rents in ▶ SoHo to the north. As in other areas, so too in TriBeCa: the lofts, whole floors in former warehouses and factories, serve as residences and studios. Meanwhile an infrastructure has developed for which SoHo had become famous: TriBeCa boasts some of the best restaurants in all of Manhattan, as well as bars, discos, jazz and rock clubs; also some galleries have opened, for the most part in the upper floors.

Attractions

The most striking buildings in TriBeCa include the eight built between 1804 and 1828 in the Federal Style on **Harrison Street**, though six of them were »imported« from other streets. The **New York Telephone Company Building** (32 Ave. of the Americas) was built in 1918 to designs by Ralph Walker in the Art Deco style and has an opulent lobby. Another Art Deco building is the **Western Union Building** from 1928 (60 Hudson St.). In the south, between Chambers and Greenwich St., is the small **Washington Market Park**, which gives an impressive view of the high rises in ►Battery Park City.

✶ ✶ United Nations Headquarters

F 13

Location: First Ave. between E 42nd and E 46th St.   **Subway:** Grand Central Terminal

The United Nations (UN or UNO, both expressions are acceptable) was founded in 1945 in San Francisco as the successor organization of the League of Nations in order to secure world peace and to promote international cooperation. The UN headquarters are in New York, and in addition there are other »UN cities« such as Geneva and Vienna.

The main organizations are the General Assembly (UNGA; it meets once a year from mid-September, but cannot pass any laws); the Security Council (UNSC) with the five permanent members USA, Russia, People's Republic of China, Great Britain and France, and ten other members from the General Assembly who are elected for two years; the Economic and Social Council (ECOSOC); the International Court of Justice (IJC) with its seat in The Hague (Netherlands); and the Secretariat (UNSG) headed by the Secretary General. The original 51 states have now become 191 member states. On 24 October, the official founding day, the »Day of the United Nations« is celebrated.

Tours

When the assembly is in session there are tours in English: Mar–Dec daily 9.30–4.45pm, Jan, Feb Mon–Fri only; children under five years are not admitted. General information: tel. 212-963-7713; information on tours: tel. 212-936-8687; www.un.org.

Buildings

The UN headquarters stands in an area which was once the domain of slaughterhouses and small industry. It was bought with money

UN headquarters, with the Chrysler Building in the background

donated by John D. Rockefeller Jr., while the construction costs of $67 million were paid by means of an interest-free loan from the United States. The land is exterritorial – neither the USA nor the City of New York have any say there – and has its own police and post office.

The building complex was built in 1949–1953 according to plans by an international team of architects, including Le Corbusier from France, who later distanced himself from the project, the Brazilian Oscar Niemeyer and the Swede Sven Markelius. The American Wallace K. Harrison was in charge of the project. Four individual buildings were built, which are decorated with the flags of all member states displayed in alphabetical order according to the English alphabet.

The glass front of the relatively narrow 39-storey **Secretariat Building** (154m/505ft) dominates and is the seat of the UN administration and the Secretary General, whose office is on the 38th floor. In the conference room there is a remarkable Swiss world clock. In the pool in front of the building is the abstract sculpture *Single Form* by Barbara Hepworth (1963).

The flat **Conference Building** connects to the curved **General Assembly Building** (for sessions of the General Assembly) with the domed, elliptical auditorium in the middle. The entrance to the UN complex between E 45th and E 46th St. leads into the lobby, where several works of art can be admired, including an ancient statue of Neptune, a Russian sputnik and to the rear on the right a stained glass window by Marc Chagall. Jean Bernard Foucault's 65m/213ft-high pendulum, a gift from the Netherlands, demonstrates the revolving of Earth on its axis.

On the lower floor there is the UN gift shop, where arts and crafts and souvenirs from all member states are sold, and a bookshop. Stamp collectors will enjoy a visit to the UN post office, also on the lower floor, where letters are specially stamped and franked. However letters and cards have to be deposited in mailboxes within the building in order to be mailed.

The murals in the General Assembly are by Fernand Léger.

South-west of the General Assembly Building is the Dag Hammarskjöld Library, named after the second UN General Secretary, who was killed in an aeroplane crash in the Congo in 1961. The building was constructed in 1962 according to plans by Harrison, Abramovitz & Harris and is a gift of the Ford Foundation.

Dag Hammarskjöld Library

In the north of the UN building complex along the East River stretches a beautiful park with numerous sculptures from different countries, including the bronze statue *Reclining Figure*, a gift from the Henry Moore Foundation (1982), the sculpture *Swords to Ploughshares*, a gift from the former Soviet Union (1958), the bronze sculpture *Climber* by the East German Fritz Cremer, the *White Horse* by the German artist Elisabeth von Janota-Bzowski, the *Statue of Peace* from Yugoslavia as well as the peace sculpture *Non-Violence* by the Swedish artist Karl Frederik Reutersward, a gift from Luxemburg in the year 1988.

Sculptures

Anyone visiting UN headquarters should also take a look at some of the surrounding buildings and plazas, such as 1 UN Plaza (First Ave./44th St.), built in 1976 by the architects Roche, Dinkeloo and Assocs. as a hotel and office high rise, Tudor City and the building of the Ford Foundation on 42nd St. (►Grand Central Terminal).

Surroundings

At United Nations Plaza and 46th St. is the African-American Institute, where exhibitions of African art are held on the ground floor. Sculptures are displayed in rotation on Dag Hammarskjöld Plaza.

◄ African-American Institute

** Whitney Museum of American Art

F 9

Location: 945 Madison Ave./75th St.   **Subway:** 77th St.

The Whitney Museum of American Art is the only museum in New York dedicated exclusively to American art of the 20th century. It's origins go back to the studio founded in 1908 by the wealthy sculptress and patron Gertrude Vanderbilt Whitney (1877–1942).

⊙
Opening hours:
Wed, Thu, Sat, Sun
11am–6pm
Fri 1pm–9pm

www.whitney.org

In 1918 she opened the Whitney Studio Club and the Whitney Studio Gallery in Greenwich Village. Her aim was – in a time when museums, galleries and collectors in the United States still preferred European art – to acquaint a broader public with works by American artists. The first studio museum, which showed predominantly the private collection of the founder, was opened in 1931 in Greenwich Village. The current museum building was built in 1966 according to plans by **Marcel Breuer** and Hamilton Smith. Breuer began working in the Bauhaus in Dessau, Germany as a designer of furniture and came to the USA in 1937 as a professor of architecture, while Philip

Whitney Museum, the most representative collection of American art

Johnson, Edward Larrabee Barnes and others were his students. The main building, which projects outward in steps like an inverted pyramid, is covered with grey granite plates. The strictness of the north face on E 75th St. is loosened up by irregularly distributed prism windows. The building is entered from Madison Ave. across a bridge, from which visitors can look down on a sculpture garden and a popular restaurant, Sarabeth's. Since 1932 the »Whitney Biennale of American Art« has been held here every two years in May. The sales exhibition is at the same time a chance to judge the direction of current creative art work. Beyond that there is a museum shop on the ground floor and a cafeteria on the lower floor. Currently Renzo Piano is planning an extension, which will enlarge the exhibition space considerably.

◄ Whitney Biennale

The Whitney has over 12,000 paintings, sculptures, prints, drawings, photographs, films and videos by all important American artists (► Art in New York, p.50). On permanent display are Alexander Calder's *Circus* (1926–1931) in the foyer as well as an exhibition with works by Edward Hopper, Georgia O'Keeffe and Alexander Calder on the fifth floor. All other treasures of the museum are shown in rotating exhibitions. In addition, special exhibitions are held regularly.

Collection

✶ ✶ World Trade Center Site

A 18

Location: Between Church, Vesey, West and Liberty St.

Subway: Cortland St., World Trade Center, Chambers St.

Until 11 September 2001, the two towers of the World Trade Center were New York's tallest buildings and together with the five side buildings symbolized American financial power. Today the area is a giant building site, and the construction of the Freedom Tower is underway.

The twin towers, both built 1966–1977, 417m/1,368ft high and with 110-storeys, were masterpieces of engineering (plans: Minoru Yamasaki & Assocs. and Emery Roth and Sons). They stood on foundations that were sunk 21m/69ft deep into the slate bedrock (the excavated ground was dumped into the river and ► Battery Park City was built on it). Around 50,000 people worked there, and 80,000 visitors came every day. The two towers, in which a total of 180,000 tons of steel were used, stood 101 and 56 minutes respectively, after the aeroplanes had crashed into them. The north tower collapsed first, followed by the south tower (moreover, ultimately all of the side buildings were destroyed). Their steel scaffolding could not stand up to the temperatures of thousands of litres of burning kerosene. About 3,000 people lost their lives in the attack. Six weeks before 11 September 2001 the real estate tycoon Larry Silverstein had signed the lease for the WTC for 99 years – the total cost was $3.2 billion.

The reconstruction progress is sluggish. In the first years Larry Silverstein was opposed to a rebuiliding. While having secured the construction and commercial rights to the five planned skyscrapers, he failed to get the necessary financing. In 2006 he had to give the Port Authority, the corporate body of the city and the state of New York that owns the site, at least the construction control of Freedom Tower (1 World Trade Center) and a second skyscraper. Then in fall of 2008 the financial crisis began.

The new WTC The master plan for the new WTC is by David Libeskind, the builder of the Jewish Museum in Berlin. Five high rises are planned, which will stand in a semicircle open towards the west, and which will increase in height from south to north. Construction work on the northernmost and tallest building began in 2004. Great value was placed on building security. The steel used was subjected to special fire protection treatment; the stairwells are extra wide etc. What was originally called »Freedom Tower« is now called **1 World Trade Center**. The new tower is a compromise between competition winner Daniel Libeskind's original design, and the recommendations made by David Childs, high rise specialist from the architecture factory S.O.M. Additionally, lengthy negotiations concerning the design took place with Larry Silverstein, leaseholder of the WTC site. Libeskind's design contributed the height – 1776 feet (541m) – which commemorates the year of American independence, and the asymmetrical top of the tower. The shaft of the 70-storey building, which winds on its own axis and recedes as it gets higher, is Childs's contribution. On completion, planned for 2013, it will have cost $3.2 billion. The name was changed because of the first confirmed renter, the Chinese Vantone International company, which wants to have a »China Center« here. **7 WTC** (228m/748ft high) was already completed in 2006.

2 WTC (200 Greenwich St.), designed by Norman Foster, is supposed to be completed in 2012, and to be 382m/1,253ft high. The angled roof of the glass giant, reminiscent of a diamond, is already considered to be an enhancement for the New York city skyline. **3 WTC** (175 Greenwich St.) is based on the design by Richard Rogers and is supposed to be 352m/1,155ft high. The building is a little fur-

? DID YOU KNOW …?

■ Until 11 September 2001 the term Ground Zero was used by the military for the place where an atom or hydrogen bomb had exploded, or the place where the greatest damage occurred. Soon after 9/11 the desert of ruins in south Manhattan and then the bottom of the gigantic crater that was created when the masses of rubble from the WTC were removed were called Ground Zero.

ther away from the others, but will contribute to the harmonious picture from a distance. The same applies to **4 WTC** (150 Green St., 297m/974ft) with its narrow silhouette (design Fumihiko Maki). In the center of the area will be the **National September 11 Memorial & Museum**, an underground memorial (memorial design by Michael Arad, Peter Walker), in which the remains of the unidentified victims will be laid to rest. It will be a worthy tribute to the victims of the attack.

The plans for the new transport terminal **PATH**, an ultra-modern subway in an airy design of glass and steel (completion in 2013), come from a Spanish architect: the famous bridge, airport and railway station designer Santiago Calatrava.

Tribute WTC Visitor Center ⏱

Relatives of the victims of 9/11 established the Tribute WTC Visitor Center in 2006, a visitor centre and museum (120 Liberty St., at Ground Zero, opened Mon, Wed–Sat 10am–6pm, Tue noon–6pm, Sun noon–5pm). It offers **tours of Ground Zero**: »Tribute Center Walking Tours« take place daily at11am, noon, 1pm, 3pm, Sat also at 2pm and 4pm. Ordering tickets in advance is advisible: www.tributewtc.org, tel. 1-866-737-1184, 212-393-9160 ext. 138.

The daring, more than 500m/1650ft high tower of 1 WTC is supposed to dominate the skyline.

INDEX

LIST OF MAPS AND ILLUSTRATIONS

PHOTO CREDITS

PUBLISHER'S INFORMATION

Illustrations etc: 216 illustrations, 22 maps and diagrams, one large city plan
Text: Achim Bourmer, Monika Hausner-Schönfelder, Ole Helmhausen, Wolfgang Liebermann, Carin Drechsler-Marx, Henry Marx, Anja Schliebitz, Barbara Schmidt-Runkel, Jörn Trümper, Wolfgang Veit, Jens Wassermann
Revision: Thomas Jeier
Editing: Baedeker editorial team (Anja Schliebitz, Robert Taylor)
Translation: Barbara Schmidt-Runkel
Cartography: Christoph Gallus, Hohberg; Franz Huber, Munich; MAIRDUMONT/Falk Verlag, Ostfildern (city plan)
3D illustrations: jangled nerves, Stuttgart
Design: independent Medien-Design, Munich; Kathrin Schemel

Editor-in-chief: Rainer Eisenschmid, Baedeker Ostfildern

2nd edition 2012
Based on Baedeker Allianz Reiseführer
»New York« 15. Auflage 2011

Copyright: Karl Baedeker Verlag, Ostfildern
Publication rights: MAIRDUMONT GmbH & Co; Ostfildern

Printed in China